PRESIDENTIAL GRAVE HUNTER

One Kid's Quest to Visit the Tombs of Every President and Vice President

ISBN: 9798218141738 (paperback)
ISBN: 9798218141745 (ebook)

Library of Congress Control Number 2023525703

Printed by IngramSpark, of La Vergne, Tennessee.

Excerpt from *Who's Buried in Grant's Tomb* by Brian Lamb, copyright © 2003. Reprinted by permission of PublicAffairs, an imprint of Hachette Book Group, Inc.

Excerpts from *So You Want to Be President?* By Judith St. George, illustrated by David Small, copyright © 2000. Reprinted by permission of Penguin Random House LLC. Cover art reproduced by permission of David Small.

The author cannot take responsibility for changes to exhibit contents and interpretation, nor location accessibility. Travelers are encouraged to contact individual sites ahead of visitation to verify information.

Cover design by SusansArt@99D

Interior book layout by Marcy McGuire and Kurt Deion

Ebook formatting by Formatted Books

Photographs by Paul and Lynne Deion, except where otherwise noted

Author photograph by Steve Stewart

James Leavelle photographs by Dylan Hollingsworth

"Equal parts charming and informative, this book will appeal to anyone from the avid historian to the casual reader alike."

> \- **Thomas J. Balcerski**, author of *Bosom Friends: The Intimate World of James Buchanan and William Rufus King*

"I've been pretty open in interviews that graves and live interpretation aren't really my jam, but I am violently supportive of anything that gets people interested in history. I think his story is pretty cool."

> \- **Lindsay M. Chervinsky**, executive director of the George Washington Presidential Library and co-editor of *Mourning the Presidents: Loss and Legacy in American Culture*

"In the tradition of recent writers like Sarah Vowell or Nathaniel Philbrick, Deion gives readers a vivid and encyclopedic retelling of his various travels, mixed with the history of the sites he visited, and the people those sites commemorate. Deion has an attention for detail that comes through in recounting the various sites he has visited, and communicating the atmosphere for those who have not."

> \- **Joe Faykosh**, professor of history at Central Arizona College and host of *Visiting the Presidents* podcast

"In *Presidential Grave Hunter*, Kurt Deion combines his wide-eyed boyhood obsession to visit every American president and vice-president's grave with an accomplished scholarship of the public historian he became. Parts memoir, history, and madcap adventure, *Presidential Grave Hunter* offers a unique, informative, and entertaining lens into presidential history. From the solitude of Martin Van Buren's Kinderhook tombstone to the national spotlight on C-SPAN, I enjoyed every page and every grave."

> \- **Louis L. Picone**, author of *Grant's Tomb: The Epic Death of Ulysses S. Grant and the Making of an American Pantheon* and *The President Is Dead!: The Extraordinary Stories of the Presidential Deaths, Final Days, Burials, and Beyond*

"*Presidential Grave Hunter* provides an extraordinary look at American history that is at once highly unique and thoroughly captivating. It's a must read for every student of our nation's narrative and everyone who loves exceptional, unusual adventures."

> \- **Donald M. Stinson**, author of *Downstairs at the White House: A teenager, an Oval Office, and a ringside seat to Watergate*

"It's not just that Kurt Deion takes us on visits to presidential gravesites. It's adventures he takes us on, lots of them, as he revisits a childhood passion through his skills as a now grown-up writer/historian. Kurt's writing is lively and informed, and some of the stories he shares with us are deeply personal and moving."

- **Steve Buckley**, senior writer, *The Athletic*

"Blending fresh, historical research with his personal experiences, Deion brings readers along for the journey, sharing his extensive knowledge and insight along the way."

- **Matthew R. Costello**, director of the David M. Rubenstein National Center for White House History and co-editor of *Mourning the Presidents: Loss and Legacy in American Culture*

"Kurt Deion's *Presidential Grave Hunter* is an inspiring journey of a kid with a mission, and when I say inspiring I don't just mean it inspires me to go out and achieve my goals, because Deion does something even better-- he inspires the reader to help anyone who's young at heart complete their passion projects. A vivid American travelogue and a road map for making idiosyncratic dreams come true."

- **Howard Dorre**, co-host of *Plodding Through the Presidents podcast*

"Digging into the backstory of Kurt's extensive travels was such a treat. His account deepened my appreciation for the final resting places of our former leaders. And, as an added bonus, it provided an unexpected opportunity to draw a pantless Eisenhower."

- **Heather E. Rogers**, presidential doodler, potuspages.com

"I'm impressed by your obsession, by your dedication to its fulfillment resulting in this well-written book! [...] Above all, of course, I was stunned by your introductory remarks about my and Judy St. George's book being the original inspiration for your years-long quest. [...] This is your real gift to me: proof that a book can have its impact at unpredictable times and in unpredictable ways."

- **David Small**, Randolph Caldecott Medal-winning illustrator of *So, You Want to Be President?*

In Memory of Jessica Sultaire

1988-2017

Advisor and Friend

Contents

Presidential Directory

George Washington (1732-1799) – 1st president, 1789-1797. No party affiliation. Interment at George Washington's Mount Vernon, Mount Vernon, Virginia.

John Adams (1735-1826) – 2nd president, 1797-1801. Federalist Party. Interment at United First Parish Church, Quincy, Massachusetts.

Thomas Jefferson (1743-1826) – 3rd president, 1801-1809. Democratic-Republican Party. Interment at Thomas Jefferson's Monticello, Charlottesville, Virginia.

James Madison (1751-1836) – 4th president, 1809-1817. Democratic-Republican Party. Interment at James Madison's Montpelier, Montpelier Station, Virginia.

James Monroe (1758-1831) – 5th president, 1817-1825. Democratic-Republican Party. Interment at Hollywood Cemetery, Richmond, Virginia.

John Quincy Adams (1767-1848) – 6th president, 1825-1829. Democratic-Republican Party. Interment at United First Parish Church, Quincy, Massachusetts.

Andrew Jackson (1767-1845) – 7th president, 1829-1837. Democratic Party. Interment at Andrew Jackson's Hermitage, Nashville, Tennessee.

Martin Van Buren (1782-1862) – 8th president, 1837-1841. Democratic Party. Interment at Kinderhook Reformed Church Cemetery, Kinderhook, New York.

William Henry Harrison (1773-1841) – 9th president, 1841. Whig Party. Interment at Harrison Tomb State Memorial, North Bend, Ohio.

John Tyler (1790-1862) – 10th president, 1841-1845. Whig Party. Interment at Hollywood Cemetery, Richmond, Virginia.

James K. Polk (1795-1849) – 11th president, 1845-1849. Democratic Party. Interment at Tennessee State Capitol, Nashville, Tennessee.

Zachary Taylor (1784-1850) – 12th president, 1849-1850. Whig Party. Interment at Zachary Taylor National Cemetery, Louisville, Kentucky.

Millard Fillmore (1800-1874) – 13th president, 1850-1853. Whig
Party. Interment at Forest Lawn Cemetery, Buffalo, New York.

Franklin Pierce (1804-1869) – 14th president, 1853-1857. Democratic
Party. Interment at Old North Cemetery, Concord, New Hampshire.

James Buchanan (1791-1868) – 15th president, 1857-1861.
Democratic Party. Interment at Woodward Hill Cemetery, Lancaster,
Pennsylvania.

Abraham Lincoln (1809-1865) – 16th president, 1861-1865.
Republican Party. Interment at Oak Ridge Cemetery, Springfield,
Illinois.

Andrew Johnson (1808-1875) – 17th president, 1865-1869.
Democratic Party. Interment at Andrew Johnson National Cemetery,
Greeneville, Tennessee.

Ulysses S. Grant (1822-1885) – 18th president, 1869-1877. Republican
Party. Interment at General Grant National Memorial, New York,
New York.

Rutherford B. Hayes (1822-1893) – 19th president, 1877-1881.
Republican Party. Interment at Rutherford B. Hayes Presidential
Library & Museums, Fremont, Ohio.

James A. Garfield (1831-1881) – 20th president, 1881. Republican
Party. Interment at Lake View Cemetery, Cleveland, Ohio.

Chester A. Arthur (1829-1886) – 21st president, 1881-1885.
Republican Party. Interment at Albany Rural Cemetery, Menands,
New York.

Grover Cleveland (1837-1908) – 22nd and 24th president, 1885-1889
and 1893-1897. Democratic Party. Interment at Princeton Cemetery,
Princeton, New Jersey.

Benjamin Harrison (1833-1901) – 23rd president, 1889-1893.
Republican Party. Interment at Crown Hill Cemetery, Indianapolis,
Indiana.

William McKinley (1843-1901) – 25th president, 1897-1901.
Republican Party. Interment at McKinley National Memorial,
Canton, Ohio.

Theodore Roosevelt (1858-1919) – 26th president, 1901-1909. Republican Party. Interment at Youngs Memorial Cemetery, Oyster Bay, New York.

William Howard Taft (1857-1930) – 27th president, 1909-1913. Republican Party. Interment at Arlington National Cemetery, Arlington, Virginia.

Woodrow Wilson (1856-1924) – 28th president, 1913-1921. Democratic Party. Interment at Washington National Cathedral, Washington, D.C.

Warren Harding (1865-1923) – 29th president, 1921-1923. Republican Party. Interment at Harding Memorial, Marion, Ohio.

Calvin Coolidge (1872-1933) – 30th president, 1923-1929. Republican Party. Interment at Plymouth Notch Cemetery, Plymouth Notch, Vermont.

Herbert Hoover (1874-1964) – 31st president, 1929-1933. Republican Party. Interment at Herbert Hoover Presidential Library and Museum, West Branch, Iowa.

Franklin D. Roosevelt (1882-1945) – 32nd president, 1933-1945. Democratic Party. Interment at Home of Franklin D. Roosevelt National Historic Site, Hyde Park, New York.

Harry S. Truman (1884-1972) – 33rd president, 1945-1953. Democratic Party. Interment at Harry S. Truman Presidential Library and Museum, Independence, Missouri.

Dwight D. Eisenhower (1890-1969) – 34th president, 1953-1961. Republican Party. Interment at Dwight D. Eisenhower Presidential Library, Museum & Boyhood Home, Abilene, Kansas.

John F. Kennedy (1917-1963) – 35th president, 1961-1963. Democratic Party. Interment at Arlington National Cemetery, Arlington, Virginia.

Lyndon B. Johnson (1908-1973) – 36th president, 1963-1969. Democratic Party. Interment at Lyndon B. Johnson National Historical Park, Stonewall, Texas.

Richard Nixon (1913-1994) – 37th president, 1969-1974. Republican Party. Interment at Richard Nixon Presidential Library and Museum, Yorba Linda, California.

Gerald Ford (1913-2006) – 38th president, 1974-1977. Republican Party. Interment at Gerald R. Ford Presidential Museum, Grand Rapids, Michigan.

Jimmy Carter (1924-2024) – 39th president, 1977-1981. Democratic Party. Interment at Jimmy Carter National Historical Park, Plains, Georgia.

Ronald Reagan (1911-2004) – 40th president, 1981-1989. Republican Party. Interment at Ronald Reagan Presidential Library & Museum, Simi Valley, California.

George H.W. Bush (1924-2018) – 41st president, 1989-1993. Republican Party. Interment at George Bush Presidential Library and Museum, College Station, Texas.

Bill Clinton (1946-present) – 42nd president, 1993-2001. Democratic Party.

George W. Bush (1946-present) – 43rd president, 2001-2009. Republican Party.

Barack Obama (1961-present) – 44th president, 2009-2017. Democratic Party.

Donald Trump (1946-present) – 45th and 47th president, 2017-2021 and 2025-present. Republican Party.

Joe Biden (1942-present) – 46th president, 2021-2025. Democratic Party.

Vice Presidential Directory

John Adams (1735-1826) – 1st vice president, 1789-1797. Federalist Party. Interment at United First Parish Church, Quincy, Massachusetts.

Thomas Jefferson (1743-1826) – 2nd vice president, 1797-1801. Democratic-Republican Party. Interment at Thomas Jefferson's Monticello, Charlottesville, Virginia.

Aaron Burr (1756-1836) – 3rd vice president, 1801-1805. Democratic-Republican Party. Interment at Princeton Cemetery, Princeton, New Jersey.

George Clinton (1739-1812) – 4th vice president, 1805-1812. Democratic-Republican Party. Interment at Old Dutch Churchyard, Kingston, New York.

Elbridge Gerry (1744-1814) – 5th vice president, 1813-1814. Democratic-Republican Party. Interment at Congressional Cemetery, Washington, D.C.

Daniel D. Tompkins (1774-1825) – 6th vice president, 1817-1825. Democratic-Republican Party. Interment at St. Mark's Church in-the-Bowery, New York, New York.

John C. Calhoun (1782-1850) – 7th vice president, 1825-1832. Democratic-Republican Party. Interment at St. Philip's Episcopal Church, Charleston, South Carolina.

Martin Van Buren (1782-1862) – 8th vice president, 1833-1837. Democratic Party. Interment at Kinderhook Reformed Church Cemetery, Kinderhook, New York.

Richard M. Johnson (1780-1850) – 9th vice president, 1837-1841. Democratic Party. Interment at Frankfort Cemetery, Frankfort, Kentucky.

John Tyler (1791-1862) – 10th vice president, 1841. Whig Party. Interment at Hollywood Cemetery, Richmond, Virginia.

George Mifflin Dallas (1792-1864) – 11th vice president, 1845-1849. Democratic Party. Interment at St. Peter's Episcopal Churchyard, Philadelphia, Pennsylvania.

Millard Fillmore (1800-1874) – 12th vice president, 1849-1850. Whig Party. Interment at Forest Lawn Cemetery, Buffalo, New York.

William Rufus DeVane King (1786-1853) – 13th vice president, 1853. Democratic Party. Interment at Live Oak Cemetery, Selma, Alabama.

John C. Breckinridge (1821-1875) – 14th vice president, 1857-1861. Democratic Party. Interment at Lexington Cemetery, Lexington, Kentucky.

Hannibal Hamlin (1809-1891) – 15th vice president, 1861-1865. Republican Party. Interment at Mount Hope Cemetery, Bangor, Maine.

Andrew Johnson (1808-1875) – 16th vice president, 1865. Democratic Party. Interment at Andrew Johnson National Cemetery, Greeneville, Tennessee.

Schuyler Colfax (1823-1885) – 17th vice president, 1869-1873. Republican Party. Interment at City Cemetery, South Bend, Indiana.

Henry Wilson (1812-1875) – 18th vice president, 1873-1875. Republican Party. Interment at Dell Park Cemetery, Natick, Massachusetts.

William Wheeler (1819-1887) – 19th vice president, 1877-1881. Republican Party. Interment at Morningside Cemetery, Malone, New York.

Chester A. Arthur (1829-1886) – 20th vice president, 1881. Republican Party. Interment at Albany Rural Cemetery, Menands, New York.

Thomas A. Hendricks (1819-1885) – 21st vice president, 1885. Democratic Party. Interment at Crown Hill Cemetery, Indianapolis, Indiana.

Levi P. Morton (1824-1920) – 22nd vice president, 1889-1893. Republican Party. Interment at Rhinebeck Cemetery, Rhinebeck, New York.

Adlai E. Stevenson I (1835-1914) – 23rd vice president, 1893-1897. Democratic Party. Interment at Evergreen Memorial Cemetery, Bloomington, Illinois.

Garret Hobart (1844-1899) – 24th vice president, 1897-1899. Republican Party. Interment at Cedar Lawn Cemetery, Paterson, New Jersey.

Theodore Roosevelt (1858-1919) – 25th vice president, 1901. Republican Party. Interment at Youngs Memorial Cemetery, Oyster Bay, New York.

Charles Fairbanks (1852-1918) – 26th vice president, 1905-1909. Republican Party. Interment at Crown Hill Cemetery, Indianapolis, Indiana.

James S. Sherman (1855-1912) – 27th vice president, 1909-1912. Republican Party. Interment at Forest Hill Cemetery, Utica, New York.

Thomas R. Marshall (1854-1925) – 28th vice president, 1913-1921. Democratic Party. Interment at Crown Hill Cemetery, Indianapolis, Indiana.

Calvin Coolidge (1872-1933) – 29th vice president, 1921-1923. Republican Party. Interment at Plymouth Notch Cemetery, Plymouth Notch, Vermont.

Charles G. Dawes (1865-1951) – 30th vice president, 1925-1929. Republican Party. Interment at Rosehill Cemetery, Chicago, Illinois.

Charles Curtis (1860-1936) – 31st vice president, 1929-1933. Republican Party. Interment at Topeka Cemetery, Topeka, Kansas.

John Nance Garner (1868-1967) – 32nd vice president, 1933-1941. Democratic Party. Interment at Uvalde Cemetery, Uvalde, Texas.

Henry A. Wallace (1888-1965) – 33rd vice president, 1941-1945. Democratic Party. Interment at Glendale Cemetery, Des Moines, Iowa.

Harry S. Truman (1884-1972) – 34th vice president, 1945. Democratic Party. Interment at Harry S. Truman Presidential Library and Museum, Independence, Missouri.

Alben Barkley (1877-1956) – 35th vice president, 1949-1953. Democratic Party. Interment at Mount Kenton Cemetery, Paducah, Kentucky.

Richard Nixon (1913-1994) – 36th vice president, 1953-1961. Republican Party. Interment at Richard Nixon Presidential Library and Museum, Yorba Linda, California.

Lyndon B. Johnson (1908-1973) – 37th vice president, 1961-1963. Democratic Party. Interment at Lyndon B. Johnson National Historical Park, Stonewall, Texas.

Hubert Humphrey (1911-1978) – 38th vice president, 1965-1969. Democratic Party. Interment at Lakewood Cemetery, Minneapolis, Minnesota.

Spiro T. Agnew (1918-1996) – 39th vice president, 1969-1973. Republican Party. Interment at Dulaney Valley Memorial Gardens, Timonium, Maryland.

Gerald Ford (1913-2006) – 40th vice president, 1973-1974. Republican Party. Interment at Gerald R. Ford Presidential Museum, Grand Rapids, Michigan.

Nelson Rockefeller (1908-1979) – 41st vice president, 1974-1977. Republican Party. Interment at Rockefeller Family Cemetery, Sleepy Hollow, New York.

Walter Mondale (1928-2021) – 42nd vice president, 1977-1981. Democratic Party. Interment pending at Lakewood Cemetery, Minneapolis, Minnesota.

George H.W. Bush (1924-2018) – 43rd vice president, 1981-1989. Republican Party. Interment at George Bush Presidential Library and Museum, College Station, Texas.

Dan Quayle (1947-present) – 44th vice president, 1989-1993. Republican Party.

Al Gore (1948-present) – 45th vice president, 1993-2001. Democratic Party.

Dick Cheney (1941-present) – 46th vice president, 2001-2009. Republican Party.

Joe Biden (1942-present) – 47th vice president, 2009-2017. Democratic Party.

Mike Pence (1959-present) – 48th vice president, 2017-2021. Republican Party.

Kamala Harris (1964-present) – 49th vice president, 2021-2025. Democratic Party.

JD Vance (1984-present) – 50th vice president, 2025-present. Republican Party.

Prologue

*"…I have long believed there is more drama in a
graveyard than a textbook."*
Richard Norton Smith in *Who's Buried in Grant's Tomb?*

This story ends with a plane ride to Minnesota, a locale any sane person would strive to steer clear from in the bitter cold of January. But my father and I haven't led the most conventional of lives. The apparent ill-timing of the trip was necessitated by a gap in my busy schedule – namely winter break from college. The success of our mission was certain to negate any misgivings generated by the frosty weather, anyway. After all, how many sophomores got the chance to meet an *actual* United States vice president?

We didn't plan to introduce ourselves until the next morning, but we were so excited that we couldn't help but drive straight from the Minneapolis-Saint Paul International Airport to meet the veep. The two of us found his address easily enough, and the adrenaline coursed through our bodies as we passed through the front gate. I took no time to compose myself as I jumped out of our rental car and trudged through a foot of accumulated snow over to our predetermined meeting spot. Much to our chagrin, the VP was nowhere to be found. This elusiveness wasn't appreciated, but it was not unexpected, either. My dad and I had been dodged by many a politician in our time. Yet the two of us did not travel 1,100 miles to pack it in the moment we were given the cold shoulder. So we started kicking away the snow.

Our desperation-fueled digging quickened as the sun dipped below the horizon. Dusk threatened to ruin my photo op, though I knew my father was certain to press for a picture no matter how dark it was outside. After 15 minutes of searching, I was the one who finally found the vice president. Introductions were made, and my father pulled out his cell phone to take a commemorative picture as I posed beside the VP. Then we said our goodbyes, and I cast one last look in his direction to read the inscription by his feet.

HUBERT H. HUMPHREY
1911 – 1978

At long last, after ten hardscrabble years that consumed over half my lifespan, I had achieved a feat *perhaps* no other person could claim: I'd met all 66 deceased U.S. presidents and vice presidents.

The 2014 venture to Minneapolis was the culmination of an unusual quest that started under unlikely circumstances. My long-standing fascination with presidential and vice presidential burial sites can indirectly be traced back to my mother, Lynne. It was she who in the early months of 2002 perused the Scholastic Book Clubs order form I received at Hope Highlands Elementary School and purchased a paperback about U.S. presidents. At seven years old, my primary interests at school were that of a typical second grader: recess and lunch, rather than anything academic. I initially protested the book's acquisition, preferring to keep my literary interests confined to the Caped Crusaders and lasagna-loving felines that graced the comics, but my mother prevailed. When *So You Want to Be President?* arrived, my antipathy gave way to my innate desire to be an obedient offspring and I made the pivotal decision to pick it up. Over the next few years, I scarcely laid it down.

As I look at the book now, I can see all the wear brought on by the innumerable hours I pored through its pages.[1] The historical nuggets presented by author Judith St. George fascinated me, but I was drawn in primarily by artist David Small's illustrations. William Howard Taft, the heaviest president at over 300 pounds, bathed in a tub that could hold four average-sized men. *So You Want to Be President?* depicts Taft being lowered into an oversized bathtub by a construction worker-operated crane as the corpulent POTUS downs a beverage and clutches a turkey leg. Two page turns later, the reader comes across a beauty contest in which Warren Harding is crowned the handsomest chief executive. Ten of his presidential peers stand on stage behind him, all clapping and cheering (with the exception of a dour Richard Nixon).

---

[1] See Figure 1.

Some facts and caricatures evoked visceral responses from me. "The President has lots of homework," the book notes. Hey, same here! "Do you have pesky brothers and sisters?" it queries. Affirmative! Not as many as George Washington, who is shown enduring the tugging, kicking, and biting of eight screaming siblings, but I had one four-year-old sister who was adept enough to take on *all* of those responsibilities. And I enjoyed swimming like John Quincy Adams, although I received lessons at the YMCA and he routinely skinny-dipped in the Potomac River. St. George and Small took these historical giants and presented them in a way that a seven-year-old could relate to.

So You Want to Be President? is thin and flimsy, but the heft of its impact on my life is immeasurable. My mother thought she was order-ing me a book, but she actually bought a springboard that propelled me on my life trajectory. Had I never read and been captivated by the paperback, my father, Paul, might have paid no mind when he stum-bled upon a C-SPAN book talk about presidential burial sites. He may have never told me about network founder Brian Lamb's quest to visit them all, and I wouldn't have had the stimulus to ask to follow in his footsteps.

But why visit historical gravesites? Why visit history-based places at all? The nature of my interests and travels has evolved since this all started two decades ago, but my answer to these questions remains effectively unaltered: practicing "hands-on history" enables the visitor to become immersed in the story, as opposed to relegating them to the role of spectator. Seeing, feeling, and experiencing the sites connected to historical figures and events adds another facet to historical learning that is non-replicable.

Despite the ease with which St. George and Small achieve relat-ability in their book, understanding the presidents is no simple task. With the possible exception of the Founding Fathers, it is reasonable to argue that no collection of Americans has been more mythologized than its commanders-in-chief. The presidents, both those who have been venerated and vilified, can seem untouchable. When we hold a five dollar bill and look at the portrait of Abraham Lincoln, what first crosses our minds? Do we think of the emotional turmoil that consumed him after his eleven-year-old son, Willie, succumbed to typhoid fever, or as tens of thousands of Americans slew each other on battlefields? Can we extract from that two-dimensional visage his sense of humor, or the apprehension he must have felt leaving his home in Springfield for the White House as secession was underway? For me, anyway, the answer is no. On that piece of paper he seems more than a man, with a canyon separating his qualities and accomplishments from my own.

The feeling of distance between us and the presidents may also be caused by the significant power they wield, as well as the passage of time. The longer it has been since a president's death or tenure of office, it stands to reason that they would be less prominent in public memory. Understandably, far more people still mourn the loss of John F. Kennedy – whose assassination sixty years ago is embedded in extant memories – than James A. Garfield, who languished for two and a half months during the summer of 1881 before his body gave out. Garfield continued to suffer in death. The site of his shooting in D.C. was unmarked and unacknowledged until temporary waysides were unveiled in 2018, whereas his twentieth-century successor has long been commemorated with a museum and a 30-foot memorial near where he was struck down in Dallas.

Even for me, a devotee of history, the not-far-removed assassination of JFK at times can feel as distant as the 1799 death of Washington. By the time I was born in 1994, 36 presidents were deceased, our paths never to cross. I have learned about these figures from books and documentaries that provide exceptional analysis and insight – sources that paradoxically stir up feelings of deprivation and want. Why couldn't I have met these heads of state and gotten to know them, or at least been present to witness their triumphs and follies? Hands-on history fills that void for me. I never had a chance to dine on clam chowder with Kennedy, nor could I stroll with Harry S. Truman, or simply shake hands with Lincoln. I *have*, however, gotten the opportunity to eat at Kennedy's favorite Boston restaurant, to trace the path of Truman's daily walk through his hometown in Missouri, and to rest my hand on the staircase railing in the only house Lincoln ever owned. Hands-on history, or at least my version of it, is tactile.

Unless they are a component of a historical institution or tour program, presidential resting places are typically devoid of historical interpretation. Yet while they may look like unexplained monoliths at first glance, they can still offer insights.

With the family burial vault at his beloved Virginia estate in disrepair, George Washington stipulated in his last will and testament that a replacement be erected a few yards away. Though there were repeated efforts to remove the president's remains to a repository in the center of the U.S. Capitol, in 1831 the general and his relatives were relocated to the belatedly-constructed new tomb at Mount Vernon, per his request. GW's great-nephew, John Augustine Washington, Jr., laid the matter to rest in 1832, telling Congress he refused to disturb his ancestor from his "perfect tranquility" and violate his wishes. George Washington wanted nothing more than to live in peace at his farm on the Potomac River, a dream he put on hold several times to serve his country. No one was going to keep him from Mount Vernon in death.

Herbert Hoover lived out his last years in a luxury Park Avenue suite at Manhattan's Waldorf Astoria. But in a fashion that rang true to his humble Quaker origins, his progeny arranged for him to be buried on a small hill near his quaint birth cottage in Eastern Iowa. Calvin Coolidge's basic headstone, fitting for the laconic Republican, contrasts with the grand edifices of Grant, McKinley, Harding, and others. It'd be incongruous for someone with the sobriquet "Silent Cal" to have a mortus memorial rife with pomp and circumstance. Just his name, birthday, and date of death? 'Nuff said.

A president's grave can provide insights on how they wished to be remembered – or instead how Americans chose to show their affection toward them. Although Lincoln coveted a place in the annals of history, I personally find it doubtful that the often self-effacing POTUS would have approved of the grandiosity of his tomb, which is laden with statuary and rises over 100 feet in the air.

I was nine years old the fateful day my father watched that C-SPAN book talk about presidents' tombs, and over eight years passed until April 2012, when, as a high school senior, I had my picture taken at my 38th and final presidential gravesite. It took another 21 months to fully complete my objective. Over the course of my odyssey, my intentions morphed from duplicating Mr. Lamb's feat to topping it. He was one of several people to trek to each president's grave, but, to my knowledge, no one had achieved the same for every vice president. The one roadblock for all other grave hunters appeared to be Nelson Rockefeller, interred on his private family estate in the Hudson Valley. Pushed by my force of nature father, I gained access to the Rockefeller Family Cemetery on my way to becoming, possibly, the only person to have seen all 66 collective presidential and vice presidential burial sites in existence at that time.

Primarily a memoir, *Presidential Grave Hunter* is a story about a child's hunger for historical learning, but also about discovering America through travel, overcoming objections and obstacles, and the bond that strengthened between me and my parents as they helped facilitate my journey. Neither one has a background in history – my father is a former toy dealer, while my mother has made a career as a nurse specializing in substance use disorders and mental health. Yet, just as they forged their own paths, they encouraged me to find my passion and, in my father's case, forced me to push boundaries and advocate for myself in pursuit of that passion.

In writing this book, my goal is to inspire people – young and old – as Judith St. George, David Small, Brian Lamb, and historian Richard Norton Smith inspired me. No matter what area of history you find relatable or interesting, be it individuals like the presidents, campaigns like the civil rights movement or women's suffrage, or something entirely different, I hope when you finish reading about my journey to historic sites and tombs you will be determined to embark on your own pilgrimage. Walk the Edmund Pettus Bridge in Selma as activists did on Bloody Sunday. Behold the scores of "I Voted" stickers left by enfranchised women on Susan B. Anthony's grave in Rochester, New York, or Belva Lockwood's headstone in Washington, D.C.

Hands-on history complements traditional historical education methods such as classroom studying, books, and documentaries, and I encourage that, when possible, they be employed in tandem in order to develop a well-rounded understanding of how we remember the past.

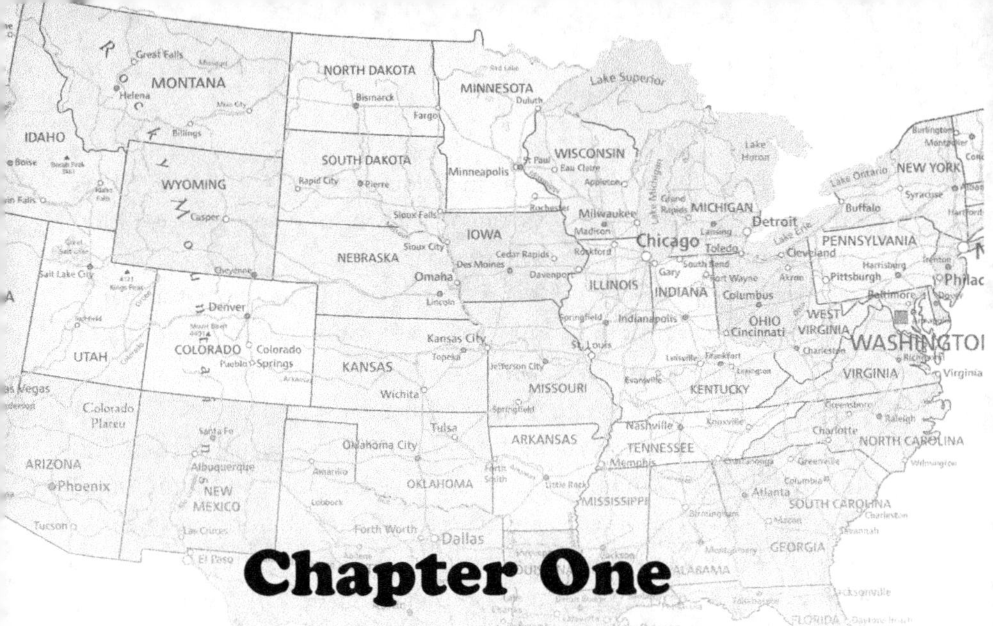

Chapter One
Before the Beginning
~ 2003 ~

This story begins in summer 2003, roughly six months before my father accidentally channel surfed his way into committing to spend a decade's worth of vacations at cemeteries. The place was Quincy, Massachusetts: the City of Presidents and, just as importantly to this account, the home of my mother's brother, Craig. My family lived nearly 60 miles south in central Rhode Island, and visits with Uncle Craig were few and far in between. That enhanced the specialness of the invitation he extended to me and my sister, Olivia, to spend a weekend with him and his girlfriend once the school year was over. At the time we arrived at Uncle Craig's condominium, I was utterly unaware of Quincy's White House connection – and no one knew that, for one of us, the weekend would be life-changing.

Many people left in charge of young children might read with them, or maybe play some games and plop them down in front of a television for a few hours. Our uncle and his girlfriend did just that, but they also threw in a field trip, one that catered specifically to me. It was a short drive – just three miles down Hancock Street – to the Adams National Historical Park (ANHP) Visitor Center. "Adams as in John and Abigail," I pondered silently before I saw the signage with a singular letter D, "or A<u>dd</u>ams as in Wednesday and Cousin Itt?" Fresh out of third grade, I was a walking anachronism – an eight-year-old in the twenty-first century who read history books and watched decades-old reruns on TV Land. Based on the name of the park, I reasoned I was about to be indulged in at least one of my interests.

It soon became evident that the Quincy Adamses were not creepy and kooky, but rather the presidential sort. The ANHP, under the aegis of the National Park Service and the Department of the Interior, preserves the birthplaces of Presidents John and John Quincy Adams, as well as the estate where four generations of their kin resided. With this knowledge, the trolley ride away from the Visitor Center was as thrilling to me as sitting aboard a flying elephant at Disney World.

The trolley unloaded us on Franklin Street in front of two side-by-side buildings with dramatically-sloped roofs that stretch down the back. A uniformed park ranger called them saltbox houses because that asymmetric feature makes them resemble the containers salt was kept in. The ranger led us inside the simple, unpainted abode on the north end of the lot, which was the site of John Adams's birth in October 1735. I deflated when I heard tours weren't allowed upstairs where he was actually born, but nevertheless I was exuberant to walk through the same space that a president did when he was my age. Now I had something in common with John Adams.

As a young adult, John inherited the abutting home, where his wife, Abigail, gave birth to John Quincy in July 1767. There too we found the second story birth room off limits, though we *were* shown the parlor where Mrs. Adams might have penned a letter pressing her husband and his colleagues in the Second Continental Congress to "Remember the Ladies" as they constructed a government independent from Great Britain.

John did not advocate for his wife's cause in the Congress, though he did make invaluable contributions during his tenure. It was Adams who nominated George Washington to command the Continental Army in June 1775, perhaps the most consequential decision of the American Revolution. Adams was also a member of the Committee of Five that crafted the Declaration of Independence, who among themselves chose Thomas Jefferson to write the first draft. Adams and others edited it.

Long after the Second Continental Congress disbanded, Adams continued to contribute – both directly and indirectly – to the United States's early development. By the mid-1780s, it was apparent that the new country's governing document, the Articles of Confederation and Perpetual Union, was ineffectual. Representatives called to a convention in Philadelphia in 1787 drafted a new constitution that provided the basis for a stronger central government. Being on diplomatic assignment in Europe at the time, Adams did not attend the Constitutional Convention, but his influence was still felt.

To illustrate this point, the ANHP positions a table with a copy of the Massachusetts Constitution smack dab in the middle of John's front parlor law office in the John Quincy Adams birthplace. As elucidated by our park ranger, the document, authored by the elder Adams in 1779, is the oldest governmental constitution still in effect in the entire world. It was a template for the U.S. Constitution in both its structure and content, partly by beginning with a preamble and establishing a bicameral legislature. The significance of its Declaration of Rights section is also evident: the right to a trial by jury, freedom of the press, and freedom of religion (for "every denomination of Christians" in this instance) are all listed. Years before these thoughts were put to parchment in our national Bill of Rights, John Adams led the charge in Massachusetts.

Neither birthplace has anything in the way of original furnishings, as the Adamses took their belongings with them when they moved a mile or so north to the farm they called *Peace field* in 1788. Alterations like the addition of the front portico make the home more reflective of subsequent generations' tastes, but the property is still categorically tied to their ancestors. Abigail's roses continue to grow in the garden beside the Stone Library, where the volumes collected by John Quincy and his heirs fill shelves two books deep. JQA was well-read and well-traveled, attributes that must have appealed to President James Monroe when he chose him to be secretary of state in 1817. The mahogany table Monroe was seated at when he informed John Quincy's parents of his selection is kept in the *Peace field* dining room. I knew *my* parents were always proud when I came home with good grades, so John and Abigail must have been elated that their son was going to be in the presidential cabinet, I reasoned as I marveled at the woodwork.

Abigail died of typhoid fever in her upstairs bedroom just over a year later, in October 1818. John Quincy was elected president six years later, and his father, John, stayed alive for nearly two years after that – until July 4, 1826. Our tour group was led over to his second-floor study, where the chair in which he collapsed at age 90 is nestled in the corner. His passing a few days later coincided with the fiftieth anniversary of the adoption of the Declaration of Independence, which he signed and helped draft.

I was overwhelmed to be immersed in so much personal history, but it was at the Adams family's final resting place, ironically, where they truly came to life for me. Down the street from the ANHP Visitor Center is the United First Parish Church, which the four of us investigated upon hearing that the Adamses were congregants. The church is still active, which prohibits it from being taken over by the National Park Service. A guide greeted us inside the entryway and presented us with a choose-your-own-tour scenario: for a small donation, we could tour the whole building and sit in the John Quincy Adams pew; if we chose to forgo a donation, however, that wouldn't preclude us from seeing the crypt.[2]

I was unsure what the word "crypt" meant, but that's where I found myself headed after Uncle Craig and his girlfriend kept their wallets pocketed. My companions and I managed not to tumble down the steep steps into the basement, where down a hallway a wrought iron gate is hinged to the stone walls. Between the bars I discerned what appeared to be two large stone tables, one with a 15-star Amer-

---

[2] Nowadays, visitors cannot go down to the Adams Crypt without making at least a nominal cash donation. The History and Visitors Program run at the Church of the Presidents is highly-dependent on financial contributions in order to keep the gravesites open to the public.

ican flag draped over it. We were told that they were sarcophagi, or coffin containers. These particular ones held the bodies of John and Abigail Adams.

To my astonishment, our guide asked if we wanted to enter the crypt. You mean that I can actually go right up to John and Abigail Adams? *Of course* I'm going to take that offer! The gate was summarily unlatched, and it was as if a new world had been opened for me. I walked between the granite sarcophagi, guiding my fingers along the sunken letters in the names chiseled atop the lids. On the other side of the chamber, not visible from the outside, were two more dark gray sarcophagi. One of them, too, was covered with a flag. It was John Quincy Adams. Beside him was his wife, Louisa Catherine Johnson. The Episcopalian Louisa wasn't a member of the church, which had long been Unitarian. Nonetheless, when the tomb was expanded in 1852 to accommodate JQA, his late bride journeyed with him from their vault in Hancock Cemetery across the street.

The entirety of the situation was blowing my young mind. Not only had I learned about the Adamses, I invited myself over their house and now was meeting them, sort of, even though they hadn't been alive for almost two centuries. (Eat your heart out, Disney World!) Yet despite the ecstasy, it didn't enter my mind that these could be just the first of thousands of interment sites I would clamor to visit in the coming years.

Receptive to a glowing report about the transformative visit to the Adams sites, my parents decided there was no better place to take a family vacation later in the summer than Washington, D.C., a veritable smorgasbord of history-related attractions where I could satisfy my burgeoning desire to make presidential pilgrimages. I delighted in exploring the city's most famous sites, from memorials and museums to the White House, where every president from John Adams to George W. Bush had worked and lived. "If only I could go in there, like the Adams homes," I privately yearned as my mother snapped the requisite picture of my sister, my father, and me alongside the fence on Pennsylvania Avenue.[3]

I reclaimed my insider status at the U.S. Capitol, where a tour leader let my family in on some of the building's rich history. In Statuary Hall, which was the meeting place of the House of Representatives from 1819 to 1857, I stood astride a small square plaque that marks the former location of John Quincy Adams's desk. Adams was first elected to the House in 1830 — one of just two presidents to serve in Congress after leaving the White House, and the only one to serve in the lower chamber. Our tour leader told us JQA represented Massachusetts until February 1848, when, right where my feet were planted, he suffered a fatal stroke.

I couldn't have been more intrigued, a stark contrast to my ever-restless sister. As young as we were, our respective positions in the dichotomy of Deion children were already evident. I had inherited our mom's reserved demeanor and by-the-book attitude, as well as elements of our father's sense of humor and nostalgia for things before my time (namely music, comics, and television shows of the 1960s). Outburst-prone Olivia was a more impetuous version of my dad, but shared very little of his impishness and not an ounce of his affection for cultural relics of bygone eras. Looks and a common residence aside, my sister and I had very few things in common, and it was quickly becoming apparent that she was growing to resent anything history-related. Luckily, she was placated through her affection for animals with a day at the National Zoo and a photo op with the statue of famous presidential pooch Fala at the Franklin Delano Roosevelt Memorial.

Arlington National Cemetery, across the Potomac River in Virginia, presented another opportunity for me to become acquainted with a dead president: John F. Kennedy. The Bay Stater survived the sinking of his PT boat in World War II and went on to become the youngest elected president, only to be assassinated at age 46 (which didn't seem that youthful from an eight-year-old's perspective). His plot is awash with symbolism, from the slate tombstone that sits flush

---

[3] See Figure 2.

with rectangular granite rocks quarried from his beloved Cape Cod, to the iconic eternal flame lit by the widowed Jacqueline Kennedy at his funeral. Mrs. Kennedy chose to be buried with the president, even though she remarried to businessman Aristotle Onassis in 1968. The first couple's markers are flanked by two smaller stones that belong to their infant son, Patrick, and a stillborn child. A chain cordoned off the grave from visitors, who all stood solemnly. I'd yet to read much about the Kennedy assassination, but I could tell that the vibe in Arlington's Section 45 was much more somber than the Adams crypt in Quincy.

The plot, where a prescient President Kennedy remarked he could stay forever during a March 1963 visit, is at the base of a hill with the mansion of Mary and General Robert E. Lee at its apex. The U.S. military confiscated the Greek Revival house and the rest of the Lees' 1,100-acre estate in May 1861, toward the start of the Civil War, for its strategic placement overlooking Washington. The property was put up for auction in January 1864 and was promptly purchased by the Federal Government. The first military burial on the grounds occurred four months later. Hundreds of thousands would follow.

I held no sympathy for the Lee family about the loss of their land, for they used it as a slave plantation. My family was guided through Arlington House's halls by a National Park Service ranger who explained that its original proprietor, George Washington Parke Custis, had arranged for the people enslaved there to be emancipated upon his death. When the time came in 1857, Custis's daughter, Mary Lee, inherited the plantation and her husband, Robert E. Lee, countermanded his father-in-law's orders. This triumphant-feeling northerner couldn't help but believe that Robert E. Lee had gotten his just desserts for helping lead the Confederate cause and perpetuating slavery throughout the nation and in his own home. For that, the general lost the panoramic view of D.C. and the Potomac River that I now embraced as I stepped onto his former front lawn. The vantage point from the Lee-Custis Mansion is unparalleled in my opinion, with the Capitol, Library of Congress, and the largest memorials dotting the skyline.

Later in our trip we experienced another satisfying glimpse of the Potomac at Mount Vernon, the palatial home of Mary Lee's great-grandmother, Martha Washington. Mrs. Lee's father, George Washington Parke Custis, was the first lady's grandson through her first marriage, which was to Daniel Parke Custis. After Daniel's death in 1757, widowed Martha married George Washington and lived with him at Mount Vernon, the property he inherited from his half-brother's widow.

Martha resided at Mount Vernon, of course, but truly the home is the living embodiment of her husband, George. In the 45 years that he operated the estate, he had the house renovated and rebuilt repeatedly so it matched his wishes for his family, as well as the standards befitting their growing social status in eighteenth century Virginia. By far, it was the most lavish house I'd seen in my short life. I was particularly struck by the New Room – a green-walled, two-story space decorated with plaster molding ceilings and the president's collection of paintings. It was the perfect setting, I imagined, for him and Martha to entertain guests like Revolution ally, the Marquis de LaFayette. The white cotton-covered canopy bed upstairs, in which the general passed away after a two-day illness, impressed as well. "Washington even *died* in style," I thought to myself. In July 2003, I was fortunate enough not to know about the bloodletting and enemas that consumed George's final hours.

George put equal thought into the mansion's exterior aesthetics, which I learned about courtesy of an adventure map for young visitors. One side of the paper displayed an illustration of the plantation with numbered locations, while the other side bore nine corresponding *Wheel of Fortune*-type educational puzzles for each site. I deciphered, for example, that s a n d was mixed in the paint used on the home's façade to mimic the look of expensive white stones Washington originally wished to use. The mansion's most distinctive feature – the cupola that protrudes from its red roof – is topped with a weathervane shaped as a twig-carrying dove, a representation of peace. The general used this metal attachment to determine the direction of the w i n d. With each solve I felt like Sherlock Holmes, uncovering the mysteries of GW's past.

Beyond Mount Vernon's physical appearance, the puzzles also taught me about the property's functionality as a plantation and the enslaved populace that maintained it. One puzzle said that some of the 314 Black people held in bondage at the estate "lived together in one large room." The literature's misstep of making their living situation seem more sociable than forced slipped by me at the time. "For entertainment at the end of a long work day," it continued, "they sometimes played music and sang." Those words were accompanied by a lone drawing of a cheerful, unnamed Black man, singing and clapping. I wondered how he could be enslaved but look so happy. Maybe it was because, as the puzzle concluded, "By the end of his life Washington realized that slavery was wrong and freed his slaves."[4]

Technically George's will ordered that they be freed after the death of Martha Washington. He asserted that he feared emancipating them during Martha's lifetime would create "insuperable difficulties" because of intermarriage. Many of the people enslaved by GW married people enslaved by the Custises, the family of Martha's first husband. Mrs. Washington manumitted the Washington slaves ahead of schedule in 1801, perhaps out of fear that they might want to induce their freedom by hastening her demise. Upon the matriarch's death the following year, those considered Custis property were kept in bondage and divided among her grandchildren. In both instances, intermixed families were separated.

Blissfully unaware of this over-simplification, I moved on to the next puzzle convinced George Washington was the Grinch of slavery — he had done something bad, but his heart grew three sizes and he made amends. At eight years old, while I was already a hardliner with Confederates like Robert E. Lee, who would rather rebel and start a civil war than live in a country without slavery, I was more willing to

---

[4] An internet search revealed that Mount Vernon subsequently updated its Adventure Map to be more historically accurate. This version also illuminates young adventurers about the lives of specific people enslaved at Mount Vernon, such as William Lee, Alce, Dolsey, and Vina.

forgive Washington, Thomas Jefferson, and other leaders who I reasoned did a lot of good deeds otherwise.

When Martha Washington died in May 1802, the former first lady's body was initially placed in Mount Vernon's deteriorating burial vault. She was moved with the rest of the family in spring 1831 to the new tomb constructed under the provisions of George's will. Per the president's wishes, the second brick structure is larger in scale and situated at the foot of the property's vineyard, which my family found using my adventure map.

Between the oppressive heat and near-paralyzing awe, I struggled to move toward the tomb. Yet I forced myself to push onward. I couldn't believe I was just feet away from *the* George Washington – fêted for his service as commanding general of the Continental Army in the American Revolution and as the precedent-creating first president. We were unable to get right next to him, as a gate blocked the antechamber, but at least the first couple's marble sarcophagi were plainly visible. The enclosures are less bulky than the Adamses', and the lid on the president's sarcophagus incorporates a carved eagle and shield. A black metal door on the back wall leads to the rest of the tomb, where relatives such as Supreme Court Justice Bushrod Washington (a favorite nephew) rest out of view.

Washington was eulogized by Robert E. Lee's father, Major General Henry "Light Horse Harry" Lee, as being "First in war, first in peace, and first in the hearts of his countrymen." On that hot and humid day he also became the first president whose gravesite I had my photo taken at. Dripping with sweat in my sleeveless green t-shirt, I did my utmost to muster a smile while one of my parents took a picture for posterity with our intermittently-used camera.[5] 'Twas a momentous occasion.

✠ ✠ ✠

Even as I notched my fourth presidential burial site with Washington's tomb, the thought didn't register that I could visit the

---

[5] See Figure 3.

grave of every individual who had taken the presidential oath of office. Such an undertaking required further inspiration, and that spark ignited on the evening of December 21, 2003 – a date I can pinpoint thanks to the immaculate airdate records the Cable-Satellite Public Affairs Network (C-SPAN) keeps on its website.

Searching aimlessly for something to watch on TV, my father came across a repeat broadcast of a National Press Club event originally recorded in March 2000. C-SPAN chairman and CEO Brian Lamb and historian Richard Norton Smith were discussing the publication of *Who's Buried in Grant's Tomb? A Tour of Presidential Gravesites.* The book was primarily written by C-SPAN staffer Carol Hellwig, woven together with vignettes and a foreword penned by Smith, an afterword from historian Douglas Brinkley, and photos taken by Lamb. The purpose of *Grant's Tomb* was to give readers historical accounts of the deaths and final resting places of American presidents, as well as provide directions and other information pertinent to visitation (such as addresses, cemetery hours, and potential admission fees).

The origins of the project arose in February 1993, when Lamb interviewed Smith on the show *Booknotes* about his recent work, *Patriarch: George Washington and the New American Nation.* In the course of their dialogue, it came up that Smith had a "lifelong habit of dragging his family from grave to grave of the United States presidents." It was a hobby Smith took up at eight years old, the same age I was a few months earlier when I ventured into the Adams crypt. The historian's account impressed Lamb, who was motivated to begin a similar endeavor. He consequently traversed to each president's final resting place, asking fellow tourists to photograph him so he could show Smith proof of his accomplishment.

Lamb wanted to surpass his friend, though, and set out to see every deceased vice president as well, a goal Smith jokingly derided in the National Press Club program as "pathological." The only gaps in Lamb's collection were Hubert Humphrey, whom he planned to visit in Minneapolis shortly after the recording, and Nelson Rockefeller at his private family cemetery in Sleepy Hollow, New York. "I tried," said the wistful Lamb. "I wrote Mrs. Rockefeller a letter, and I got a very nice letter back from her saying, 'Sorry.' But I got a picture of the gate."

I was not within earshot of the television when the book talk aired, but later in the evening my father relayed to me Smith and Lamb's quests. I reflected back on the emotions I experienced visiting those four president graves during the summer. By going inside a president's home, I could see how they lived. By going to a president's grave, I could see *them*. And what if I could see them all?

With childlike innocence, unaware of the funds and effort such a slog could require, I gazed up at my father.

"Can *we* do that?" I inquired.

"Do what?" was the befuddled reply.

"Go to every presidential burial site!"

As I readied for bed, my dad jumped on the internet to get better grounded on the locations of the presidents' final resting places. He hollered up to me when he found a website called Travelin-Tigers, run by an average Joe who, like Smith and Lamb, had been to all 36 sites that existed at that time. His website included a chart that listed all the cities and towns where the presidents were interred, and individual pages incorporated photographs of each locale. Whereas my father had the benefit of watching the *Grant's Tomb* book talk and its accompanying imagery, the Travelin-Tigers pictures were the first I'd ever seen of any president graves apart from those I'd already visited, and thus I was completely captivated. At my direction, my father clicked on the small camera graphics beside each chief executive's name, and one by one the differing designs of their final resting places were unveiled. I was probably the only nine-year-old staying up past their bedtime to fawn over pictures of Franklin Pierce's gravestone. Even his bland monument, which pales in comparison to the Art Deco interior of Abraham Lincoln's towering tomb, was enticing in my eyes.

Eventually I was ordered up to bed, but stepping away from the computer didn't slow my mind. I was able to drift to sleep only because I had no clue about the scope of the adventures that would be in store over the next decade.

Chapter Two
R.I.P. the Gipper
~ June 2004 ~

A person can't control when inspiration hits them, but winter proved not to be the prime season to assume a graveside crusade, what with many of the presidents buried beneath an extra snowy layer in the Northeast and Midwest. The anticipation ate away at me for months as I waited for warmer weather to pave the way for my quest to officially begin. Come the thaw, I was beyond ready to spring into action. My father, self-employed through his collectibles business, The Wayback Machine, Inc., was a stay-at-home dad with the flexibility to chauffeur me to cemeteries during school break that April. My mother's more traditional work situation at the hospital made her unavailable to watch my sister, and so Olivia became an unwilling companion to Kinderhook, New York, hometown of Martin Van Buren.

Lindenwald – the Little Magician's ritzy post-presidency residence, which was disappointingly closed when we arrived – contrasts with the bleak and uninspired obelisk atop his grave in the local cemetery. Mundaneness notwithstanding, I was nearly as excited to see Van Buren as Chester Arthur, who is perpetually mourned by a patina-covered angel in Menands. Posing next to the figure, who rests a palm frond across the Republican's granite sarcophagus, admittedly made for a more compelling picture, however.

Unlike Washington or the Adamses, Arthur isn't actually inside his sarcophagus, but underneath it. The monument and statue were placed posthumously in June 1889. It's surprising that Arthur, a stuffy New Yorker who refused to move into the drab Executive Mansion until it was renovated, apparently had no similar stipulations about his permanent residency at Albany Rural Cemetery. Arthur's protracted period of ill health adds to the perplexity. His fatal kidney affliction, Bright's disease, was a major factor in Arthur's decision not to actively seek the Republican presidential nomination in 1884, and he left office in March 1885. Though his retirement was brief, surely he had the time to contemplate what he wanted his grave to look like. Yet after his death in November 1886, it fell upon friends to hire sculptor Ephraim Keyser and raise $10,000 for his gravesite monument, which was placed over his buried body three years later. When we visited the 21st commander-in-chief, I believed he was inside the black granite box, but the knowledge that he was beneath it would have made no difference in my excitement. Either way, I was near a president.

Even retreading old ground was electrifying. Brian Lamb's account impressed upon my father the importance of photographically documenting these visits, and that meant going back to see my first three commanders-in-chief. The close proximity of the United First Parish Church made calling on the Adamses again easy enough, and we managed to squeeze them into our plans while we were in Quincy for a Mother's Day lunch. The revelation that William Howard Taft was interred in Arlington National Cemetery necessitated a return trip, at which time I could revisit JFK. Nevertheless, Virginia was hundreds of miles away from our Rhode Island home, and I was unsure when an opportunity to rectify the Taft-Kennedy oversights would arise.

The answer came sooner than expected, unfortunately through subtraction from the fraternity of living presidents. On Saturday, June 5th, I was visiting my mother's parents' house next door when my grandfather switched on the television. "Welp, Reagan died," he announced, which summoned my immediate attention. A picture of the Gipper with the years 1911 and 2004 beneath it graced the screen. Stunned, I sprinted home. I burst through our front door and found my father napping on the couch. I woke him up with the news.

After they conferred that evening, both parents sat down with me to ask if I wanted my dad to drive me to Washington to pay my respects when Reagan lay in state in the Capitol Rotunda the next week. Reagan was the first president to pass away in my lifetime, as I was born several months after Richard Nixon's death in April 1994. Even then, Nixon's family eschewed a grand send-off in the nation's capital. It was a decision Tricky Dick made himself – possibly in relation to his resignation in the wake of the Watergate Scandal that cast a pall over not only his last two years in office but the presidency itself. According to the media coverage, no president had lain in state since Lyndon Johnson in 1973. How could I decline such an offer, lest an additional three decades pass before another such opportunity?

Just one day after our huddle, complications set in during a pickup game of flag football. As my father reached for the fumbled pigskin on the ground, another player dove for the recovery and landed on my dad's left arm. Each time this story is brought up, my father brags that, despite his limb breaking, he recovered the football. But with his dominant arm wrapped in a cast up past his elbow, an eight-hour trek to D.C. became a daunting exercise. Our new game plan was to see how the week panned out, but with each passing day the prospect of going grew bleaker. Luggage was left unpacked. The crowd accumulating on the Capitol grounds looked gargantuan on the TV. All four of my grandparents voiced concerns that we would be driving toward certain doom, a product of post-9/11 anxiety. I attempted to cling to any thread of hope.

All such threads were severed when an airplane flew over the Capitol on June 9th, the first of Reagan's three scheduled days in the Rotunda. The subsequent evacuation of the building and grounds, albeit brief, was enough for my mother and father to cancel our plans. The assaults on the Pentagon and World Trade Center were just three years in the past, and, with prominent leaders scheduled to attend Reagan's services, the prevailing fear was that the incident was part of another terrorist attack. In actuality the aircraft was carrying the governor of Kentucky and had experienced a radio malfunction, but the damage was done. Tensions were just too high on all fronts. I was informed that the trip was off, and I climbed into bed at night with tears cascading down my cheeks.

As I prepared for school the following day, my main mission was to research the identity of my new archenemy, Kentucky's governor. With the name Ernie Fletcher seared into my brain and a backpack full of books on presidents, I begrudgingly boarded the school bus.

But Governor Fletcher was spared from incurring the eternal hatred of a fourth grader. In the middle of recess, I realized I had a pair of scissors from a morning activity in my pocket and rushed to return them to my classroom. Before I could properly deposit the scissors, my teacher, Ms. DeFelice, informed me that I had just been summoned to the main office. I scampered to the front of the building, where I found my father waiting in the middle of the foyer. When I asked why he was there, his eyes widened. He and my mother had a change of heart.

"We're going to D.C.!"

A swarm of ineffable joy overwhelmed me, as all of the excitement that had eroded since Sunday was instantly rebuilt.

Despite the impediment of his fractured arm, my father guided us safely during the 400-mile journey from my school to Dupont Circle. I only *moderately* freaked out when he used his knees to steer as he turned the radio knob and completed his ritual of tapping the dashboard to the Crosby, Stills & Nash song, "Suite: Judy Blue Eyes." The two of us checked into the same hotel on Connecticut Avenue NW where we stayed the previous summer, after which we wolfed down dinner and hailed a taxi to transport us to Capitol Hill. Our arrival was right around 9:00 p.m. As we secured our spot in line, a wave of optimism led me to believe the wait wouldn't be more than an hour or so.

It was wishful thinking, likely precipitated by an urge to escape the weather. The Washington heat was overbearing, but not more so than the humidity. Moisture dripped from my forehead as the queue slowly proceeded toward the Capitol. The monotony was interrupted by some unexpected and unwelcome excitement when I stuck my hand in my pocket and realized that, in the frenetic turn of events at school, I neglected to give back the scissors. Luckily I became aware of the situation before we reached the security checkpoint, and my father directed me to discard the scissors as we passed by a trash can. I had reservations about throwing out school property, but the prospect of being reprimanded by authorities didn't appeal to me either. Ms. DeFelice, I owe you some scissors.

As the minutes multiplied, so did the beads of sweat sticking to our skin. The thousands of dead Brood X cicadas that littered the ground near Garfield Circle added to the unpleasantness, as the sound of crunching carcasses beneath tired feet became ubiquitous for the rest of our five-hour wait. It was 2:00 a.m. when the two of us finally passed through security and into the Capitol. We walked between statues of Ulysses S. Grant and Abraham Lincoln as we entered the Rotunda.

Flanked by inward-facing service members, President Reagan's flag-draped casket was planted in the center of the chamber on a cloth-covered catafalque originally constructed to hold Abraham Lincoln's remains in 1865. Earlier, my father and an affable fellow line-goer tried to prepare me for the possibility of an open casket. As much as I wanted to connect to the presidents, I was relieved to be spared from looking upon my first dead body. I wasn't that desperate.

Like the 104,682 other mourners who passed through over the three-day viewing period, we glided along the velvet ropes and stanchions in silent contemplation. The majesty of the Rotunda distracted me, even though our family toured the Capitol not eleven months prior, and my eyes wandered to the surrounding statuary and the Apotheosis of Washington that hovers from the Dome 180 feet above. My father realized where my attention had gravitated, and with a nudge he refocused my attention on the intent of the trip.

Good thing, because our viewing allotment was brief. As we exited and a suited event employee handed us white visitation cards, my dad remarked to me that the two of us walked around Reagan's casket for exactly 60 seconds. To some, the brevity may have made the endeavor feel like a waste of time, but we were more than satisfied with our results. That was, if the Republican was truly in the closed box, my father qualified.

"After all we went through… he better not be at home watching football."

I *could* have noted that it was 11 p.m. California time on a Thursday in June, and that there would have been no football on TV to watch, but I would have just been chided for "deconstructing the joke."

As rain dampened the streets of D.C. hours later, a hearse carried President Reagan's body from the Capitol to the Washington National Cathedral for his funeral service. While my father showered, I watched the ceremony on the hotel television. Reagan's vice president, George H.W. Bush, delivered a moving eulogy, and a stoic, pre-recorded message from former Prime Minister Margaret Thatcher of the United Kingdom played. When my father was dressed, we set out to the National Mall to see the recently-dedicated World War II Memorial, and then to the grave of one of the Great Communicator's predecessors.[6]

We located William Howard Taft in Section 30 of Arlington National Cemetery, at the end of a long brick path north of the Military Women's Memorial. Carved from reddish Stony Creek granite that originated in Connecticut, the 14-and-a-half-foot monument he shares with First Lady Helen Taft towered over all the other graves I'd

---

[6] See Figure 4.

seen at the cemetery the year prior. Old Bill's major accomplishments — his service as both president and Supreme Court chief justice — are etched into the narrow sculpture in gold lettering.

The artist behind the Taft monument was none other than James Earle Fraser, who also sculpted *The Contemplation of Justice* and *The Authority of Law* — the statues that flank the front staircase of the Supreme Court Building. Taft did not live to see the construction of the building, but he was largely responsible for its existence. During his SCOTUS tenure, the Court was confined to a series of crowded rooms in the Capitol. Taft swayed the House Public Buildings Committee to press for funding for a separate structure. Congress allocated $9,740,000 for the project, and President Hoover approved it in December 1929 — two months before Taft's failing health forced his resignation, and three months ahead of his death.

After I saluted the Tafts, we called on the Kennedys for a second time in less than a year. With the click of a button on our new digital camera, I no longer lacked documentary proof for any presidential gravesite visits.

Being in the D.C. area allowed us to play catch-up at other sites as well, like Ford's Theatre. The brick building where Abraham Lincoln was shot was closed for renovations in 2003, but now I was able to enter and have a clearer vision of what happened that April night nearly a century and a half prior. Even though the original playhouse was devastated by a fire in 1893 and the current interior is essentially a rebuilt facsimile, it was unsettling to climb the staircase to the second floor and see the president's box festooned with bunting, just as it was in 1865. My father positioned me for a picture next to the doorway through which actor John Wilkes Booth was permitted to enter after he showed Lincoln's personal attendant, Charles Forbes, a calling card or some paper. Moments later, Booth became the first presidential assassin, and bedlam ensued.

In the basement museum, I tiptoed as silently as JWB over to the Philadelphia Derringer he used to commit the foul deed.[7] How

---

[7] See Figure 5.

could such a small weapon, capable of holding just one bullet, irrevocably alter the course of history? I had equal difficulty fathoming the insignificance of the exalted Lincoln's place of death, a boarding house across 10th Street NW, where his limp body was carried and then perished at 7:22 the following morning. The Petersen House was closing by the time we were finished touring Ford's Theatre, so we had to return the next day to navigate through the narrow hallway to the back room where the president expired. It is much more confined than nineteenth-century depictions indicate. Some, like Alonzo Chappel's painting *The Death of Lincoln*, characterize his deathbed vigil as a rite dozens of people participated in simultaneously, which would've been spatially impossible I realized – even at nine years old. The quarters measure at 9 1/2 feet by 17 feet.

The original bed was auctioned off in the 1870s and was acquired by the Chicago History Museum in 1920, leaving the Petersen House with only a replica to display. I wanted my picture taken with the substitute anyway.

As newly-minted octogenarian George H.W. Bush prepared to celebrate his milestone birthday skydiving in Texas, my dad and I took a taxi to the building where, just the day before, he eulogized Ronald Reagan. Our intentions in exploring the National Cathedral had no correlation to Reagan, although my enthusiasm about him certainly had not ebbed in the previous 24 hours. My clothing ensemble for the day included an oversized, white t-shirt with a black-outlined, chest-up image of the late POTUS above the words "Remember President Reagan" in all caps and his lifespan.[8] My father bought it for me the day before from a vendor near Ford's Theatre. The shirt would remain a featured item in my wardrobe for north of four years, long after it should have been retired to a shadow box as a casualty of adolescent growth spurts.

Though I later posed standing beside leftover funeral wreaths and was photographed sitting in the same front row seat President George W. Bush used during the ceremony, our mission was centered on a different chief executive. The National Cathedral contains the

---

[8] See Figure 6.

body of Woodrow Wilson, the only president to remain in the capital city in death.[9] On his website, the Travelin-Tigers proprietor discussed the travails of locating Wilson's sarcophagus, which he and his son found only after inadvertently resting a coffee mug on top of it in the midst of their exasperated search. I had my concerns, but we picked up a map and guided ourselves to the 28th chief executive without difficulty. The Tigers must not have looked down at the floor, where a golden presidential seal marks the Wilson Bay.

The Gothic Revival church makes sense as the president's place of interment, and the Crusader cross carved into his sarcophagus is logical as well; he was the son of a minister. Yet Wilson didn't always adhere to the Golden Rule to do unto others as you would have them do unto you. Born in the Antebellum South, Wilson carried white supremacist beliefs with him to Princeton, where as university president he strove to bar Black people from campus. When he was in the White House years after, Wilson's administration applied Jim Crow segregation policies to the civil service system, and he declared that appointing an African American as an official in the South would be "a social blunder of the worst kind." At the time I stood at his grave, however, my knowledge of Wilson was limited to his role in World War I and – thanks to Judith St. George – that he "liked to do the jig step while singing silly ditties."

An inscription carved into the wall at the end of the president's marble box conveys that First Lady Edith Wilson is interred in a vault under the bay, though her relegation to a literal footnote is not indicative of her stature in American history. In fact, Mrs. Wilson became one of the most powerful presidential spouses after her husband's incapacitating stroke in 1919. She controlled who was allowed to meet with Woodrow and decided which memos required his attention. "I, myself, never made a single decision regarding the disposition of public affairs," the first lady wrote years later. "The only decision that was mine was what was important and what was not, and the very important decision of when to present matters to my husband." This

---

[9] Wilson was also the last president to live in Washington after his administration, until Barack Obama in 2017.

gatekeeping proved consequential for U.S. membership in the League of Nations, as the president's ignorance of its plight in Congress and inability to compromise with the opposition contributed to its demise in the Senate. An international partnership organization was one of President Wilson's Fourteen Points he asserted would lead to sustained peace in Europe in the aftermath of World War I. Ironically, his own country never joined up.

While we fared well at finding the Wilsons' graves, deaf-blind activist Helen Keller – another deceased cathedral resident – eluded us, as did the first couple's home on S Street NW. The Woodrow Wilson Service Area in Hamilton Township, New Jersey, appeared destined to be my lackluster consolation prize, but I made a fortuitous decision to withdraw my father's atlas from under the front passenger seat in the Dodge caravan during our return drive up I-95.

To pass the time, I thumbed through the book and circled the various communities across the country where the presidents were buried, all of which I already knew by heart, not yet six months since I started analyzing the Travelin-Tigers website. At some point my father remembered that we were going to pass through New Jersey, home state of Grover Cleveland, and asked Princeton's proximity to the highway. Not far at all it turned out, so we diverted to the Princeton Cemetery of Nassau Presbyterian Church.

The clock was ticking as sunset encroached on our mission, the first of many times it threatened to do so over the years. Failure to find Cleveland before dark would jeopardize my chances at having decent photos, but I was spared from such misfortune as I pulled the last remaining cemetery map from the metal box by the gate. Locating the president's monument turned out to be a breeze; it's head and shoulders above all others in its vicinity. First Lady Frances and daughter Ruth lie beneath unadorned headstones, whereas the only president to serve two non-consecutive terms is remembered with a boxy memorial topped with a bulbous ornamental urn.

Though the president's gravestone was barren that day, occasionally it is decorated with shell necklaces and leis left by native Hawaiians. In January 1893, at the tail end of Benjamin Harrison's presidency, white American capitalists backed by the U.S. minister and a contingent of Marines overthrew Hawaii's constitutional monarchy. The outgoing Harrison transmitted a treaty of annexation with the new provisional government to the Senate, but Cleveland withdrew the treaty once he took over. He described the deposition of Queen Lili'uokalani as "the lawless occupation of Honolulu under false pretexts by the United States forces" and "an act of war, committed [...] without authority of Congress." Unwilling to reinstall the Indigenous Lili'uokalani as monarch, the provisional government designated Hawaii as a republic until it was annexed anyway in 1898 during the McKinley administration. Over a century later, some islanders leave mementos to commemorate Cleveland's support for their sovereignty when they visit Princeton Cemetery.

My father and I first learned the bulk of that information in 2010, on our second trip to Princeton. A fellow graveyard guest educated us about what we first believed was non sequitur décor. Neither then nor during our first visit did we stand much of a chance of being confused by tributes lain at neighbor Aaron Burr's gravesite. Burr's plot bore no mementos in the years preceding Lin-Manuel Miranda's 2015 *Hamilton* musical. When I initially scoured the cemetery map for the Clevelands in 2004, Burr's name on the list of notable interments caught my eye, though – no Broadway needed.

There are multiple reasons why Aaron Burr's name has retained an air of notoriety through the centuries. Most infamously, he killed former Treasury Secretary Alexander Hamilton. The death was the result of a pistol duel that occurred on July 11, 1804, while Burr was vice president under Thomas Jefferson. It was evident that Burr was going to be replaced on the 1804 re-election ticket, owing to his disagreements with Jefferson, and he launched an unsuccessful gubernatorial bid in New York. During the run, Hamilton condemned Burr as "a dangerous man" at a private dinner party. A witness recalled the offending words in a letter which later found its way into the *New-York Evening Post*, and, eventually, into the hands of Burr himself. The prickly exchange that followed between Burr and Hamilton resulted in the former challenging his critic to a duel.

Hamilton had no designs of firing at Burr, at least during the initial bout. Leading up to their confrontation in Weehawken, New Jersey, he wrote of his intention "to *reserve* and *throw away* my first fire." His goal was to inspire Burr to "pause and reflect," at which point he likely hoped Burr would throw away his shot as well. Then the quarrelers could determine whether an additional round of dueling was necessary, or if they could verbally end their feud. Hamilton's bullet struck a tree limb twelve feet high and four feet to the side of where Burr stood. With his shot, the vice president aimed a smidge lower. His ammunition entered Hamilton's torso and damaged a rib and multiple organs. The projectile lodged in his spine, rendering him paralyzed. He expired the following afternoon in Manhattan.

The unrepentant Burr was indicted for murder in both New York and New Jersey, though neither charge stuck. He spent a large chunk of the remainder of 1804 in the South, where he avoided the harshest scrutiny. Upon his return to Washington in November he received a mixed reception that largely fell upon party lines — Hamilton's Federalists were angered and unsettled by his presence, while a number of officials from Burr's Democratic-Republican Party cozied up to him. He presided over the Senate as vice president until his term ended the following March.

Burr's status as second banana in the Executive Branch was of little importance to me at the time, but the bizarreness of a sitting VP fatally shooting someone was too much of a draw to ignore. His grave is a short walk from the Cleveland plot. One of the last surviving Founding Fathers, Burr was buried in 1836 near his father, who served as head of Princeton University when it was called the College of New Jersey. My head came about a foot shy of the top of his somewhat degraded white tombstone. The epitaph remained mostly legible, but a transcription on a plaque placed at the base by the Aaron Burr Association in 1995 made the reading easier. His service as vice president and colonel in the Continental Army during the American Revolution receive mention. His killing of Hamilton is tastefully omitted.

Just as Burr's duel marked the end of Hamilton's life, his gravesite punctuated the end of our tumultuous trip. I was glad to deboard the emotional rollercoaster, what with the trek being canceled and then salvaged at the eleventh hour. But I was simultaneously energized to continue my unconventional quest and grateful to have the best parents in history, who were making this journey possible.

Chapter Three
I ♥ NY Gravesites
~ August 2004 ~

Because my mother and sister were kept in Rhode Island by work and school, respectively, while my father and I went to Washington, fairness demanded that we still take a summer vacation that the whole family would join and enjoy. My parents selected New York, where we could all conduct some obligatory sightseeing, I'd cross some more graves off my list, and my animal-loving sister had ample opportunity to drool over the countless canines being walked on the streets.

Our first evening in town, my sister and I had our inaugural taste of stereotypical NYC tourism atop the Empire State Building, where from the 86th-floor observation deck we gazed at the millions of lights that set Midtown below aglow.[10] With the aid of coin-operated binoculars, I was able to *just* make out the Statue of Liberty off in the

---

[10] See Figure 7.

distance. From 86 stories high, Lady Liberty and the rest of the world seemed insignificant.

Up close and personal, Frédéric Bartholdi's copper creation was far more imposing. At noon the next day we were ferried over to Liberty Island, the first sight many immigrants had of the United States, including our own ancestors. The immense stature of the viridescent woman was evident as we crossed the harbor, but was best illustrated inside her pedestal, where exhibits included castings of her foot and face; Olivia's head fit comfortably inside a full-scale nostril![11] Security fallout from September 11th left the interior of the statue itself off limits, so the top of the base was as high as we were allowed. That limitation didn't put any damper on my perspective of the visit. Before we took the boat back to Manhattan Island, my father used our new camcorder to document as I alternated between narrating our experience and playing with the rubber torch replica I'd just been bought. My sister used her airtime to lament she was unable to pet a dog she saw hours earlier.

Even with the scope of my quest parochially confined to presidents, certain names were notable enough for me to deviate from the norm, like Aaron Burr two months prior. Add to that list of exceptions his duel opponent, Alexander Hamilton. Hamilton's contributions to the structuring of the United States during its early days as a republic are difficult to overstate. Along with James Madison and John Jay, in 1787 and 1788 he authored a series of essays which successfully advocated for the ratification of the Constitution – known today as The Federalist Papers. As the premier secretary of the Treasury under George Washington, he was the driving force behind the creation of the Bank of the United States. He also helped establish the fledgling country's line of credit by negotiating a deal in which the Federal Government consolidated the debt of individual states and assumed responsibility for its repayment. That same agreement resulted in the relocation of the nation's capital from New York to a federal district south. That area is none other than Washington, D.C. Hamilton was one of the most consequential Founding Fathers, and

---

[11] See Figure 8.

with his killer, Burr, already in my collection, it felt appropriate to complete the set.

Records show that Hamilton rented a pew at Trinity Church in Lower Manhattan, not far from where his office was when he became Treasury secretary in September 1789. Five of his eight children with wife Eliza Schuyler were baptized at Trinity. Upon the dying duelist's request in July 1804, Right Reverend Benjamin Moore – the rector of that Episcopal house of God – administered Holy Communion to him. And, two days after, Alexander the Late was buried in the south churchyard.

The monument subsequently placed atop his remains is a white marble box that rises up to form a pyramid, with four ceremonial urns positioned at its corners. Knowing myself, I presume my thoughts as we approached the Financial District were something along the lines of, "Did Hamilton leave instructions about the design of his grave, or did his family have to figure that out after he died?" I was 200 years too late to ask this information, and apparently too tardy to even get a decent photograph with his marble monument. It wasn't yet four o'clock by the time we arrived from Liberty Island, but the gate to Trinity, found at the intersection of Wall Street and Broadway, was already locked. Hamilton's memorial is situated beside the fence along Rector Street at least, so I got my picture with it, albeit with bars between us.[12] The grave portion of the trip was off to an unfortunate start.

The next day, it got worse.

New York has long been America's most populous metropolis, and though many presidents have resided there, only two have ever been laid to rest within its confines. Financially hampered in his post-White House years, James Monroe moved in with his daughter's family in Manhattan, where he died in 1831. Monroe's remains were kept in the New York City Marble Cemetery until they were exhumed and transported to his native Virginian soil in 1858. Then, in 1885, Ulysses S. Grant was entombed in a temporary vault in Riverside Park, uptown

---

[12] See Figure 9.

from the brownstone where he lived for four years. Before he succumbed to throat cancer, Grant listed New York as one of three potential places for his interment. The Riverside Park vault housed his remains until 1897, when construction finished on his gargantuan permanent repository. It is the largest mausoleum on the continent in terms of square footage. Officially named the General Grant National Memorial, it has been cared for by the National Park Service since 1959.

The question posed in the title of C-SPAN's presidential grave bible – *"Who's Buried in Grant's Tomb?"* – has a tricky answer. No one is *buried* in the building, but the eponymous POTUS and his first lady, Julia Dent, are entombed in its sublevel crypt. This riddle was popularized by Groucho Marx, game show host and legendary comedic actor. Yet there was nothing funny as my family stood upon the tomb's granite porch. A sign attached to the door ominously stated, "Photography prohibited inside of the memorial." My father taped with the video camera as I stood at the entryway, mouth agape.

Historically, Grant has not been characterized by scholars as a successful president. In the win column, he used federal troops and the newly-established Department of Justice to crush the terroristic Ku Klux Klan in the South. Black Americans made great strides early in Grant's first term, which ran from 1869 to 1873. The Fifteenth Amendment, ratified in 1870, proclaims, "[t]he right of citizens of the United States to vote shall not be denied or abridged by the United States or by any State on account of race, color, or previous condition of servitude." Also that year, Black men took seats in Congress for the first time: Hiram Rhodes Revels of Mississippi in the Senate, and Joseph Rainey of South Carolina in the House. But those political and civil rights gains receded as Reconstruction fizzled out during Grant's second term. After the country was hit with the economic Panic of 1873, support dropped among white northerners for financing protective measures for Blacks in the South. With the Federal Government willingly turning its back, it became much easier for aggrieved former Confederate officials to regain power and find new ways to oppress Black people. In Washington, meanwhile, Grant's administration was under fire for a series of scandals, though the president himself was not among the corrupt perpetrators.

That being said, it's of no surprise the components of his looming shrine lean heavily on his status as commanding general of the Union Army rather than his eight years as president. Inside, I craned my neck to look up at a mosaic mural of Grant shaking hands with Confederate General Robert E. Lee. Lee's surrender of the Army of Northern Virginia at Appomattox on April 9, 1865 meant U.S. victory in the Civil War was all but assured. The circular opening beneath the mural allowed me to peer into the crypt below, where matching dark red sarcophagi hold the remains of President and Mrs. Grant. They are encircled by bronze busts of five other Union generals: James B. McPherson, Edward Ord, Philip Sheridan, William Tecumseh Sherman, and George Henry Thomas.

I couldn't readily make out the busts from above, and it didn't appear I was going to get a chance to inspect them up close. Compounded with the photography embargo, I was dismayed to discover the staircase by the far wall leading to the crypt was blocked off. The park ranger my parents inquired with informed them these measures were instituted in response to the terrorist attacks three years back. My father attempted to entreat the NPS employee into letting us downstairs to take a picture, explaining that Grant was my tenth president grave and I just wanted to document my visit. The ranger stonewalled us (Civil War pun intended).

In a stroke of luck, he soon left for his break, at which point a sympathetic co-worker approached us. The second ranger was going to allow us to enter the crypt and take our photos, with the caveats that we be quick and refrain from using the flash feature. While my mom and sister kept watch with the ranger upstairs, my father and I advanced quietly through the blockade and down the marble steps into the chamber. My father snapped several photos of me in front of the sarcophagi, but the lack of lighting made everything indistinguishable. Even so, as men of our word, we adhered to the parameters of our compact and swiftly returned to the upper level.

When the replacement ranger asked how the pictures turned out, he received an honest answer. Without any additional convincing, he relented and permitted us to use the flash. There was urgency in his voice, and we spent little time downstairs the second go-around. Though I was largely bleached out, the sarcophagi and I were far more discernible than in the previous photos.[13] We rushed upstairs mere moments before the original, glowering ranger returned.

Just as Manhattan can claim only one dead president, it can boast only one presidential birth: Theodore Roosevelt, who was born on E 20th Street in 1858. The trustbuster spent many of his early years in the city, but also summered with his family 40 miles away in Oyster Bay, on Long Island. In his adulthood he had a home constructed in Oyster Bay called Sagamore Hill, Sagamore being the Algonquin term for "chieftain." It served as the Summer White House during his seven and a half years as president, and was where the "old lion" expired in 1919 at the age of 60. Roosevelt was laid to rest atop a knoll at the nearby Youngs Memorial Cemetery, where he took joy in listening to birds. Signage simplified our search for TR, whose 26 steps leading up to his resting place symbolize his position in the sequence of presidents. Like at Grant's Tomb, we encountered a hurdle, this time in the form of a tall fence.

The four of us briefly detoured to the neighboring bird sanctuary which carries Roosevelt's name. There, my mother was able to contact the cemetery caretaker to let us into the president's plot. Back at Youngs a short while later, we were approached by a gregarious man in a sleeveless Cancun shirt and a USS *Theodore Roosevelt* hat. The loquacious Nick LaBella, a former art teacher, was the superintendent and passionate about all things TR. Right away, Nick delved into vast details about the cemetery and its most noted resident. He pointed out the tombstone of the Roosevelt family nurse and waxed poetic about a quotation on a plaque at the presidential gravesite. Nick also revealed why later in life TR usually kept his left hand clenched or in his pocket: he was blind on that side and didn't want to react to something he couldn't see.

---

[13] See Figure 10.

As he began to tell how the Rough Rider was posthumously awarded the Medal of Honor for his actions during the Spanish-American War, Nick unlocked the gate to the shared stone of Theodore and Edith Roosevelt, the first lady. Before I posed for some pictures beside their memorial, Nick and I engaged in a friendly squabble over the semantics of who was the first president to ride in an automobile.[14] He maintained it was Roosevelt, whereas I was steadfast in my belief that his predecessor, William McKinley, held that title because he rode in an electric ambulance after he was shot in 1901. I conceded out of deference – and my father's prodding – though the potential historical inaccuracy gnawed at the stickler in me.

When I emerged from the plot, Nick re-locked the entrance and resumed demonstrating the breadth of his knowledge of Roosevelt and anything tangentially-related to the president. My father switched the video camera on and recorded as Nick glowingly showcased the rest of the cemetery: the grave of the chaplain who was with TR in Cuba during the war, local plants, and so on. With what little time Nick took to catch his breath between monologues, it took my family the better part of an hour to find an opening to depart for Sagamore Hill.

Nick may have been long-winded about TR, but as a relative newbie it was invigorating to meet someone who was as passionate about the presidents, or at least one of them, as myself. His position as cemetery superintendent was surely bringing him much joy in his retirement. It is befitting that when Nick passed away from a "sudden, massive heart attack" in September 2011 he died "doing the thing that he loved the most," according to one obituary: "talking to a group of people at the Theodore Roosevelt gravesite at Youngs Memorial Cemetery."

Nick's ardor for his favorite historical figure seemed rivaled possibly only by Roosevelt's love of nature, which is reflected in his house a mile and a half from Youngs. Though he was a conservationist who protected many species and millions of acres of land, TR was also a big game hunter who mounted the heads of his fallen prey on the walls of Sagamore Hill. Our guide educated us that if a mounted

---

[14] See Figure 11.

animal's mouth was closed, it was an herbivore, whereas an open mouth indicated a carnivorous diet. As for the creatures that were kept as pets at the hilltop home, she disclosed that there was a room that the Roosevelt children were forbidden from entering but the exotic animals had free rein in. The family might have been a tad eccentric.

In the North Room, I took interest in the president's cribbage board because I enjoyed playing the game with my grandparents. Unlike my grandparents' board, however, TR's was carved from a walrus tusk. It was fascinating to see the tusk and mounted animal heads, but it weighed on my conscience that the reason I was able to see them was because they were killed. When my family encountered a jolly Teddy impersonator outside later on, I elected not to confront him about my concerns.

The Roosevelt theme carried over to the following day, although the focus shifted to Theodore's fifth cousin and niece, Franklin and Eleanor.[15] Approximately two hours from Oyster Bay in Hyde Park, their Hudson River home originally belonged to FDR's parents. He was born there in 1882, lived there with Eleanor (and his mother) part-time as an adult, and was laid to rest in its rose garden in 1945, followed by the first lady in 1962. I'd spent all of my nine years living in one house, and based on my own emotions I couldn't blame the president for not wanting to leave the home where he grew up.

While our visit to the garden later on was going to be self-guided, our tour leader went into detail about the gravesite and remarked that, per request, the cuboid stone the president and Eleanor share was carved of white marble from Vermont. She surveyed the children on the tour to see if any of us knew who was buried by the sundial behind the monument, and she noted that my hand was raised before she even finished posing the question. The answer my sister and I correctly offered was Fala, the Roosevelts' beloved Scottish Terrier. Impressed, the guide relayed a melancholy story from the dog's post-White House life: after Eleanor returned to Hyde Park with Fala in 1945, whenever guests drove up toward the house, the Scottie took off down the road

____

[15] In addition to being husband and wife, Franklin and Eleanor were fifth cousins, once removed.

anticipating the return of FDR, but was always greeted instead by disappointment. Right in the heart strings.

The home itself was once "a sprawling farmhouse," and Franklin's father asked his wife on his deathbed to maintain Springwood as it looked during his lifetime. Although she adhered to the request for years, Sara Roosevelt's only child ultimately swayed her to renovate. In 1916, the farmhouse was enlarged to a Georgian Revival home with 35 rooms. One of the grander spaces is the dining room, where on the evening of November 8, 1932, FDR learned he had won the White House and defeated the incumbent president, Herbert Hoover. I was more taken by the small elevator down the hall, which contains one of the wheelchairs the New Dealer used after an illness – diagnosed as polio – stripped him of his ability to walk at age 39. In order to move from floor to floor under his own power, the president manually hoisted the elevator up and down by pulling on a rope. His upper-body strength undoubtedly surpassed ours, so we were stuck using the staircase to reach the second floor.

You would think that of all the areas upstairs we might have spent the most time lingering near the president's boyhood room or the bedchamber where he was born, but that distinction belonged to one of the mansion's nine bathrooms. Standing in the hall, the guide regaled us with a story of how Sara Roosevelt had Springwood's bathrooms remodeled prior to a visit from King George VI and Queen Consort Elizabeth of the United Kingdom in June 1939. It was the first time in history that a reigning British monarch visited America, and it was important to make a good impression: FDR wanted to strengthen diplomatic relations between the U.S. and the U.K. The Roosevelt matriarch did her part by improving the loos.

Sometime after the esteemed guests left, Sara received an over-priced bill from the plumber and realized he was taking advantage of either the Roosevelts' wealth or the royal visit. As a matter of principle, she refused to pay the sum. The plumber responded by removing the accoutrements. He planted a repossessed toilet in his front store window with a sign that read, "The king and queen of England sat here."

Given that Springwood was directly under Roosevelt family care until it was turned over to the National Park Service in 1945, the furniture is original, including the bed where Sara Roosevelt gave birth to the president. The continuous presence of Eleanor's domineering mother-in-law, coupled with her unfaithful husband's lifelong residency at Springwood, likely contributed to the emotional distance she felt between herself and the mansion. She "never felt at home" there, we were informed. Starting in the 1920s, she used a cottage named Val-Kill on the eastern section of the Hyde Park estate as a retreat. It was a space where Eleanor could formulate her policy recommendations and host foreign heads of state.

After Franklin died of a cerebral hemorrhage during his unprecedented fourth presidential term, Eleanor's public service continued. She served as a delegate to the United Nations and also as chairperson of the Presidential Commission on the Status of Women from its inception in 1961 until her passing in November of the subsequent year. Owing to a visceral fear of being buried alive, the former first lady requested that her veins be slit to verify her death.

Fortunately, Eleanor's nightmare-inducing insurance policy was nowhere on my mind as I sauntered from Springwood to her grave. As our family passed under the trellis in the southeast corner of the rose garden, my eyes fell upon the chiseled, marble marker. Two raised mounds parallel to the front of the stone indicate the exact burial locations of the president and first lady, whose full name, Anna Eleanor Roosevelt, is carved into the monument. The mound closer to the stone is decorated with a small U.S. flag for the 32nd chief executive. I scuffled clockwise along the rectangular, gravel path with my father, while my sister and mother walked in the opposite direction. I tried to call Olivia's attention to the sundial that marks the site of Fala's resting place, but yelling across the expanse was not met with a pleasant reaction from my father.

Once I was admonished and we regrouped, I showed my sister how the sundial stands beside the round stones for Fala and Chief (another Roosevelt pet), which are flush with the ground, out of view. A chain is strung around the perimeter of the inner garden, so Olivia had to be content with the upright sundial being 30 feet away in the background of her picture. Same went for me with Franklin and Eleanor.[16] Such compliance with gravesite barriers would not be standard procedure on future adventures.

The grounds of Springwood also house FDR's presidential library, which opened in 1941 as the first of the federally-operated presidential libraries. In times past, the papers from previous administrations were sometimes lost because there was no place to deposit them, so President Roosevelt established his library to preserve his presidential documents and private papers. Public opinion among patrons has been impacted almost solely by the museum exhibits, however — less than one percent of guests to presidential libraries utilize the archives.

Had I wanted to dig through Franklin and Eleanor's paperwork as a rising fourth grader, I probably would have been gently rejected by library staff. No matter — I was sated envisioning myself cruising with the president in his 1936 Ford Phaeton, which was outfitted with manual hand controls that allowed him to drive around the countryside in spite of his partial paralysis. A large photo reproduction behind the vehicle showed Roosevelt and Fala in the car, which my father mentioned as he videotaped the exhibit. My six-year-old sister interpreted this as her cue to drop down to the floor and start panting in imitation of the terrier. "And, of course, the Deion family is *so* proud of the dignity we have when Olivia is *acting* like Fala in the museum. It's a nice touch," our dad uttered, exasperated yet amused.

Composure and decorum were exercised for some of the more touching artifacts, like the pen Roosevelt used to sign the Servicemen's Readjustment Act of 1944 — aka the G.I. Bill. At their worst, historic museums can whitewash their subject's life story. At their best, they can show a diverse audience the ways, for better or for worse, that a person or group of people are relevant to their own experiences. My father's Uncle Raymond, who flew 38 combat missions over Europe as a B-24 ball turret gunner in the Second World War, was one of the millions of veterans who invoked the benefits of the G.I. Bill to further

---

[16] See Figure 12.

their education. Subsequent to his graduation from Boston University School of Law, he built an esteemed law practice, and with his guidance his firm later became the first in Rhode Island to bring in a female partner. Sometimes people underestimate the impact that Washington politicians have on their everyday lives. For my family, all notions of that were written off by a pen.

Chapter Four
Land of Lincoln
~ August 2004 ~

A remarkable thing about presidents is that, no matter how mediocre or controversial their administrations are, the towns they hail from don't hesitate to advertise their White House connection.

Take North Bend, Ohio, a small community 22 miles from Cincinnati. The village was once the home of William Henry Harrison, a Whig president who was lauded as a military hero for his 1811 victory over Tecumseh's Confederacy at the Battle of Tippecanoe.[17] Harrison made an infinitesimal impact on the presidency other than bringing into question the line of presidential ascension. He developed an apparent cold three weeks after his March 1841 inauguration, and soon after was diagnosed with pneumonia by the White House physician. The array of contemporary medical practices used to heal the new president failed. Harrison died on April 4th, exactly one month after

---

[17] Harrison's feat would be unlikely to earn him wide-spread accolades in the twenty-first century. The Battle of Tippecanoe in Indiana came after an unsuccessful attempt to coerce Shawnee leader Tecumseh to cede tribal lands. Tecumseh himself was absent from the skirmish; he was in the South recruiting allies for his fight to maintain sovereignty.

he was sworn in. That unprecedented vacancy was filled by Harrison's vice president, John Tyler, who was called "His Accidency" by critics who did not accept the legitimacy of his claim to office. The Twenty-Fifth Amendment to the Constitution, which stipulates the vice president be elevated to the office of president in the event of removal, death, or resignation, was not ratified until 1967.

Leaving the legacy of the shortest and most ineffectual presidency behind in Washington, Harrison was laid to rest on his property in North Bend. The family tomb is all that remains of the estate, but the Harrison-Symmes Memorial Foundation preserves and operates the memorial, probably so that President Harrison won't be overlooked more than he already is.

Before we even left to see Grant and the Roosevelts in New York, my father was already planning a Midwest trip, scheduled just three days after our return. It was to be our most ambitious trek to date: five presidents, five states, and just three full days. President-for-a-month Harrison was going to be the first domino to fall.

In his internet research, my dad observed that all the pictures he found of visitors to the Harrison Memorial indicated they were unable to access the inner brick repository where the president slumbers. Instead, many of them posed at the gated entrance to the room and photographed Harrison's vault through the iron bars. That wouldn't suffice for us. My father contacted the president of the Harrison-Symmes Memorial Foundation, Bev Meyers, who agreed to set aside time to meet us and grant us entry.

Our schedule was disrupted by a flight delay, but Mrs. Meyers was more than willing to push back our appointment. A few hours late, our drive from the airport in Cincinnati culminated when we crossed the Brower Road overpass and Harrison's limestone tomb burst into view. Its most distinguishing feature, the 60-foot obelisk, isn't original to the tomb, but rather a 1924 addition. It bears an engraved list of Harrison's posts (e.g., secretary of the Northwest Territory, delegate of the Northwest Territory to Congress, territorial governor of Indiana, U.S. representative, Ohio state representative, U.S. senator, minister to Colombia and, of course, U.S. president). Once parked, we passed through eagle-topped columns and climbed to the summit of a knoll named Mt. Nebo. Harrison favored that spot because of its proximity to the intersection of three states: Ohio, Indiana, and Kentucky, seen across the Ohio River.

The iron gate at the obelisk's base hung open, and from the antechamber my father peered through the inner fence into the tomb. Mrs. Meyers and her husband, Terry, arrived soon after and bestowed upon me the honor of unlocking the final entrance. It required several shoves for my scrawny, nine-year-old frame to generate enough force to push the doors open, but I finally succeeded and dropped down a step into the tomb. Just as I was in the Adams crypt, I found myself entranced as I ran my fingers over the gold-leaf tablet that covers the side-by-side slots of the president and his wife, Anna Symmes Harrison.[18] Mrs. Harrison's story is unique among post-Martha Washington first ladies in that she never set foot in the White House. She intended to journey from North Bend to the nation's capital once she recovered from an illness, but her husband's death interceded. Out of respect, Congress voted to bequeath the widow a one-time $25,000 payment and free postage for life.

Mrs. Meyers directed our attention to the marble-covered niche to the left of Anna Harrison, which belongs to one of her offspring with the president, John Scott. I knew that William Henry Harrison's grandson, Benjamin, was also a commander-in-chief and that his father signed the Declaration of Independence. What I *didn't* know until Mrs. Meyers told me was that his son, the second President Harrison's father, served two terms in the U.S. House of Representatives from 1853 to 1857. She used that gap in my Harrison family knowledge as an opportunity to enlighten me and my dad about John Scott Harrison's ghastly post-death fate. During his burial at North Bend's Congress Green Cemetery in May 1878, attendees discovered that a nearby grave had been disturbed. Its freshly-dead occupant, 23-year-old Augustus Devin, had been poached by resurrectionists. Resurrectionists stole bodies from graves and sold them to medical institutions, which were in need of cadavers to dissect and study. Harrison's mourners feared

---

[18] See Figure 13.

that the body snatchers sold Devin's carcass to the Ohio Medical School in Cincinnati.

During an investigation at the institution the next day, one of John Scott's good Samaritan sons used a crank to pull up a rope that led into a basement shaft. When he did so, he discovered the rope was tied around the neck of a nude corpse — but not Devin's. To his horror, it was his own father, John Scott Harrison! The son reclaimed Harrison's remains, which were briefly interred at Spring Grove Cemetery in Cincinnati until their final disposition next to his parents at the family tomb in North Bend. Devin's remains were recovered in Ann Arbor, Michigan. As much as I felt out of place in the twenty-first century, I was glad to live in a time without pervasive body-snatching.

The journey of John Scott Harrison's body seemed unusual, but he was far from the only Washington politician whose quest to rest in peace was interrupted. The second president on our itinerary that day, Zachary Taylor, was also disinterred, albeit under more legitimate circumstances. On Independence Day 1850, in the second year of his administration, the parched president returned from a ceremony at the Washington Monument construction site and consumed iced milk and cherries, which he topped off with a prodigious amount of water. Taylor took ill hours later, and on July 9th he became the second chief executive to die in office, following William Henry Harrison just nine years prior.

Although the consensus was Taylor died from a natural ailment such as cholera morbus or gastroenteritis, a theory eventually emerged that he was poisoned. The president opposed the Compromise of 1850, which, in part, proposed that states and territories choose for themselves whether or not to permit slavery under the principle of popular sovereignty. The Compromise passed after his death. Was it possible that he was poisoned for his opposition to the deal?

Retired University of Florida professor Clara Rising believed so. Her notion was tested in 1991, when she received the blessing of Taylor's descendants to have their ancestor exhumed from his mausoleum in Louisville, Kentucky. Samples such as fingernails and hair were taken from his body and examined for traces of arsenic, the only poison that stood a chance of being detected in a 141-year-old body, according to Rising. In the end, a forensic expert found no suspicious amounts of arsenic. Rising was resolute that another, undetectable poison was used to off Taylor, like cyanide or a deadly mushroom. Most other people were satisfied that Abraham Lincoln retained his title of America's first assassinated president.

1991 marked the third time Taylor was disinterred. The first occasion was in October 1850, when his body was removed from the Public Vault at Congressional Cemetery in D.C.[19] By then, the Senate had allocated funds to have President Taylor's corpse transported to Kentucky, as widowed former First Lady Margaret Taylor requested. On November 1st he was laid to rest on the 700-acre farm purchased by his father decades prior, within a vault embedded into a hill. The late president resided there for close to 76 years. In May 1926, he and Mrs. Taylor were moved – for what was thought to be the last time – to a neoclassical mausoleum of limestone, granite, and marble a few yards southeast.

Like the Harrison property in North Bend, the Louisville Taylor farm was partitioned long after the president's death. A large amount of the acreage is now occupied by a residential neighborhood. The family burial ground has changed as well: an act of Congress transformed it into the Zachary Taylor National Cemetery in 1928. Most of the graves that fill its green spaces are the short, white stones that typify military burial grounds, so my father and I had no difficulty finding the president's final resting place. From the entrance, I could already see the towering monument that commemorates his service in the U.S. Army.

Before he was president, Taylor was Old Rough and Ready, an oft-disheveled military officer who was willing to fight alongside the troops under his command and endure their hardships, no matter how

---

[19] Previously, that same Aquia Creek sandstone sepulcher had temporarily stored the mortal remains of William Henry Harrison, John Quincy Adams, and former Vice President John C. Calhoun. Taylor's five months within its walls overlapped with the extended stay of former First Lady Dolley Madison. Her body was kept there from July 1849 to February 1852.

high his rank. He was commissioned as a lieutenant in 1808 and was a brigadier general by the time President James K. Polk ordered him and his units to advance on the Rio Grande in January 1846. Texas had recently become the 28th U.S. state, and there was a dispute with the neighboring nation of Mexico as to where the border between the two countries lied. Polk latched onto the notion that it was the Rio Grande, which if true would provide the U.S. with more territory. It aligned with the president's vision that the U.S. would and should expand throughout the continent – a mantra newspaper editor John O'Sullivan termed "Manifest Destiny."

General Taylor and his troops were charged with maintaining the border at the Rio Grande. Efforts by Mexican forces to cross east over the river were to be considered an act of war. An April 25th attack upon two U.S. companies by Mexican cavalry kicked off the fighting. When word reached Washington, D.C. two weeks later, Polk asked legislators to declare war. It can be argued that was what he was hoping for – a way to wrestle more land from Mexico's hands. By the time Congress approved the war declaration, Taylor had already led his outmanned forces to victory at the battles of Palo Alto and Resaca de la Palma. These battles and others are carved into the plinth of his monument at the cemetery. At its top, a stony General Taylor stands in his army uniform, though that wasn't necessarily his usual military attire. The general was known to sometimes don farm clothes instead.

Narrating for the camcorder, I walked with care backwards from the monument down the walkway to the handsome 1926 mausoleum. An earlier visitor had lain flowers in front of the column-flanked doorway, which was sealed tight. My forlorn gaze pierced its glass panels and fell upon the twin sarcophagi. My father photographed me pressed against the doors, looking longingly at the forbidden interior.[20] Nobody with a key was there to let us in this time.

This wasn't our only missed opportunity in Louisville. Since Taylor is not among the most recognizable U.S. presidents, my father was more personally interested in another notable burial elsewhere in town: Kentucky Fried Chicken entrepreneur Colonel Harland Sanders.

---

[20] See Figure 14.

The idea must've just come to him on a whim, as he didn't conduct any advanced research and didn't know where Sanders was, except within the city limits. Thus I had the unique experience of witnessing my father wait in line to ask a bewildered KFC employee where Colonel Sanders was buried. That information evidently wasn't part of the teenager's training, so we were forced to forge ahead to Indiana.

Another repercussion of our delayed flight arose when we reached Indianapolis, by which time it was dusk – too late to visit Benjamin Harrison at Crown Hill Cemetery. Rather than retire for the evening, we ventured down 38th Street to the Indiana State Fair, the first such festival my father and I had ever gone to (Rhode Island does not hold a state fair). We got our money's worth at the funhouse, which I re-entered time and again even after I used up all my tickets, at the encouragement of the blatantly-inebriated attendant.

Friday morning was a more sobering affair. Rain trickled to the earth as we set off in search of Benjamin Harrison. Crown Hill prides itself as the third largest privately-operated cemetery in the nation, so it was in our best interest to request a map rather than try to find the Republican on our own.

Coincidently, it was August 20th – Harrison's birthday. To honor each deceased president, a wreath-laying ceremony on behalf of the sitting commander-in-chief is held at their gravesite for their respective birth dates.[21] This tradition started in 1967 during Lyndon Johnson's administration. Some festivities occur on the actual anniversaries, but an administrative employee informed us that Crown Hill had opted to hold the celebration the following day, a Saturday, instead. Officials likely figured they would see better attendance on the weekend. Sound logic – how many people were going to take a day off work to hang out with Ben Harrison?

---

[21] I'll use this as an opportunity to brag that, in July 2019, I participated in the ceremony for John Quincy Adams's 252nd birthday as an intern with the History and Visitors Program at the United First Parish Church. I read an excerpt from his 1845 essay "Society and Civilization" and joined the wreath-laying procession down to the crypt.

I would have, of course, had I been of employment age. Bummed to miss the wreath-laying, I was still eager to put another presidential notch on my belt. We thanked the office worker for the map and handout about the cemetery's history.

With the camcorder covered in a plastic sheet to protect it from the rain, my father videoed as I marched up the path to the 23rd president's grave, situated at the base of the cemetery's namesake hill. The monument is a sight different from the Harrison tomb in Ohio. It's a mere ten feet tall and six feet square, with a few carved embellishments wrapping around its rectangular body, which tapers to a slight pyramid at its head. In comparison, in North Bend, William Henry Harrison's exploits are chiseled so big they take up more than ten feet of real estate on his 60-foot obelisk. Of course, with that feature of the tomb being erected in the 1920s, William Henry had no say in that enlarged tribute to his career. Contrastingly, his grandson personally selected the smaller, unostentatious monument in Indianapolis himself. He had done so after his wife, First Lady Caroline Harrison, died in 1892 during his re-election campaign.

The first lady's headstone is third in a row of four inclined markers that sit in front of the monument. The one immediately to the left belongs to Ben, who joined her in 1901. Further left – first in line – is the stone for Mary Lord Dimmick, Caroline's niece and secretary. Mary wed her widower uncle in 1896 to the disapproval of his two children, Russell B. Harrison and Mary Harrison McKee, who were both slightly older than their father's new bride. Rather than suffer the indignity of watching their father's nuptials to their cousin, whom Mrs. McKee professed to *"thoroughly* despise," the pair removed their belongings from the family home. The former president, nicknamed "the human iceberg" for his social acumen, responded by disinheriting his offspring in his last will and testament. Remarkably, Russell is also buried in the family plot – fourth in line, beside his mother. His sister is interred in an adjoining lot. "Oh boy," my dad quipped, "that should be a fun eternity."

We wished Ben Harrison a happy 171st birthday and sallied forth to the next gravesite. Although I still had yet to officially incorporate vice presidents into my quest, it seemed foolish to skip over them if we were already at the cemetery they were interred in, and Crown Hill contains the remains of three VPs: Thomas Hendricks, Charles Fairbanks, and Thomas Marshall. We momentarily paid our respects to each of them before we moved to the outskirts of the grounds. I took my father's picture crouching next to the nondescript grave of John Dillinger in section 44, but I was uninterested in the notorious criminal and declined a reciprocal photograph. If Dillinger had the good sense to enter politics rather than rob banks, maybe I'd have felt differently.

From Indianapolis, it was a journey of over 200 miles to the most-anticipated grave of my endeavors thus far. To be sure we'd see the monument that day and not have to squeeze it in the following one, my father turned into a speed demon on the highway to Springfield, Illinois. "We drove like crazy to get here. I won't even say how fast I drove," he confessed to the camera once we reached Oak Ridge Cemetery. By that point, I'd already jumped out of the rental car and was practically floating ahead of it toward the tomb of Abraham Lincoln.

The rail-splitter is often considered the most venerable president, and that is reflected in his final resting place. The soaring 117-foot structure features an immense obelisk that serves as the backdrop for a twice life-size statue of the president. Bronze representations of military figures flank their commander-in-chief from four sides. A bas-relief of an eagle clutches a broken chain in its beak, symbolizing Lincoln's overly-mythologized role as "the Great Emancipator." Yes, his January 1863 executive order (the Emancipation Proclamation) provided the legal framework for freedom in rebellious states as the Union Army took back territory from its Confederate counterpart. And yes, as president he was the key government official in securing the Thirteenth Amendment's passage through Congress. But his contributions, though significant, were not the end-all-be-all of abolition. Chattel slavery's end was brought about in large part by Black people who escaped plantations and by the 215,000 African Americans who served in the Union's military during the Civil War.

But Lincoln's tomb was not intended to be an interpretive site that delves into the nuances of his views on race and the many parties that enabled abolition. Lincoln's tomb symbolizes his stature in the nation's collective memory and is the perfect embodiment of the narratives propagated about him as the Great Emancipator and martyr of the Union.

That was the version of Lincoln that nine-year-old me envisioned as he approached the tomb, bouncing with nervous excitement. I found the building's entranceway guarded by a large bronze Abe head designed by Gutzon Borglum, the sculptor who oversaw the creation of Mount Rushmore. The bust's nose has been rendered a dull gold by all the visiting hands that have rubbed it for good luck since its installation in the 1930s.[22] I sprung upward in my best attempt to do the same, but all I managed was to brush his chin.[23] Even though his broken arm was still in a brace, my father lifted me up so I was able to reach the metal proboscis.

Stepping into the tomb's rotunda, I had no trouble recognizing the next piece of art to greet us: sculptor Daniel Chester French's sitting Lincoln in miniature form. Being familiar with the 19-foot original at the Lincoln Memorial in D.C., I saw no reason to dawdle in the foyer. I'd waited long enough to meet America's greatest president. My dad and I set off down the right-hand side corridor and followed the archipelago of statuary that leads to the family crypt. Mary Lincoln – the complicated if not misunderstood first lady – and her three youngest children are interred inside the wall on the left, but my eyes locked on the elongated stone opposite them. It goes without saying who that was made for.

Though the Arkansas marble sarcophagus appears long enough to contain the 6'4" president's remains, it is purely ceremonial. Lincoln is hidden underneath the floor, safe in a vault of concrete and steel ten feet down. This delayed precautionary measure was taken in 1901 after

---

[22] One previous nose-rubber was Ronald Reagan, who visited Springfield in May 1980 while he was on the campaign trail.

[23] See Figure 15.

would-be thieves nearly absconded with his coffin a quarter century prior, on election night in 1876.

A velvet rope separated us from the reddish stone, and the dim lighting was burdensome for photography, but my father did what he could and I was beyond pleased. At the back of the room, the words reputedly uttered by Secretary of War Edwin M. Stanton after Lincoln's last breath are immortalized atop the wall: "Now he belongs to the ages."[24] The opulent tomb as a whole is enough of a statement on the 16th president's legacy, so the inscription on his barren sarcophagus is as simple as can be:

ABRAHAM LINCOLN

1809 – 1865

The tomb is the main attraction at Oak Ridge Cemetery, but it's not the sole Lincoln site on the grounds. When the president was assassinated at the start of his second term, he had voiced no thoughts on how or where he would like to be interred. Faced with a list of potential locations that included Chicago and Washington, Mrs. Lincoln chose Springfield since it had been her husband's home from 1837 to 1861. The National Lincoln Monument Association formed and set about collecting funds for a proper shrine. The organization selected a design in 1868.

In the meantime, Lincoln's embalmed body had to be kept somewhere. When he finally reached Oak Ridge Cemetery on May 4th after weeks of unprecedented pageantry, he was placed in a receiving vault at the bottom of the hill upon which the permanent tomb was subsequently built.[25] He was joined by his late son Willie, who died in the White House in 1862. For three years, eleven-year-old Willie was sheltered in a tomb owned by Supreme Court clerk William Thomas Carroll at Oak Hill Cemetery in Georgetown. At Mary Lincoln's direction, Willie was exhumed and accompanied his slain father on the winding 1,654-mile train route from Washington to Springfield. The pair was then transferred to a second temporary repository halfway up

---

[24] Some sources maintain that Secretary Stanton said Lincoln "belongs to the ages," while others claim he eulogized him as belonging "to the angels."
[25] See Figure 16.

the hillside on December 21st. Edward Lincoln, Abe and Mary's second child, was waiting for them there. Eddie died in 1850 at age three, likely of pulmonary tuberculosis. He was originally laid to rest at Springfield's Hutchinson Cemetery. According to an interpretive sign at Oak Ridge, he was disinterred a week before his father and the brother he never knew were moved. The three of them stayed in the second vault until 1871, at which point they were relocated inside the permanent tomb, which was still a work in progress. It took another three years to finish.

The first tomb survives. The second was dismantled, but its location is signified by a small tombstone-shaped marker. I took note of the appropriate tributes left upon it.

"Millions of pennies on it," I exclaimed quite hyperbolically.

"I don't know about millions," my dad chuckled, "but enough to tip the maid" at the hotel. "Okay, after I shut the camera, this stash is up."

I grasped one of the coins, intent on picking up those with the reverse side displayed and flipping them so that the obverse side with Lincoln's profile was featured instead.

"No!" my dad scolded, prompting my hand to recoil. "I said *after* I shut the camera. Bye, everybody!" He turned off the camcorder to cover our tracks.

Rest assured, he was joking. We left the pennies where they laid and my dad tipped housekeeping a couple of his own Lincoln five dollar bills when we checked out of our hotel the next morning. Our day started downtown outside Honest Abe's yet-to-be-dedicated presidential library, which was slated to open in April 2005 under the auspices of the state of Illinois rather than the National Archives. My picture was taken out front, and then with statues of the Lincoln family a block away. The figures stand across from the Old State Capitol State Historic Site, where Lincoln served as a state legislator from 1836 to 1842. In 1858, he stood in its halls as a U.S. Senate candidate and delivered his renowned House Divided Speech, in which he predicted the United States would either universally permit slavery or abolish it entirely.

The address occurred in the House chamber on the second floor, in which a bespectacled guide explained the room's layout to us. A stovepipe hat and shawl in the second row of desks marked where Lincoln sat as a representative, just feet away from where the docent said his body laid in state in 1865. My experiences during Ronald Reagan's ceremonies in Washington two months earlier rushed back to me as the docent clued us in. "In 24 hours, son," he proclaimed, "*75,000 people* walked through this room," and an additional 20,000 to 25,000 mourners were shut out.[26]

The Old State Capitol was disassembled and reconstructed in the mid-twentieth century to make it appear just as it did during Lincoln's lifetime, and his neighborhood half a mile away was renovated to achieve the same effect. Several buildings from the time period line the historic district's unpaved streets, including the only house Abe ever owned. He purchased it for $1,500 in 1844. He and Mary raised their family there until they left for Washington in February 1861.

Around 10:15, my father and I convened with other visitors on the sidewalk for a guided tour. The pigtailed park ranger delivered a brief introduction before she paraded us up the front steps. I was too excited to allow anyone else the privilege of being the first tourist to enter the home, and she directed me and all who followed into the parlor on the left. That's the room where the family entertained guests, and where Abraham Lincoln formally received the Republican Party's nomination for the presidency in 1860.

Outside, the ranger had informed us that the family sold most of its furniture when it said goodbye to Springfield, and that a majority of the items in the house were period pieces. She noted that many surviving furnishings original to the Lincolns are covered in black upholstery, including the sofas and chairs I spotted in the parlor. In a different downstairs room, the ranger pointed out an item that belonged to one of the Lincoln sons — a stereoscope, akin to the

---

[26] In February 2007, two and a half years after our visit, U.S. Senator Barack Obama drew a less lugubrious crowd at the site when he announced his candidacy for the presidency.

Batman View-Master I had back home, though one device's slides were less crime-fighting-focused than the other.

The second floor houses other effects, such as the president's desk and shaving mirror. Yet it was neither upstairs nor downstairs where I experienced my grandest thrill, but in between. Our group was advised to use the banister as we scaled the steep staircase, and I was overtaken with awe when the ranger remarked that it was the actual railing the Lincolns used. Mouth wide in astonishment, my hand clutched the rail for the entire climb so that there was no chance I'd miss where Lincoln's grip had been. Hands-on history, literally.

While the president did not personally select Springfield as his resting place, there's no doubt Mary Lincoln made the correct call. So much of his world was centered there, and as my hand touched the figurative shadow of Abraham Lincoln's hand, I couldn't help but feel in that moment that I was part of it. With the luxury of more time, it would've been nice to explore the numerous other Lincoln-related sites in Springfield. It was the last full day of our trip, however, and we still wanted to pay our respects to Herbert and Lou Hoover at the Hoover Presidential Library another 200 miles away.

Herbert Hoover was born in West Branch, Iowa, and although he left the state as an eleven-year-old, his upbringing there made an indelible impact on him. The museum exhibits discuss that early part of his life, including how he was orphaned by age nine – my own age, I shuddered to think! Other displays cover his career as an engineer and his humanitarian efforts across the world. A granite map spans the floor, highlighting the fifty-plus nations that he aided and fed over the decades as the head of non-profits, such as the American Relief Administration. Another room showcases flour sacks that were returned to Hoover by beneficiaries of his benevolence from Belgium. The Commission for Relief in Belgium that he founded in 1914 fed 9.5 million needy people from Belgium and Northern France. I was unaware of Hoover's magnanimous contributions around the globe, and of his role in standardization during his seven years as secretary of commerce between 1921 and 1928. According to one sign, Hoover "exhorted American industry to standardize products ranging from milk bottles and auto tires to kitchen plumbing and gas meters." He was even responsible for the homogenization of red and green lights for traffic signals!

These accomplishments were dimmed after the stock market crash of 1929 and the Great Depression. As president, Hoover didn't favor direct federal action, which hampered chances of economic recovery. "Nobody is actually starving," the Republican spuriously stated. Hoover clearly never met the unemployed Rhode Islanders my great-grandmother made sandwiches for in exchange for menial labor. Reality forced the president to reluctantly permit the establishment of the Reconstruction Finance Corporation, the purpose of which was "to shore up weak banks, railroads and insurance companies" via loans. That was as far as the POTUS was willing to compromise. "It is not the function of the government to relieve individuals of their responsibilities to their neighbors," he proclaimed, "or to relieve private institutions of their responsibilities to the public, or the local government to the states, or the responsibilities of state governments to the Federal Government." Hoover lost his re-election bid to Franklin Roosevelt by a margin of 413 electoral votes.

Before we ventured over to Hoover's burial site, my father and I browsed the museum gift shop, where he initiated two purchases. One was a small photo album with a presidential seal for me to hold my gravesite pictures in. The other was a copy of *Who's Buried in Grant's Tomb?*, the subject of the book talk that set my quest into motion eight months earlier, to the day. Why did we wait so long to pick it up?

As we exited the library, I scanned the brochure to see where Hoover's grave was located. I determined it was a short distance from where we were and wanted to walk, but my dad intimated that the map probably wasn't drawn to scale and ordered me into the car. I sported a smug expression when my mildly-embarrassed father pulled into the gravesite parking lot seconds later. It was just a few hundred feet away.

Once he ate crow, my father switched on the camcorder as we walked uphill to the stark white marble slabs that mark the graves of the president and his wife, Lou, who was as much of a humanitarian as her spouse.[27] She tended to injured individuals when she and Herbert were in China during the Boxer Rebellion in the late nineteenth century and founded the American Women's War Relief Fund during World War I. Mrs. Hoover preceded her husband in death by two decades and was buried in Palo Alto, California, the site of the couple's shared alma mater, Stanford University. Upon Herbert's passing in 1964, Lou was disinterred and brought to the hilltop there in West Branch.

The younger of the couple's sons, Allan, chose that sublime spot for their final resting place because it overlooks the two-room cottage where his father was born. The National Park Service says President Hoover romanticized the cottage as "physical proof of the unbounded opportunity of American life. In no other land could a boy from a country village, without inheritance or influential friends, look forward with unbounded hope." We snapped some pictures of the gravesite and rushed over to the birthplace, part of the Hoover National Historic Site. I entered just one minute before it was set to close for the day, though it was of no apparent bother to the ranger inside. On the left, she showed us the room in which Herbert was born and where he and his siblings slept with their parents. Jesse and Hulda Hoover slumbered in a bunk with a trundle bed beneath it that the president and his brother stayed in. They were joined by their younger sister when she outgrew her cradle.

Few presidents had beginnings as modest as the "Great Humanitarian" did. Heck, my bedroom back home wasn't much smaller than the whole Hoover house. It took two minutes to examine the dwelling in its entirety before we left through the back door.

---

[27] See Figure 17.

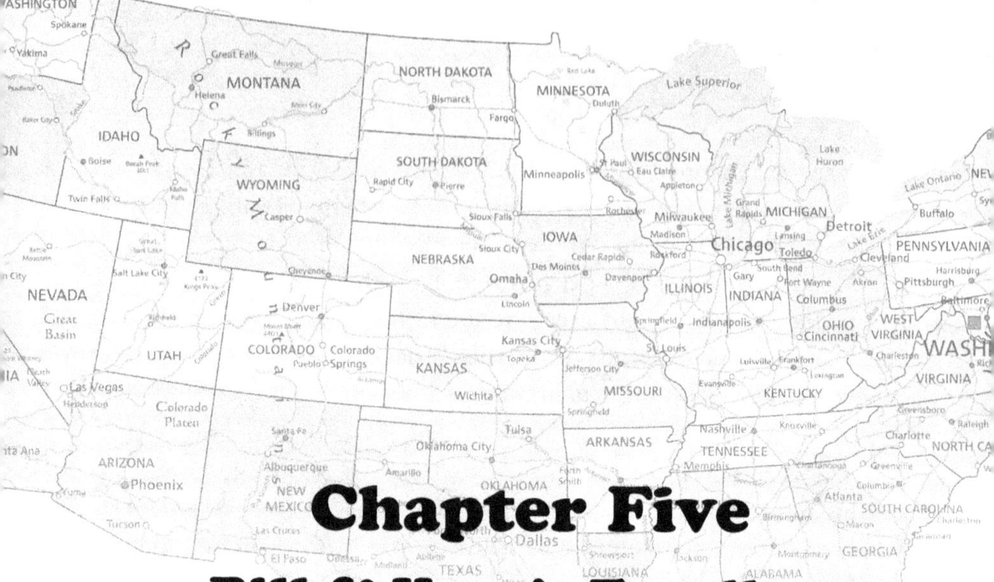

Chapter Five
Bill & Kurt's Excellent Adventure
~ April 2005 ~

Sitting at the kitchen table one day in late April 2005, my father perused the *Providence Journal* and read that former President Bill Clinton was set to deliver a lecture on foreign and domestic policy at Brown University later in the week. He would participate in a book signing at the campus bookstore beforehand. Later on, my parents, neither of whom voted for Clinton in 1992 or 1996, jointly presented to me the idea of attending the book signing and meeting him.

Recent history was not my forte, and my knowledge of the 42nd president was myopic. One of the few books I owned that mentioned Clinton was the presidential volume from Dorling Kindersley's youth-oriented *Eyewitness Books* series, published in association with the Smithsonian Institution. The book said that Clinton was accused of having an "inappropriate relationship" with Monica Lewinsky, a 21-year-old White House intern. Clinton originally lied about what happened, then later copped to a cover-up. I also read that Congress held a trial to decide if he should be removed from office, but acquitted him the following month. At ten years old, that was probably all I needed to know.

After my parents' presentation, I was reticent about my decision-making process and grappled with my moral compass. Honesty was very important to me, and Bill Clinton had lied. But I also had to be honest with myself – I really wanted to meet a living commander-in-chief. In the end, I decided not to get in my own way – I would go see the Comeback Kid.

Of course, an interaction with a former president was something my family wanted to document with a picture. Attendees, however, were forbidden from taking photos. Always determined to find a workaround, my father explored a few angles. Three years prior, he was featured in an article in the *Journal,* for which his picture was taken by a staff photographer. My father still had the shutterbug's contact information and reached out to him for help, but heard back that the paper's photographers could release pictures only if they appeared in print or on the *ProJo* website, which he was unable to promise. Other avenues turned into dead ends as well.

With all lifelines extinguished, my dad made an audacious decision: we'd attempt to sneak a disposable camera into the bookstore. Compact and plastic, it would probably escape Secret Service scrutiny. Since I was far more likely to be treated with kid gloves if caught than my 45-year-old father, I was tasked with smuggling the camera into the signing. As a typically circumspect child I was ambivalent about this course of action, but my urges to be an obedient son and get my coveted photograph won out.

On Thursday, April 28th, the eve of the event, my mother brought me to Providence Place Mall to pick out some formal attire for the occasion. While I tried on dress shirts and clip-on ties at an anchor store, my father bundled up heavily in preparation for a night camped outside the Brown Bookstore. The erstwhile president was scheduled to be at the shop for two hours, which would allow him to autograph an estimated 500 copies of his autobiography, *My Life.* With no idea how many people planned on attending the book signing, my father figured the best way to guarantee I got to meet former President Clinton was to wait in line overnight. He reached Thayer Street around eleven o'clock, over three hours after the first people arrived, but he was still among the first ten waiting.

The wind chill factor outside the bookstore simulated a temperature in the 30s, but I was snuggled up nice and toasty in my bed ten miles away. My parents wanted me to look my best when I met the former president, so I stayed fresh and rested at home. My mother had work early in the morning, but she and my father arranged that my grandmother would drop me off in Providence by 9:30, which was when the shop was set to open.

Gram and I had to wait until the school bus picked up my sister before we could depart the next day. We were cut loose at 8:50 – ten minutes after the bus typically arrived – which was inauspicious because the doors to the Brown Bookstore were unlocked early. When people started being ushered inside, my father had no choice but to step aside and wait for me at the entrance. "I'm slipping quickly," he bemoaned to a journalist from the *ProJo*. By the time I arrived on Thayer Street, around 80 people had passed him by. I bounded out of the vehicle toward my dad, who lifted me over the barricade and reintegrated into the line.

As we entered the building, my accomplice swiftly handed off the disposable camera, which I jammed into my pants pocket. We immediately came upon the station at which to purchase Clinton's autobiography, and with our print of *My Life* in tow we pressed on to the security checkpoint. Before I was wanded, a Secret Service agent inquired if I had anything in my pockets. As I mulled over the ethics of sneaking in the camera, I swiveled my head to look at my father for guidance. He anticipated my move and turned away to maintain a semblance of plausible deniability. It was a tacit indicator of what my response should be. I whirled back around to the Secret Service agent and replied, "No." Miraculously, this poorly-orchestrated exchange aroused no suspicion. The plastic device wasn't detected by the wand, and we were permitted to ascend upstairs. We resumed our wait in a line that snaked between bookshelves.

The event was not supposed to start until 10:30, so to help pass the time I brought along two items: my *Eyewitness Books* hardcover on presidents, and the photo album I got from the Hoover Library the previous year, in which I'd inserted images of my presidential gravesite adventures. Two pictures of Franklin Pierce's granite monument were the most recent additions – we trekked through the snow in Concord, New Hampshire, to visit him and his family in February.

Reading the book and reminiscing with the album occupied me during the next hour-plus, although even something as benign as that wasn't without drama. On multiple occasions, event workers approached us and attempted to confiscate my book. Each remarked snippily that former President Clinton was signing *only* his autobiography, and, every time, my father explained that I was not going to ask Mr. Clinton to sign the book – I simply wanted to alleviate the boredom. After a third employee tried to relieve me of it, I was almost convinced it was illegal to read in a bookstore.

I was thankful to have maintained possession of my book, because the signing was delayed beyond the planned 10:30 start time. Apart from the *Providence Journal,* we were interviewed by the *Brown Daily Herald* and *Brown Alumni Magazine,* which helped to break up the monotony.

An interminable time later, applause enveloped the store. Although my vision was blocked by the tall shelving, I knew Bill Clinton had arrived.

As the clapping halted, the line began to move. Slowly but surely, the scores of people ahead of us advanced, one at a time. When we emerged past one set of shelves, former President Clinton entered into our view. He was ensconced at a table stockpiled with *My Life,* and a man next to Clinton presented him with uniformly open copies that he affixed his signature to. My father commented on the fact that the 6'2" Arkansan was standing as he autographed the books, whereas most people sat at such lengthy events, and speculated that he symbolically didn't want anyone above him. Around this time, my father also asked me for the disposable camera, which upon the transfer he discreetly slid into his jeans' rear pocket.

Moments later it was our turn in the spotlight. My father introduced me to Mr. Clinton as a ten-year-old who had visited the burial sites of 18 of his presidential predecessors. I was mortified, as this essentially told the former president that we were going to travel to his grave someday in the future. But Clinton looked at me and exclaimed, "That's amazing, Kurt!"

One of my father's hands pushed into my back as he steered me forward, surreptitiously using his other hand to remove the disposable camera from his back pocket as he did. I was positive that he was going to be gunned down or tased by the Secret Service detail, but the agents were either incisive enough to recognize the Kodak wasn't a weapon or were positioned at an angle that they couldn't see his actions at all. When my dad then asked the former president if it'd be okay for me to pose for a picture with him, he enthusiastically agreed! Bill Clinton placed his left hand on our copy of *My Life* and his right on my shoulder as my father prepared to take the forbidden photograph. I'd heard numerous people comment that Bill Clinton's rapt attention and charisma could make you feel like you were the only person in the room with him, and I was now able to attest to that.

The button on the camera was depressed, the picture was snapped, and the film was wound.[28] Despite the odds, my father and I had circumvented the obstacles and come out on top. We grabbed the autographed autobiography, thanked its author, and prepared to leave when he lobbed us a most satisfying question:

"Kurt, would you like me to sign your other book for ya?"

After we had *thrice* staved off attempts to take my *Eyewitness* presidents book by people who wanted to ensure he wouldn't be asked to sign it, Bill Clinton, pen at the ready, offered to do so without prompting.

We returned and I handed Clinton the hardcover, which was bookmarked at his section because I had read it in line. As the former president signed and dated one of the pages of the book staffers insisted he *would not* autograph, my father announced he was going to take an insurance shot in case the first picture didn't turn out well.[29]

---

[28] See Figure 18.

[29] In private later, my father observed that the former president didn't sign the page with the subheading "Clinton Confesses."

When he heard this, Clinton, a consummate professional, raised his head to mug for the camera. The two of us left for good after that. We exited by the press area, where one of the reporters who interviewed us earlier gave me two thumbs up.

After I checked into school tardy, still sporting my dress clothes, I hit an inside-the-parker in kickball – my second home run of the day.

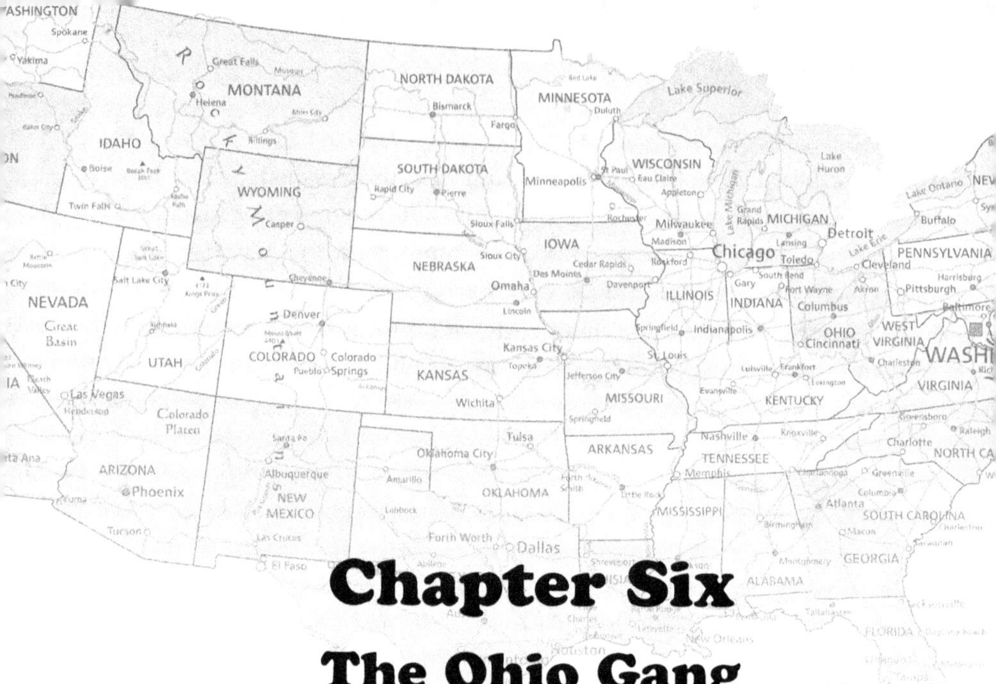

Chapter Six
The Ohio Gang
~ June 2005 ~

❝How many kids have skipped their last day of elementary school to visit Millard Fillmore's gravesite?" I contemplated as my father pulled our rental car through the crown-topped gate of Buffalo's Forest Lawn Cemetery. "There can't be many of us, right?"

It was Friday, June 17th, and while my fellow fifth graders were saying their fond farewells to one another before the crossover to middle school, I was in New York hunting the final resting place of a man none of them had ever heard of, odds are. It was just as well, because I probably wasn't missed all too much. My knowledge of people such as Fillmore hadn't made me the most popular student at either of the two elementary schools I'd attended. Many of my sensibilities and interests had already put me on a divergent path from a lot of my classmates even before I started visiting dead people in fourth grade. This recent quest sure didn't do anything to change that. Say what you want about Millard Fillmore, but at least he couldn't bully me – if there was a mean bone in his body, it was buried under six feet of dirt with the rest of him.

That being said, no one would confuse Fillmore with a great president. After John F. Kennedy was assassinated, Lyndon Johnson urged Congress to pass civil rights legislation in tribute to his late predecessor, who he said had fought so long for it. When Fillmore took over from illness-stricken Zachary Taylor, he fired his entire cabinet within two weeks' time and approved the Compromise of 1850, which Taylor had bristled at. Fillmore's intent was to give both pro-slavery and anti-slavery factions wins to prevent additional sectional feuding. For example, slavery proponents received an updated Fugitive Slave Act, which required that formerly-enslaved escapees be returned to their masters, even if they were found in a free state. Meanwhile, the slave trade was barred in Washington, D.C., which thrilled abolitionists and roiled slavery proponents. The compromise's endorsement of popular sovereignty – the doctrine that enabled a new state to decide for itself whether or not the "peculiar institution" of enslavement would be legal within its borders – eventually resulted in violence between warring factions at the border of Missouri and Kansas Territory after Fillmore left office. Not only did the president and Congress appease white enslavers at the expense of the Black population with the Fugitive Slave Act, but the Compromise of 1850 in its totality deepened the fissures that split the nation in two a decade later. Fillmore achieved the opposite of what he wanted.

The stances held by the 12th and 13th presidents on the Compromise are profoundly ironic. Taylor, a southern slaveholder, opposed the deal because he was adamant California's admission into the Union should not be contingent on the passage of other pro-slavery measures. Fillmore, who eagerly signed the five bills the deal was broken up into, was from Western New York, which was a hotbed of anti-slavery activity in his day. In fact, Fillmore proved to be more than many Whigs bargained for. In June 1852, the incumbent president finished second in the delegate count at the party's nominating convention, falling to General Winfield Scott. He spent the last nine months of his White House tenure as a lame duck. Despite his divisiveness within the crumbling Whig Party, Fillmore remained popular in Buffalo until his death, owing to his local philanthropic endeavors.

Our three-hour trek from the Cleveland airport to rainy Buffalo was eased by GPS, a godsend that unexpectedly came with our rental car.[30] My father and I had flown from Rhode Island to Cleveland since the majority of our trip itinerary was set in the Buckeye State, but we decided to get Fillmore out of the way first, before my four remaining Ohioan presidents. The GPS was useful for navigating streets, but we still required help from the Forest Lawn Cemetery office to locate President Fillmore. Once equipped with a map, we wound our way toward his plot. Beside Section 9, my father brought the vehicle to a halt when he spotted a hawk perched upon a gravestone. With the digital camera in hand, he climbed out of the vehicle and crept toward the bird of prey. He snapped one picture, but wanted to see how close he could get before the hawk flew away. He inched nearer and took another picture, then nearer and took another. And then he heard a loud slam.

I jumped out of the car to get a good look at the hawk myself, but shut the door too aggressively. The creature couldn't get away quick enough, much to my father's chagrin. Perturbed, he slumped back into his seat and drove us deeper into the cemetery. Nearly two decades later, my father still won't let me live down this blunder.

Atop a hill in Section F we recognized the pink obelisk in the Fillmore plot. The former president was buried there in 1874, and Caroline, his second wife, was laid to rest at his side seven years later. Their small headstones were slightly obscured by shrubbery, so I held the branches back when my father captured my photo.[31] The marker for First Lady Abigail Powers Fillmore, the president's first spouse, is set apart, away from the brush. She passed away a mere 26 days after vacating the White House in March 1853, having become ill after attending Franklin Pierce's inaugural festivities.

Despite his modern-day obscurity, Millard Fillmore is one of the most notable residents of Forest Lawn, and yet his grave is outdone by many of his deceased neighbors. Many prominent Buffalonians chose the 269-acre park as their final resting place, and

---

[30] From then on GPS became a necessary staple in our travels. Finding more obscure sites like the statue of Ronald Reagan eating an invisible potato pancake would have been a herculean task with a regular road map.

[31] See Figure 19.

a good number of their graves are adorned with ornate monuments and sculptures. One such tomb took my breath away and assumed the rank of my number one favorite visited grave.

John and Elizabeth Blocher were a wealthy couple whose son, Nelson, was romantically inclined toward the family's young maid. There are multiple explanations for what transpired afterward, but one of the more popular versions goes as follows: Upset that their offspring was in love with someone they deemed beneath his station, Mr. and Mrs. Blocher sent Nelson to Europe in 1881. When their son returned the following year, he was heartbroken to find that his beloved was dismissed from her job and gone. His searches for her bore no fruit, and his physical and mental health declined until his death in January 1884.

Devastated, the Gilded Age parents constructed a powerful memorial for their son at Forest Lawn. John Blocher designed the tomb, which contains life-size marble representations of his family. Snow white statues of the grieving couple preside over Nelson, who reclines on a couch in the center of the glassed-in structure. The details are intricate and meaningful; Elizabeth Blocher clutches flowers while her moribund son grasps a bible, the only item left behind by the maid. An angel, whose appearance is rumored to be based on his lost love, hovers above Nelson. I read on a plaque that the deathbed scene, which covers the family crypt, is imaginative, but it symbolizes the sorrow the Blochers felt.

We spent the night at a hotel down the street from the cemetery, and our first stop Saturday was diagonally across Delaware Avenue: the Theodore Roosevelt Inaugural National Historic Site, which in 1901 was the home of TR's friend, Ansley Wilcox. On September 6th of that year, President William McKinley was in Buffalo shaking hands with patrons of the Pan-American Exposition, a six-month fair that promoted international relations and technological innovation. He was shot in the abdomen by Leon Czolgosz, an anarchist who believed the president was too powerful. Vice President Roosevelt stayed at Wilcox's house for a few days while McKinley recuperated. Roosevelt left when McKinley's health was on the upswing, but the commander-in-chief's fortune changed and TR sped back to Buffalo. McKinley died while his VP was en route. Thirteen hours later, a mournful Theodore Roosevelt took the presidential oath of office in the Wilcox home.

Roosevelt was vacationing in the Adirondack Mountains when he received word about McKinley's worsening condition, so he lacked attire befitting a swearing-in ceremony. He borrowed clothing for the occasion, and in its galleries the Wilcox house was displaying the frock coat he wore that day. The coat was scant paces away from the main attraction – the library. Within its confines, 42-year-old Roosevelt was sworn in as the youngest president in U.S. history. A narrow table near the bay window approximates the spot where TR stood during the affair. The room was poorly lit (a recurring theme at these historic sites and tombs, I was learning), and my father struggled to take halfway decent photos. If there was anyone who could have discerned my location in the dark pictures it probably would have been Nick from Youngs Memorial Cemetery, who I imagined would be envious.

A brief foray into Niagara Falls, Ontario, set us back on our return to Ohio. The drive to Canton was over 250 miles, and by the time we arrived we were exhausted and ravenous. My dad and I weren't fully aware of how tired we were until we sat down to dinner around midnight. Sophomoric jokes were not generally my cup of tea, but the flatulent noises that emanated from our ketchup bottle had both of us keeled over in our booth. Victimized by sleep deprivation, we lost all composure when we saw a family at another table staring at us as if we each had three heads.

We recovered enough by the time we left to take a late-night swing by President McKinley's tomb, which was an apposite end for the day considering where we started it. I knew we wouldn't be able to go inside, but I yearned to see a presidential grave at night. A locked gate separated us from the mausoleum by about the length of three football fields – an appropriate measurement approximation to use in Canton, the birthplace of professional football. Yet it was still thrilling to see the tomb illuminated against the darkened sky. Its rounded features and hilltop placement made it resemble an observatory with its starry backdrop.

In the daylight the next morning I was finally allowed to climb the 108 steps up to the gravesite.[32] As I reverently ascended past a bronze rendering of McKinley, a man wearing black gym shorts ran up the stairs for exercise on the statue's other side. "Now we might be able to get ten grand on *America's Funniest Home Videos* if this guy goes to the top and falls," my father joked as he taped from a distance. "Oh, oh darn it, there goes ten grand," he griped when the jogger reached the summit, whisking away our potential prize money. "Coulda paid for this trip and the next one. And the next one after that."

Unlike the Lincoln Tomb, where the crypt is situated in a back room, we found the conjoined sarcophagi of William and Ida Saxton McKinley front and center when we passed through the two pairs of double doors. The green granite base sports a pair of lion heads on two sides, just one of the many flourishes throughout the tomb, designed by Harold Van Buren Magonigle. A golden elevator door bears the presidential seal, and a quote transposed from McKinley's address the day before his shooting wraps around the room. "Let us ever remember," it reads, "that our interest is in concord not conflict and that our real eminence rests in the victories of peace not those of war."

Twenty-one wreaths from a host of organizations lined the parapet that surrounds the president and first lady. As we walked around to read the dedications on each floral arrangement, my father and I came across inscriptions for their two daughters. Three-year-old Katherine was interred in the wall with her younger sister, named Ida after their mother, who didn't make it to even five months. They passed away in the 1870s, but were exhumed from West Lawn Cemetery and placed near their parents when the tomb was completed in 1907.

The mausoleum evokes mournful feelings, but the neighboring presidential library strikes a different chord altogether. While the three libraries I previously toured are part of the NARA system, the William

---

[32] See Figure 20.

McKinley Presidential Library and Museum is operated by the Stark County Historical Society and differs vastly in tone and substance. Many of the exhibits have no correlation to the 25th president, like a planetarium and a dinosaur display. The private nonprofit historical society has created an eclectic local history and science center in the same building that preserves the world's largest collection of McKinley artifacts.

My father and I zeroed in on the room with the McKinley relics on display, but found it challenging to concentrate on anything other than the animatronic representations of him and the first lady. Ida McKinley was seated in a chair, with the president standing at her side. Like the real William McKinley, this stand-in wore his signature red carnation in his lapel. The robots moved slightly, but were almost as stiff as their dialogue. "The boys in blue were able to stop Bobby Lee's invasion of Maryland that day and preserve the Union," Mrs. McKinley explained awkwardly in reference to her husband's Civil War exploits.

Cringe.

Automaton William then announced the time had come to address visitors from Illinois who were gathered on their lawn. The missus delivered a heavily expositional talk about the benefits of William's front porch campaign, and how it allowed large numbers of people to visit "our friendly town."

My dad and I took android Ida's words to heart and explored more of Canton. We toured the Pro Football Hall of Fame, where my dad received a mug and free admission on account of it being Father's Day. When we entered a gallery where visitors could select highlights of Super Bowls to watch, I tauntingly pressed the buttons for each championship my dad's Vikings lost. Minnesota was winless in all four of its contests, whereas I was still basking in the New England Patriots' third victory from February. It was a bit out of character for me, and maybe it wasn't the best Father's Day gift I could have thought of, but I was trying to function on very little sleep.

More enlightened about the McKinley family and Los Angeles Rams star Crazylegs Hirsch, we departed Canton and headed west toward Fremont. At the motel in the evening my father and I inexplicably chose to put off a good night's sleep for a round of mini golf. I was unsure exactly how long past midnight it was, but the employee who came out to collect the clubs was certainly surprised to see them in use.

A golf prelude might have been more appropriate for an avid devotee like Dwight Eisenhower, but that was our introduction to the hometown of Rutherford B. Hayes. The 19th president lies buried on the grounds of his home, Spiegel Grove, which was built by his uncle, Sardis Birchard. Hayes inherited the estate and lived there with his wife, known as "Lemonade Lucy." Mrs. Hayes received the moniker for her opposition to alcohol consumption, though, against popular belief, it was the president who banned the substance from the Executive Mansion.

Mrs. Hayes died at Spiegel Grove in 1889, and her husband followed in 1893. We saw the chamber in which they passed away and a nine-foot portrait of the president in the main drawing room, both of which my father would have taken pictures of if photography were allowed inside. Thankfully, we were permitted to snap as many photos as we wanted at the gravesite. Rutherford and Lucy were disinterred from their original graves in the local cemetery in 1915 and returned to Spiegel Grove. The couple's granite monument, mined from the president's ancestral farm in Dummerston, Vermont, was placed at a spot on the estate where they used to relax and reflect about current events.

As I tried to relay some of these facts on tape, I was drowned out by the chattering of rambunctious squirrels. One descended from the tree overhead and planted itself beside the gravestone, holding its ground when my father stepped closer to record it. "This is our last presidential tour," he predicted, "as we get within four feet to get the cute squirrel and it's probably rabid." In vain I attempted to resume my comments, but the rodent's companion snuck over to him and my dad stopped me so we could watch the action unfold. The critter cleared a path through the greenery and pounced on its comrade, who squealed and ran off. The other squirrel pursued him up another tree, where they continued to make a racket that drowned out my history talk. I surmised these furry friends had no interest in learning about the electoral commission that put Hayes in the White House.

The trees where the squirrels pranced are an integral part of Spiegel Grove. The home's name is derived from the rainwater that pools beneath them which act like spiegels, the German word for mirrors. They also draw affection from literal tree huggers. Tradition holds that visitors either touch or wrap their arms around the giants that grace the grounds, and the more notable embraces have been commemorated with affixed markers. I was unlikely to join Grover Cleveland and William McKinley in receiving a plaque, but I offered a hug all the same.

Like McKinley, Hayes was a Civil War veteran, though RBH's service was more painful – he was wounded five times! A bullet wound sustained at the Battle of South Mountain in September 1862 put the Ohioan at risk for having his arm amputated, but such surgery didn't come to fruition. The bullet-torn coat he wore is on display at the Hayes Library, which opened next to the mansion in 1916. It was the first presidential library, but, like McKinley's museum, it has never been retroactively incorporated into the federal NARA system.

Since 1928, the estate has maintained a set of original White House gates, which we exited through as we backtracked toward Cleveland, our base of operations for the rest of the trip.[33] The vacation was planned to coincide with the Boston Red Sox's road series against the Indians and we returned in time to see Boston's 10-9 victory.

It was exciting to see the reigning World Series champions and watch my then-favorite player, Johnny Damon, swat a home run, but that couldn't measure up to what I beheld the next day. Less than a week after I declared the angelic Blocher monument to be my favorite gravesite, it was already knocked from the top billing. How could it compare to the James A. Garfield Monument? The 180-foot mass of Berea sandstone is the most elaborate grave in Cleveland's Lake View Cemetery, replete with gargoyles and life-size terracotta panels that de-

---

[33] See Figure 21.

pict key points in the president's life, such as his work as a teacher and his 1881 inauguration. At the time, the exterior stones were coated with dark residue from Cleveland's steel mills, which gave the gothic memorial an even more ominous appearance. It has since been cleaned.

I removed my baseball cap as I stepped into the castle-like structure's receiving area and through to the resplendent Memorial Hall. In the center of the rotunda an Italian marble statue of Garfield stands on a dais, illuminated by a chandelier dangling from above. Surrounding the nearly eight-foot statue are a myriad of mosaics and stained glass windows that overload the senses. As I gazed up at the golden dome, I spotted a railing indicative of another floor. Sure enough, my father and I located a staircase and ascended. At the top, we emerged onto a balcony and soaked in the spectacular view of the Cleveland skyline. The vantage point from the third floor must be even better, but access to that stairwell was cut off.

While climbing higher was verboten, we could go lower. We headed back down to the main floor and toward the front of the tomb. A mural there shows disturbed office-seeker Charles Guiteau brandishing the bulldog pistol that he used to fire into the president's back at a D.C. train station (a perplexing choice, awarding the assassin a commemorative place in the mausoleum). Beneath the artwork, a spiral staircase leads down to the crypt where Guiteau's handiwork is on full display. Well, technically infection caused by poor medical practices doomed the 20th president, but Guiteau made all that possible. Doctors wouldn't have had the opportunity to stick their unclean fingers into the president's gunshot wound without there first being a gunman.

Unlike all other dead U.S. presidents, Garfield is neither buried nor entombed in a sarcophagus or vault. When the memorial was completed in 1890, his casket was placed on a white marble catafalque in the crypt. That's what we saw when we entered the dark chamber. His flag-draped casket lies side-by-side with that of First Lady Lucretia Rudolph Garfield, who joined him in 1918. Urns containing the ashes of daughter Mollie and her husband sit upon a wooden table at the heads of the biers. An encircling gate hindered our photographic pursuits, and we asked the gray-haired docent upstairs to unlock the inner crypt. He took a hefty key ring down into the cellar with him.

From pictures I'd seen on the internet, it didn't seem that many visitors requested to saddle up next to Garfield's casket. I turned out to be right. The docent informed us that, as far as he knew, the only other visitors who asked to enter in the preceding 50 years were C-SPAN staffers. Perhaps he meant to say 15, but both my dad and I would swear under oath that he said 50. Either way, the rarity of our request became clearer after numerous failed attempts to find the right key. I grinned nervously at the video camera as the docent tried one after another, until he ran out. "I gotta go up; there's one more set of keys," he said as he retreated to the main level.

The man returned with a ring that he knew held the correct key, but it wouldn't unlock properly. He proclaimed that it was "very delicate with the moisture down here," as he seemingly suggested that we steel ourselves for the possibility that we would not be able to enter. "I've opened it before," he muttered in frustration. My father proved to be an adroit cheerleader, though, and he cajoled the keymaster to keep trying. Eventually the lock clicked and we were let in.[34] "We appreciate your perseverance, that's for sure," my dad expressed.

We finished Tuesday with another BoSox victory, and then the pattern repeated the next day: another Boston win, preceded by another locked presidential tomb. Warren G. Harding, victor of the first national election after non-intersectional women's suffrage (aka white women's suffrage) was won, is interred in an open-air memorial of Georgia marble in his hometown of Marion. The circular design forms a courtyard where the Republican and his wife rest beneath granite slabs, which most visitors view from behind a gate – yet another recurring theme among presidential sites. The entryway is generally locked to deter vandals, but, as he did with the Harrison Memorial the previous August, my father reached out in advance to get the tomb opened up. Melinda Gilpin, the historic site manager of the Harding

---

[34] See Figure 22.

Home State Memorial at the time, was unlocking the gate just as we walked up.[35]

"Looks like it doesn't get opened too often, huh?" my father bantered. Ms. Gilpin laughed. "Not too often." After introductions, the adults continued to chat as I walked to the back wall to read the inscriptions for the president and First Lady Florence Harding. Bold and assertive, Mrs. Harding was shrewd in all regards with the press. When Mr. Harding was the publisher of the *Marion Daily Star*, she ran the paper's Circulation Department and made innovations that helped enhance its sales. She was also an astute surrogate on her husband's presidential campaign in 1920, mingling with the Fourth Estate to a degree that no other candidate's spouse had done before. After he was sworn as chief executive the following year, the new first lady reportedly said to him, "Well, Warren Harding, I got you the presidency. Now what are you going to do with it?" It has sometimes been reported that – as was the case with Helen and William Howard Taft – Florence Harding foisted her White House aspirations onto her husband. That is what I had read and believed as I strolled through the tomb, but it was untrue. Warren Harding was his own driving force behind his rise from newspaperman to senator to president.

Harding was in office for under two and a half years, from March 1921 to August 1923. While he was in the midst of a cross-country "Voyage of Understanding" to promote his policies, the 57-year-old Republican took ill. With the first lady by his side, reading him a complimentary column from the *Saturday Evening Post*, he died of what is presumed to have been a heart attack. The grand memorial constructed to house his remains cost $783,103, some of which was funded with pennies donated by 200,000 school children.

Presidents who die in office have tended to receive elaborate funereal monuments, but I was confused why Harding was interred in one, and why the tomb received so many contributions. The gestures suggested popularity, and I knew Harding wasn't regarded as a good president, at least by 2005. His administration was rife with wrong-doings, which included the lease of government-owned lands to com-

---

[35] See Figure 23.

panies without competitive bidding in exchange for bribes (the Teapot Dome Scandal). But, as I learned at the Harding house later on, the disreputable episodes that plagued his presidency didn't really surface until after his demise in 1923, and members of the "Ohio Gang" were more directly to blame. This segment of the president's cabinet officials, who misleadingly did *not* all hail from Ohio, were the subjects of multiple investigations that resulted in prison sentences for some. Harding's guilt lied in trusting people he shouldn't have (here's looking at you, Secretary of the Interior Albert Fall). Nevertheless, the stress fomented by the president's cronies couldn't have been any good for him and his apparently-weak heart.

Harding was one of eight presidents to expire before their term did, and by getting him, McKinley, and Garfield, I finished off that ill-fated group. Likewise, I'd wrapped up in Ohio and New York, which left Virginia with the largest cluster of yet-to-be-visited presidents. The summer was still young, however, so they remained unvisited for no more than a few weeks.

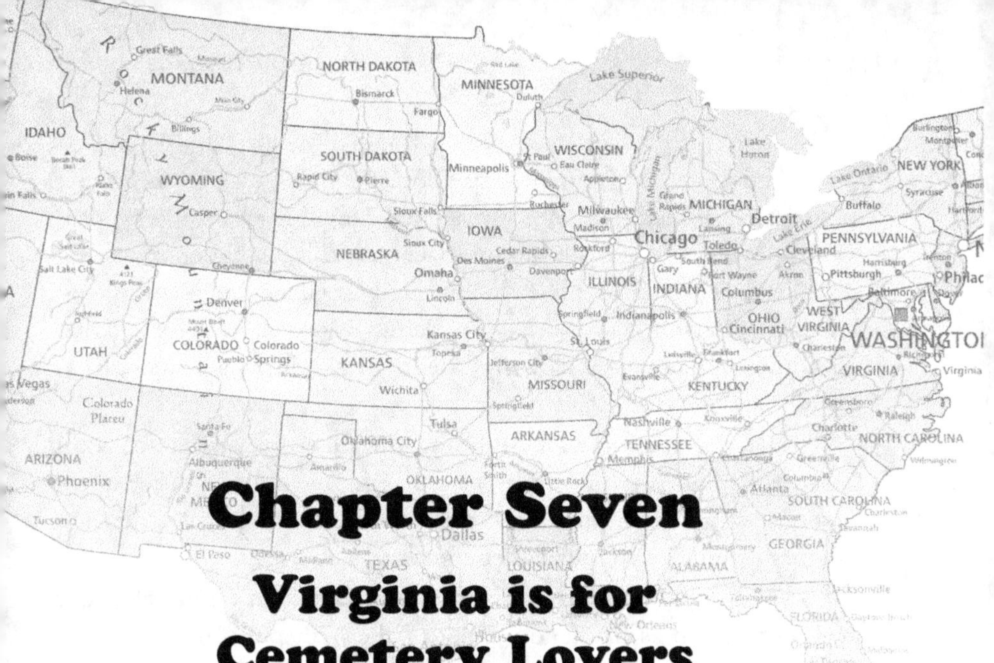

Chapter Seven
Virginia is for Cemetery Lovers
~ July 2005 ~

Part of what makes the presidency so compelling to learn about is that many of its officeholders have been colorful characters. Before their marriage, John Adams wrote Abigail Smith a list of her faults and imperfections. Warren Harding wagered a set of White House china in a poker game and lost. His successor, Calvin Coolidge, once sat next to a dinner guest who revealed she had a bet going that she could prompt him to say more than two words during the course of the evening. His only reply? "You lose."

I had quickly accumulated a smattering of presidential anecdotes from the books I read and historic sites I visited over the previous three years. Traveling had also given me the chance to encounter unique people, like Nick LaBella from Youngs Memorial Cemetery. To start off our 2005 family summer vacation, I was poised to meet another: my father's good friend, Andy. A hand puppet aficionado and one of my father's collectibles colleagues, my dad has described Andy as his "375-pound Jewish mother, Philadelphia lawyer." In visual terms, picture a larger version of the comedian Gallagher, just with fewer watermelons.

Andy lives in Pennsylvania, about 80 miles east of the state's lone dead president, the much-maligned James Buchanan. The plan was to drop in to see Andy and his daughter, Elizabeth, before visiting Buchanan, followed by my four unvisited Virginian president graves: Thomas Jefferson, James Madison, James Monroe, and John Tyler. With my sister along, though, my parents would throw in some Olivia-friendly activities to be fair.

Our clan met up with Andy and Elizabeth for supper at a local Italian restaurant the first night of our trip. But not long after introductions were made and seats were taken, Andy revealed he and Elizabeth weren't our only dinner companions.

"Hi, Kurt, I'm Richard Nixon!" he exclaimed in a guttural Tricky Dick impression as his hand puppet of the 37th president rose from beneath the table. This was the first I'd seen of Andy, but clearly, my father had kept him abreast of my interests, if not my sensibilities. I was mortified – which, granted, wasn't a difficult task to achieve given my disposition. Before I knew it, I was barraged by political puppets that included Presidents Carter, Reagan, the first Bush, and – for good measure – Vice President Spiro Agnew. The embarrassment didn't subside until long after the puppets were taken off and the eyes from neighboring tables turned away. Andy is a grade A schmoozer, however, and I was soon won over and having a ball.[36]

After a thankfully puppetless breakfast at the local Lancers Diner with Andy the next morning, we journeyed to Lancaster. Buchanan lived there almost exclusively for six decades, except when his political and diplomatic duties required his presence elsewhere. Many of his later years were spent at Wheatland, a brick mansion he purchased in 1848 when he was in President James K. Polk's cabinet. He passed away there in 1868 and was buried in Woodward Hill Cemetery three miles away.

Woodward Hill was disappointing. The cemetery appeared to be in a more rundown section of Lancaster, and numerous deteriorated

---

[36] See Figure 24.

tombstones were prostrate or leaned against one another.[37] Buchanan's grave, at least, was well-maintained. The customary flag pole made it easy to find his plot, which he has all to himself. Old Buck was America's only bachelor president, and his first lady, niece Harriet Lane, isn't buried there. Lane is interred in the same Baltimore cemetery as John Wilkes Booth, the man who killed her uncle's successor.

I found nothing too remarkable about the president's marble tombstone, which I thought fitting given his unremarkable assessment by historians.[38] Buchanan hoped to settle the slavery debate, but did so by trying to placate its proponents. In one instance, he supported a failed attempt to pass a pro-slavery constitution for Kansas Territory when it was a prospective state. An illegitimate delegation had drafted the Lecompton Constitution and submitted it for consideration without a public vote. When a referendum was held subsequently, territory residents resoundingly rejected it. Perhaps most egregiously, Buchanan then stood idly by as seven southern states seceded after the 1860 election of Abraham Lincoln, whom they considered as a threat to their slavery-based economy and way of life. The conservative strict constructionist in the White House didn't believe that the Constitution permitted states to legally leave the Union, but he also rebuffed the notion that the Federal Government had the authority to stop them. Buchanan instead left the issue to be resolved by Lincoln, whose administration was consumed by the Civil War.

None of that makes for a good epitaph though, so the Democrat's inscription is minimalistic. I read it aloud for the video camera before my father turned his attention to the Deion women.

"And, here they are. The highlight of their trip: sitting curbside at James Buchanan's gravesite," he commentated as my sister flung her arms in disagreement. "What do you think of James Buchanan, Olivia?"

"I don't like presidents."

"Fantastic! I think she said she *loves* presidents."

---

[37] These damaged stones were repaired by the time my father and I returned to Woodward Hill in June 2013.

[38] See Figure 25.

"I didn't!" she snarled through gritted teeth, unamused by our dad's playful antagonism.

Baltimore was more palatable for Olivia, with an aquarium visit, a Red Sox-Orioles game, and a two-day, city-wide scavenger hunt for fiberglass crabs to soothe her. History repeated itself, though, and her dissatisfaction began to bubble under the surface as our march toward Virginia brought us through my favorite city – Washington, D.C. 2005 marked my third consecutive summer with a trip to the capital city, but there was still a plethora of presidential sites to see. After failing a year earlier, we found Woodrow and Edith Wilson's brick house on S Street NW. Outside the National Archives Building, the four of us stopped beside a plain, rectangular tribute that was unveiled in memory of Franklin Roosevelt in 1965, on the twentieth anniversary of his death. Culled from the same quarry that produced the marble for FDR and Eleanor's gravestone, its size and location are in keeping with the wishes the president expressed to Associate Justice Felix Frankfurter in 1941. Should anyone feel the desire to erect a memorial to him, he told his friend, it should be a block roughly the size of his desk "and placed in the center of that green plot in front of the Archives Building. I don't care what it is made of, whether limestone or granite or whatnot, but I want it plain without any ornamentation, with the simple carving, 'In Memory of __________.'" The second Roosevelt Memorial near the Tidal Basin, which we'd visited in 2003, flouts that statement pretty overtly with its statues and waterfalls.

Inside the Archives Building, we viewed the Uher 5000 audio recorder that Richard Nixon used to play back Oval Office tapes. During Nixon's administration, both the Oval Office and his room in the Executive Office Building bordering the White House were rigged with voice-activated taping systems. This became public knowledge in July 1973, when former White House aide Alexander Butterfield testified as much before the Senate Select Committee on Presidential Campaign Activities. The committee was convened to investigate potential improprieties taken by the Nixon campaign during the 1972 presidential election cycle.

In the course of the overarching investigation, it was unveiled that there was a substantial gap in one of the recordings – a conversation between the president and Chief of Staff H.R. Haldeman on June 20, 1972. That was just three days after five operatives with ties to Nixon's re-election campaign were arrested during a bungled burglary at Democratic National Committee headquarters in the Watergate Office Building. Among other things, the perpetrators were found with listening devices, which were installed the previous May to obtain useful information about Nixon's potential opponent in the general election. Haldeman's uncharacteristically brief notes from June 20th indicate the break-in was among the meeting's topics of conversation, but at that point in the audio tape an eighteen-and-a-half-minute gap starts – the contents were erased. I picked up a receiver in the exhibit and retroactively eavesdropped on one of the surviving dialogues.

Unbeknownst to us, the hotel we stayed at during each visit to D.C. was across the street from the Washington Hilton, where Ronald Reagan was shot on March 30, 1981 as he left a speaking engagement. Andy informed us of this fact during a fortuitous phone call check-in with my father. Our family ambled over to the Hilton, where an employee was surprisingly eager to illustrate what happened that infamous day. He showed where the president exited the building and where he stood as shots rang out. Reagan was pushed into his limousine by Secret Service Agent Jerry Parr. Three others were wounded in the attempt, including White House Press Secretary James Brady, who was partially paralyzed. The perpetrator was John Hinckley, Jr., a mentally unwell 25-year-old obsessed with actress Jodie Foster.

As the presidential limo sped off toward the Executive Mansion, initial indications were that the POTUS was uninjured. But when Reagan started coughing up blood, Parr made the decision to reroute for George Washington University Hospital. The 70-year-old president walked into the facility unassisted, but soon fell to the floor. One of the bullets fired in the volley had ricocheted off the limo and struck Reagan. The ammo hit one of his ribs and lodged in his left lung, collapsing it. It settled millimeters from his heart. The hospital team stabilized the patient and removed the bullet during lengthy surgery. Had Parr not made the decision to seek immediate medical attention, the president almost certainly would have died.

There's a bizarre bit of trivia attached to this attack: Parr first became interested in joining the Secret Service as a child, when his father took him to see the 1939 film *Code of the Secret Service*. Its star was none other than Ronald Reagan, who acted in Hollywood before he entered politics. "It was such a strange thing," Parr later remarked, "seeing his image on a film when I was nine years old, and then I ended up helping save his life." The irony only deepens when one considers that, during a 1971 appearance on *The Dick Cavett Show*, then-Governor Reagan professed that low budget B film was the worst movie he ever made. I haven't gotten deep into Reagan's filmography, but I'm still inclined to agree with him. An ill character in the 1980 comedy classic *Airplane!* groans, "I haven't felt this awful since we saw that Ronald Reagan film!" She must have watched *Code of the Secret Service*. Those are 58 minutes of my life I'll never get back. All that really matters, however, is that Jerry Parr liked it.

In 2005, before there was a Reagan plaque at the Washington Hilton, we were lucky to have Andy and a knowledgeable hotel employee at our disposal. It's easy to miss the location of a historic event if there's no illuminating sign or plaque marking the site. You'd have to know exactly what you're looking for in advance. No one with insight rescued us from our naivety at the National Gallery of Art, which was hosting a temporary exhibit of Gilbert Stuart paintings, including his original Lansdowne portrait of George Washington. It wasn't until I read Sarah Vowell's *Assassination Vacation* years later that I learned the land upon which the gallery sits was formerly the location of the Baltimore & Potomac Railroad Station. On July 2, 1881, James Garfield intended to depart from that station and join his wife in New Jersey. Charles Guiteau had other ideas and fired upon the president.

A metal star embedded on the floor of the station once denoted where Garfield had stood that day, but the building was razed in 1908 and the shooting was forgotten. The assassination site was unmarked until November 19, 2018, when temporary waysides were installed on the 187th anniversary of Garfield's birth. The fanatic I am, I drove alone down from Rhode Island on just a few days' notice to attend. The precise location of the shooting is presently in the middle of Constitution Avenue NW, north of the Gallery building, so the other attendees and I watched the signs get unveiled on the southern face at the National Mall. Tourists can now learn the almost-forgotten presidential significance of the spot without the danger of being hit by an SUV.

13 years prior though, as I admired Stuart's work inside the Gallery, I was as unaware of my proximity to presidential history as everyone else.

I was fully cognizant of the presidential connections that remained on our trip, though not all of them unfolded as I expected them to: James and Dolley Madison's Virginia estate, Montpelier, was undergoing a massive renovation. The mansion, both inside and out, had been drastically altered by subsequent owners and we were told it was expected to cost $30 million to restore it to its Madison-era appearance and furnish it. The home was still open for tours, but standing in the barren rooms I struggled to imagine Dolley Madison hosting guests and having oyster ice cream served (this was one of the more striking/disgusting tidbits our guide told us, but its reputation as Mrs. Madison's favorite flavor may be fallacious). Though the timing was disappointing in relation to our visit, I supported refurbishing Montpelier for historical accuracy.

The Madison Family Cemetery, elsewhere on the grounds, was unaffected by the reconstruction. It had been restored in 2000, so we were lucky enough to have avoided that project. Not everyone had stones to repair, however. Several burial sites would have been unmarked, if not for makeshift signs of paper and plywood. This included the president's paternal grandfather, Ambrose, who purchased the land in 1723. For many years, his famous grandson's grave did not have a marker either. James Madison died at Montpelier in 1836, and it was not until 1857 that a tiered granite obelisk was erected over his remains.

First Lady Dolley Madison's popularity dwarfed her husband's during his administration, but she seems like an afterthought in the cemetery. Her much smaller marble obelisk is tucked into a corner behind the president's. Why the disparity, I wondered? Was it a testament to the president's political prominence in a male-focused era, or rather compensation for his diminutive stature? I noted for the camcorder that, at 5'4", James Madison was described in his day as no bigger "than half a piece of soap." It turns out that his marker was sponsored through a nineteenth-century version of crowdfunding, while the first lady's nephew was financially responsible for her stone. It's better than nothing – elsewhere on the plantation, some of the people the Madisons enslaved are buried in unidentified, clustered holes in an overgrown patch of land. The enslaved cemetery and its occupants may have been lost to history entirely if not for the 40 indentations in the settled earth and the periwinkles planted by their families and friends generations ago, per oral tradition. Montpelier's historians have added an interpretive sign at the burial ground.

Touring early presidential plantations is an experience that can rouse multiple emotions. There's solemnity and disgust over man's inhumanity to man, and the bewilderment that some of the nation's most highly-regarded proponents of liberty and freedom kept human beings against their will because of the color of their skin. At these historic sites, these leaders' ignorance and ingenuity are simultaneously on display. While at Monticello, Thomas Jefferson's plantation 30 miles southwest of Montpelier, I inspected the beautiful landscape and grieved the people of African descent that were forced to cultivate it centuries earlier.[39] Inside the stately mansion, I was inspired by

---

[39] In 2005, most of my thoughts about slavery at Monticello were rudimentary and self-generated; at that time, there was intentionally very little focus on the institution of slavery or the people enslaved by Jefferson, perpetuating an imbalance in historical interpretation. Since my first visit, the Thomas Jefferson Foundation has put serious effort into analyzing Jefferson's relationship with slavery and interpreting the lives of enslaved Monticello residents, both on-site and online, using sources such as oral histories, written records, and archaeological discoveries. For example, Sally Hemings, by far the most well-known person enslaved by Jefferson, is the subject of an exhibit that helps shed some light on her multi-faceted life, aided by the recollections of her son, Madison.

Jefferson's many talents, primarily invention and architecture. He designed his mountaintop estate, which is reproduced on the reverse side of the nickel.

Beside the foyer doorway, an elaborate clock Jefferson devised is mounted to the wall. The Great Clock uses a strand of cannonball-like weights to denote the day of the week. As the week progresses, the clock lowers the balls to correspond with wall markers for the respective days. The apparatus is too large for the room interestingly enough, and the docent showed us that Jefferson had a hole cut in the floor to allow the spheres to descend into the cellar, where the Saturday marker is affixed.

Also in the entrance hall, I was struck by the busts of Jefferson and his longtime philosophical opponent, Alexander Hamilton, which flank either side of the doorway. The tour guide advised that Jefferson positioned the sculptures that way because he felt he and the Federalist should always be in opposition to one another. "[O]pposed in death as in life," one of Jefferson's grandchildren recorded him as saying. I was indecisive as to whether the gesture was political poetry or obsessive.

The entrance hall was my favorite part of the guided tour, with perhaps the exception of Jefferson's quarters. His alcove bed has no walls at its sides, which allowed him to roll out into a different room on either his left or right. Which direction he went in depended on what tasks he wanted to accomplish that morning. That bed was where he died on July 4, 1826, the fiftieth anniversary of the adoption of the Declaration of Independence. Fellow president, vice president, and Declaration signatory John Adams passed away later that same day. One of Adams's last utterances, "Thomas Jefferson survives," was several hours too late to be true.[40]

Jefferson wasn't moved far from his deathbed – he was interred in a family graveyard downslope from the mansion. The self-penned epitaph on his obelisk recalls his authorship of the Declaration of Independence and the Statute of Virginia for Religious Freedom, and

---

[40] John Adams's very last words were directed at his granddaughter, Susanna Clark: "Help me[,] child, help me."

that he founded the University of Virginia. His service as chief executive is unacknowledged.

As expected, we found the cemetery shielded by a fence. The pictures we saw of other visitors on the internet all showed them standing outside the barricade – but they weren't ten years old. I quickly realized that I was slender enough to slip between the bars and stand right next to Jefferson's monument. Before I made my move, my family waited for other visitors to clear the area. But as the minutes drifted by, if anything there was a greater influx of tourists coming to see the boneyard. When it became evident that we weren't going to get a moment to ourselves, my father garnered the crowd's attention and enlightened everyone that I was a ten-year-old history buff visiting my 26th presidential burial site. He recited his usual spiel about my desire to get right up next to the graves for the best quality picture and polled if anyone would be offended if I slipped through the fence. His captivated audience, almost exclusively comprised of senior citizens, had no objections and even encouraged me as I slithered between the posts.[41]

Another of the early Virginia elites, James Monroe, lived at an estate a short distance away, but there wasn't enough time remaining in the day to complete the trifecta. Instead we boogied down to a hotel in Richmond, where Monroe and John Tyler's graves waited for us. Just like the Church of the Presidents in Quincy and Arlington National Cemetery, Richmond's Hollywood Cemetery holds the remains of multiple commanders-in-chief. Monroe and Tyler rest in close proximity to one another in the Presidents Circle section.

When we stopped by the cemetery office to procure a map the next day, an employee was more than willing to assist us, but when he learned we were from Rhode Island he referred to us as Yankees. I'm unsure if I was more taken aback because the Civil War had been over for 140 years or because I was a Red Sox fan. The pejorative was expressed in jest, but it was my first indicator of the cultural divide that still exists between the northern and southern states.

---

[41] See Figure 26.

On the other hand, the employee worked himself into my sister's good graces when he pointed out an image of a dog on the cemetery map. It indicated the location of a statue which stands vigil over the burial site of two-year-old Florence Rees, who succumbed to scarlet fever in February 1862. He said the cast-iron canine was placed there to save it from being melted down into ammunition during the Civil War. The four of us thanked the man for his help and made a detour to the metal Newfoundland, though it mollified my sister for only so long.[42] As we trudged up the road to Presidents Circle later, my father centered the video camera on her, apathetic as ever to historical escapades.

"Olivia, what would you rather do on vacations: go to, say, Disney World, stay at the Polynesian [Village Resort] and chase ducks," referencing a previous trip, "or go to *gravesites*?"

"Disney World," she affirmed.

"Are you sure? Olivia, you're just not like other kids, are you?"

This was one cemetery visit I hadn't been looking forward to either, actually. "We are here to see one of my least fav... no, not one of my least favorite presidents. My *least* favorite president," I stressed. I wanted future archivists who uncovered our family tapes to be acutely aware of my childhood animosity toward John Tyler. In his post-presidency, I explained, Tyler aligned himself with the slavery-defending Confederacy and forfeited his U.S. citizenship. He was elected to the Confederate House of Representatives but died on January 18, 1862, before he could assume his seat.

Given the circumstances, Tyler was the only president whose death was not officially recognized in Washington, D.C. His gravesite was once devoid of pageantry as well. It was unmarked until 1899, and even then only a small stone was placed over the tenth president's remains. Tyler had desired for his body to be laid to rest in the soil of his estate, Sherwood Forest – and while that wish was not adhered to, his initial, unostentatious marker at Hollywood Cemetery was in line with his preferences. In his last will and testament, he requested that

---

[42] See Figure 27.

his place of interment be marked "by an uncostly monument of granite or marble." Therein lied one of the few commonalities I shared with the late president – neither of us thought he should have a stupendous gravesite.

But a stupendous gravesite he got. In 1915, the small granite tombstone was replaced with a 17-foot, detailed monument with bas-reliefs, bronze eagles, and a bust of the president. The back of the shaft recounts his two marriages. His first wife, First Lady Letitia Christian Tyler, died during the second year of his presidency and was interred at Cedar Grove, her family's plantation 23 miles east in Roxbury. John soon remarried to Julia Gardiner, 30 years his junior. Their marriage in 1844 made Tyler the first POTUS to wed while in office. Julia also rests beneath the granite memorial.

My enmity for His Accidency was chiseled on my face as I posed for the pictures next to his monument. I was more than eager to move on to his neighbor and predecessor, who is entombed in what I joined many others in describing as an enormous iron birdcage.[43] It's a far cry from the small tombstone Monroe had at his original place of rest in New York. The Richmond structure's Gothic Revival design is based on the tomb of intellectual romantics Héloïse d'Argenteuil and Peter Abelard, constructed in the early eighteenth century as a repository for their remains at Père-Lachaise Cemetery in Paris.[44] Monroe probably would have approved of architect Albert Lybrock's decision to base his sepulcher off of a French Tomb. James was a Francophile, who during George Washington's administration served as minister to France. When Monroe was inaugurated as president himself in 1817, the White House was not fully restored to the level of splendor it was at before British troops burned it during their D.C. invasion in 1814. He refurnished the home with an abundance of French goods – some newly-purchased, some from his personal collection that he had amassed as a diplomat.

---

[43] See Figure 28.
[44] Whether or not Héloïse and Abelard are actually interred at Père-Lachaise Cemetery is up for debate, as is the nature of their teacher-student relationship.

The president's tomb looks different now than when my family stopped by in 2005. Back then, its 618 cast iron pieces and 2,500 fasteners had a brooding black coat. A paint analysis conducted during a $1 million restoration project that commenced in 2015 showed the original color was ivory, which is what it has now been returned to. The black layer had been added somewhere along the line and obfuscated the structural damage it had accrued since its erection in 1859. I didn't notice any fractures or corrosion at all as I reached into the canopy to touch the granite sarcophagus within.

Clearer was the disparity in lavishness between the president's grave and that of his first lady. In most cases in which a president is entombed inside a sarcophagus, his spouse rests in a similar, if not uniform, capsule. The architects behind the tombs of the Washingtons, Taylors, Grants, McKinleys, and others created egalitarian designs. The monument Albert Lybrock devised for James Monroe is large enough to contain just one body, even though the tomb he based the design on was built for two. When the fifth president's body was brought to Hollywood Cemetery in 1858, there were evidently no plans to relocate First Lady Elizabeth Monroe, who had been interred at their Oak Hill, Virginia, estate when she died in September 1830. The pair was finally reunited in 1903 when Mrs. Monroe was buried in the ground beside the birdcage. I took pity on her for the small, flush marker that designates her place of rest. Covered in an emerald patina, I could see how for some less observant visitors the plaque might blend in with the grass and evade their gaze.

I had less sympathy for our next host, buried toward the back of Hollywood Cemetery. Richmond was the capital of the Confederate States of America for the majority of the Civil War, and it makes sense that the city retains the body of its president, Jefferson Davis. He was first entombed in New Orleans, where he died in 1889. His body was removed to Richmond in 1893. Since he was the leader of the CSA he did not count toward my quest, but my parents nonetheless believed we should visit since we were there.

If a person were to try to determine the outcome of the Civil War solely by looking at Jefferson Davis's gravesite, they'd assuredly come away thinking the South was victorious. A life-size sculpture of Davis, posed heroically and with a stoic countenance, is mounted atop a plinth in a plot encompassed by cobblestone. His epitaph, carved into the plinth, lauds him as a "defender of the Constitution" and "a martyr to principle." From what I'd learned in my northern school and history books, such assertions baffled me. Further adding to my perplexity, someone had planted various banners in the soil atop the graves of the CSA president and First Lady Varina Davis – at least two iterations of the Confederacy's national flag, as well as the more famous battle flag. A full-size national flag clung to the pole towering above the statue. "And you would think they would take the Confederate flags out after all these years," I scorned as I surveyed the plot.

"Well, where are we?" my father prompted.

"Alright, we're in Virgi…" I started before he cut me off.

"We're in Richmond, Virginia. There're still some strong feelings down here. They're not taking the Confederate flags out."

My feelings were just as strong, however, and it took considerable coaxing from my mother and father before I would permit my picture to be taken with Davis's grave. Even then, I kept my arms crossed in protest.[45] To cope, I'd already set my mind on another, less controversial president.

"We will see you probably in Vermont later in the summer," I reported to the camcorder, anticipating a visit to Calvin Coolidge's final resting place in Plymouth Notch. "That's true," my father agreed – optimistic thoughts that exemplified our ignorance of the challenges that lay in wait just around the corner.

---

[45] See Figure 29.

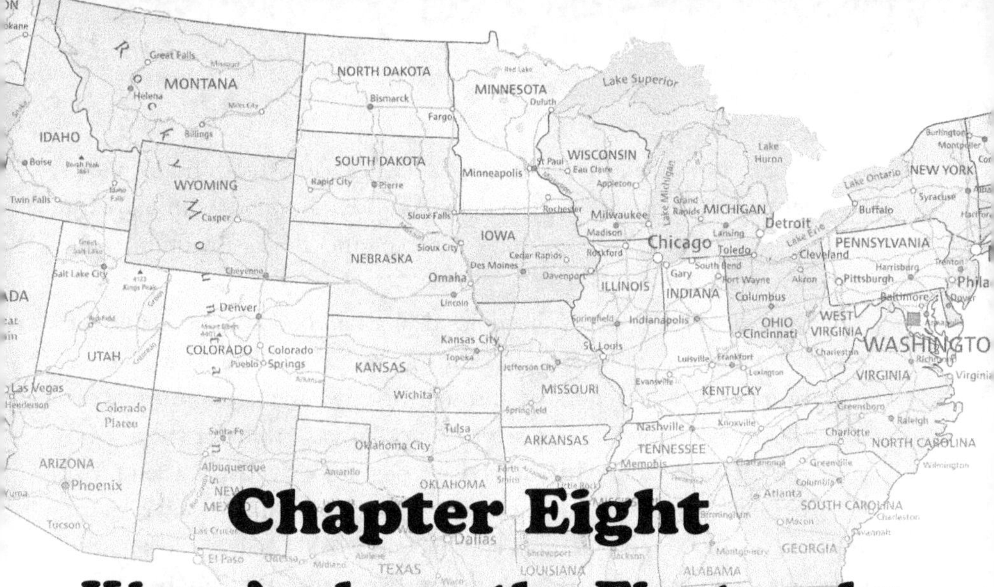

Chapter Eight
King Andrew the First and the King of Rock 'n' Roll
~ July 2006 ~

In the first few years of my quest, I was able to embark on trip after successive trip, accumulating 28 presidential gravesites in rapid fashion. It was not a sustainable pace, what with the remaining tombs scattered across the country – not every state has birthed a large litter of chief executives, like Virginia or Ohio.

Living in a household with two incomes made the endeavors financially feasible, a remarkable feat given the plummeting profitability of my father's business. The collectibles market had grown progressively unstable for middlemen like my father in the internet age. Sellers and prospective customers were increasingly connecting with one another online, via auction sites or other avenues. Previously, if someone was looking to move an item without much hassle, a dealer like my dad would take it off their hands. Often the dealer had an established, repeat customer who was likely to buy it in turn. For instance, if a painting of the *Munsters* TV characters was up for sale, my dad would purchase it and resell it to the *Munsters* collector he knew. *Now* it was easy for people to go online, research the going prices, and advertise their items themselves. For buyers, finding your long-sought-for toy, or what have you, could be as simple as typing a term in a search bar. No need to seek out a dealer or attend trade shows. Another side effect was that the market was flooded with duplicate items, which sent prices crashing through the floor. Profit margins were eviscerated.

Making a living as a collectibles dealer had become untenable for most people in my father's circle. Some stayed afloat, like Andy, whose primary income was generated through his law practice. Others were forced to try to reinvent themselves – not an easy task for those who were middle-aged and without college degrees. My dad's friend Big Mike became a scrapper, diving in dumpsters on Philadelphia's mean streets. As for my father himself, the circa 2004 sale of his entire warehouse inventory helped buoy our bank account and permitted some presidential pilgrimages, but that money lasted only so long.

The severity of our situation didn't sink in for me until the day arrived in 2006 when my dad was forced to shutter The Wayback Machine, Inc. The financial strain gave even more weight to my mother's paychecks, as my father's attempts to remake himself as an independent inventor hit a series of roadblocks. I expected I would be unable to check any presidents off my list that year. Visiting cemeteries was an unnecessary expense when you needed to pay electric bills and taxes.

Despite all the tumult, my parents *somehow* managed to arrange for a trip in late July. I was flummoxed, but decided not to look a gift horse in the mouth. There weren't enough funds to support a full family trip, so California – where my mom and sister wanted to go next – was off the table until we had more stable income.[46] That left Tennessee as the only other option if my father and I wanted to knock off multiple presidents in a singular state.

The two of us landed in Nashville and cruised in our rental car to Greeneville, 250 miles east. Andrew Jackson and James K. Polk are interred in Nashville, but since we were going to fly out from there it made more sense to visit the outlier, Andrew Johnson, first. We arrived in the evening to find the streets of Tennessee's second oldest

---

[46] As far as my interest in California was concerned, it is the final resting place of Richard Nixon and Ronald Reagan.

town empty. There didn't look to be much to do, but it was too early to retire. I asked my father to drive by a locale equally bereft of life: the Andrew Johnson National Cemetery. The president's memorial is tall, 27 feet to be exact, and I thought we might be able to see it from outside the grounds, like the McKinley tomb in Canton.

Sure enough, as we neared the cemetery we saw the marble monument on a hilltop. It was well past the five o'clock lock-up time, but my father noticed the pedestrian gate beside the car entrance was swung open. To him, this was an unfettered invitation to go inside, but I figured the gate was left unclosed by mistake and didn't want to get in trouble. We were just going to have to wait until tomorrow, because there was *no way* I was going to venture up to Johnson's creepy grave at night.

I may have acted like more of an adult than my father much of the time, but I was not in charge. So it went as I climbed the staircase to the president's monument, hands trembling. The atmosphere of a cemetery in the evening was eerie enough, but the heat lightning and dogs barking in the distance added to my agita. To top it off, like out of a suspense thriller, a car pulled up beside ours outside the property. As the auto idled, its headlights shining on the gate, my mind became deluged by worst-case scenarios. "Is it the caretaker? Is it a police cruiser, and are we going to be arrested?"

It ended up being neither of those answers, odds are, because the vehicle reversed after a minute or so and drove away. That left us with no interference as we hopped the two small fences that enclose the Johnson family plot. A spooky aura enveloped the obelisk, accentuated by the marble eagle at the top, periodically illuminated by the heat lightning. Miraculously, the two of us returned to our car a short while later unscathed, neither incarcerated nor eaten by a presidential zombie.

The cemetery is one of four components of the Andrew Johnson National Historic Site, which also encompasses two homes and a visitor center, where we started off the next day. Inside, I gravitated toward the tailor shop Johnson operated long before his White House days. In the shop, Eliza McCardle Johnson read books and documents aloud while her husband sewed. Local students and clerks congregated there and discussed political issues, and in doing so influenced the tailor's opinions on such matters. Now, in 2006, the small cabin was safeguarded from the elements – but not political discussion – within its own room in the visitor center. I was astounded because I'd never seen a building inside another building before. I was easy to impress, I suppose, but also it was fascinating to see a visual representation of one of the humblest presidential beginnings.

For juxtaposition, the center includes a reminder of how Johnson's professional career almost ended, as well. He was the first president to be impeached. Ostensibly it was a consequence of his attempt to remove Secretary of War Edwin Stanton from his cabinet, though there were other underlying causes. Johnson took over the presidency on April 15, 1865 upon Abraham Lincoln's assassination. With Congress out of session until December, Johnson had carte blanche in orchestrating Southern Reconstruction. The new president established a low amnesty threshold for southern states that cleared the way for former Confederate officials to re-enter local and national politics almost immediately after the war. He also undermined the Freedmen's Bureau, which was tasked with helping formerly-enslaved people. One of the bureau's goals was to allocate 850,000 acres of land to newly-freed African Americans. Johnson instead ordered the department to return the parcels to the pardoned Confederates they had been confiscated from. Even with chattel slavery nearing its end, the president was clearing a path for other forms of racial oppression to be implemented in the South.[47]

Johnson's views on Reconstruction ran counter to the philosophies of the Radical Republican wing of the GOP. When the Republican-led Congress reconvened, the Legislative Branch and the Executive Branch started to duke it out. The president vetoed many

---

[47] For a greater understanding of how Johnson's actions impacted the rights, financial independence, and safety of Black people in the United States, I suggest watching the 2019 two-part PBS documentary, *Reconstruction: America After the Civil War*. Another good secondary source on this saga is Brenda Wineapple's book, *The Impeachers: The Trial of Andrew Johnson and the Dream of a Just Nation*.

reform-minded bills, and Congress overrode a record 15 of them. This included the Civil Rights Act of 1866, which supplemented the Thirteenth Amendment. Another bill that passed over Johnson's veto was the Tenure of Office Act, which forbade presidents from removing members of the cabinet and other offices without the Senate's permission. In defiance of its passage, Johnson fired Secretary Stanton, who was allied with the Radical Republicans and was a holdover from Lincoln's cabinet. The House of Representatives then impeached the president, setting the stage for a Senate trial.

The exhibit at the Andrew Johnson National Historic Site had an interactive component where visitors could vote whether or not Johnson should be removed from office. I cannot recall the composition of the visitor center's exhibit and evidence, but based on the controversial nature of the Tenure of Office Act, my dad and I used our replica impeachment admission tickets to vote for his acquittal. On each of the three articles of impeachment that were put to a vote in March 1868, 35 senators cast ballots to convict President Johnson, which was one vote shy of the two-thirds benchmark for his removal. Johnson finished the last eleven and a half months of his term, then was elected to the Senate in early 1875, seven years after his trial was orchestrated by that very body. Congress repealed the Tenure of Office Act in 1887, and the Supreme Court belatedly declared it unconstitutional in 1926.

Greeneville didn't seem much livelier during the day than it was the night before. My father and I had free rein of the visitor center and no company at the homestead. We received our own private tour of the two-story brick building where Johnson lived from 1851 to 1875, his time in Washington and Nashville due to politics notwithstanding.

"Would that painting have been up there at that time?" my father questioned of a large portrait of the politician in the parlor. "That's one of the few items that survived the occupation of the soldiers," a park ranger explained. The artwork was entrusted in the care of a neighbor before the Johnsons went to Washington, and she wrapped it in newspaper. Because it was leaned up against her fireplace, the Dixie forces that passed through the neighbor's home thought it was a fire screen and "never even gave it a second look." Had they investigated, the painting likely would've been destroyed. Johnson was the lone southern senator to remain loyal to the Union, so he was singularly despised in Confederate circles. Troops occupied the Johnson residence during the war, and in Mrs. Johnson's bedroom a bare section of wall shows samples of the derisive comments the occupiers scrawled. "Eject the traitor," and "Shame on you, Andy," scream from the stripped surface.

That small section of the wall is exposed so modern-day tourists can see what the soldiers wrote, but the insults were covered up by wallpaper when the Johnsons returned from D.C. That spared Mrs. Johnson from having to read them as she sat in her recliner. "She's got a La-Z-Boy!" the guide joked of what was known in the nineteenth century as an "invalid's chair."

The first lady rarely left her quarters at the homestead or in the White House, which prompted her daughters to step in as social hostesses. Yet Eliza Johnson wasn't completely inactive; she sewed quilts, and one of her completed pieces is laid across the foot of her bed. It's likely she suffered from tuberculosis, but the exact nature of her illness and reclusiveness remained a mystery, according to the ranger. "The descendants, before they turned the home over to us, made sure every letter and record about her was destroyed," she elucidated. "So we have no information on her [illness]. It is very odd to do something like that." Beside her chair sits an ornate box that once contained 40 pounds of chocolate, a gift from the people of France. "No wonder why she never left this room," my dad deduced.

Despite her sickliness, Eliza Johnson outlived her husband, albeit for less than a year. After she passed away in January 1876, she joined him in the family plot, where we returned after our house tour concluded. The sunshine made it much easier to see the details enumerated in *Who's Buried in Grant's Tomb?*[48] A scroll that represents the Constitution is carved into the monument, and a sculpted American flag cloaks the obelisk under the eagle's talons. These were important symbols to Johnson. According to an informational sign

---

[48] See Figure 30.

downhill from the monument, the Democrat's "political philosophy was based on a strict interpretation of the Constitution, a belief in states' rights, an unshakable commitment to serve the workingman, and a conservative attitude toward government spending." In keeping with comments he made before his death, the president was laid to rest with a copy of the Constitution placed beneath his head, and his body was wrapped in the U.S. flag. Thinking about the 17th president's symbolism-infused burial was enough to distract me from the neighboring grave of son Robert Johnson, who the park ranger divulged engaged in dalliances with prostitutes in his White House office.[49]

The two of us assuredly would have learned other fascinating anecdotes at the other Johnson home in Greeneville, but we made the decision to start traversing back west instead of taking another tour. We sought refuge from the rising temperatures along the way in Pigeon Forge at Dollywood's Splash Country, singer Dolly Parton's waterpark. Again, my father wielded his parental powers as he forced me to slide down Fire Tower Falls, a 70-foot plummet. An evening excursion into a cemetery didn't seem so frightening anymore.

As recompense, I was allowed to relax in the far more docile wave pool, which overflowed with people. I couldn't understand it, but my father explained that many residents of landlocked Tennessee might not have seen the ocean before if they didn't possess the time or ability to travel. The beach was something we took for granted in coastal Rhode Island. On our drive to Memphis later, we were confronted with some other regional differences at a McDonald's drive-thru window. The employees had no idea what Diet Coke was and asked my father to go inside and point to the beverage he wanted. Even my orange juice order was lost in translation, but our competing dialects earned us drinks on the house.

Free refreshments would've been most welcome the next day in the broiling Memphis heat. The mercury levels soared to nearly 100 degrees and our air-conditioned tour of the Graceland mansion served as only a brief respite. Near the meditation garden, where musician Elvis Presley and his family are buried, my father eyed the swimming

---

[49] See? This is the history you won't learn in the classroom!

pool and gave serious consideration to jumping in. The sun was so oppressive that even *I* contemplated abandoning my typical prudence. Getting kicked out of Elvis's house would be worth it for the reprieve and the story, we both mused. In the end the better angels of our nature triumphed, and we devils in disguise kept dry.

Our time in Memphis was almost entirely Elvis-centric. Apart from his estate, we toured Sun Studio where the "Hound Dog" vocalist recorded, as did a who's who of other music stars like Carl Perkins, Roy Orbison, and Johnny Cash. Even the hotel where we stayed, the Peabody, had a connection to the King. It housed Lansky's Fine Clothing, a shop owned by Elvis's close friend and personal tailor, Bernard Lansky. The Peabody Hotel is most noted for its ducks, however. The birds were first placed in the Peabody's lobby fountain as part of a drunken prank in the 1930s, and it morphed into a decades-long tradition. Each morning at eleven o'clock, in a ceremony orchestrated by the hotel duck master, five waterfowl march down from their rooftop palace to the lobby for a six-hour swim.

Normally we steered clear of such extravagant establishments in favor of cheap motels, but even with our financial pressures my father felt the experience was going to be worth it. My sister's obsession with ducks came second only to her love for dogs, and before we left home I promised I would personally take some videos and pictures so she could see them upon our return. I panned the camcorder over to the fountain in the center of the lavish lobby. "The ducks are so special that they apparently get a red carpet and stairs to go into the fountain… wow!"

In all the pre-ceremony hubbub, a toddler separated from its parents and wandered across the busy room toward an open elevator. By the time anyone in the crowd noticed, the child was nearly at the threshold. A collective panic spread through the masses as we realized the doors might close and transport its unwitting passenger to any of the hotel's 14 floors. The only person close enough to catch the rugrat was the duck master, whose heroics earned him a round of applause.

With the hardest part of his day over, the maestro told his captive audience about the building's history and used his duck handle cane to knight the day's honorary duck masters. His duly deputized lieutenants followed him up to the rooftop, and at exactly eleven o'clock the double doors of the elevator reopened. Four hens and a drake waddled out to John Philip Sousa music, lights flashing all around. It was just like a paparazzi session at a star-studded Hollywood premiere. The ducks posed on the short steps to the fountain before they plunged one by one into the water.

One night at the Peabody was all we could afford on our otherwise shoestring budget. With no desire to profligate funds, we packed up and headed back north to Nashville to wrap up the week's presidential adventures. Andrew Jackson's grave was going to be more time-consuming because that included touring his plantation, so we chose to drop in on James K. Polk first.

The eleventh president is entombed with his wife, Sarah Childress Polk, beneath a white pillared structure on the grounds of the state capitol. It is his third "final" resting place, and her second. The former POTUS was initially buried among other cholera victims in a public cemetery when he died in 1849, just three months after he left office. He was later moved to the grounds of his home, Polk Place, which he once hoped would become a historic site. When the former first lady passed away in the 1890s, Polk Place was razed. The Polks' bodies were then interred at the statehouse. I mentioned all this in my obligatory graveside video, along with other tidbits like how Polk's administration coincided with the Mexican-American War. I was still a year or so away from reading Walter R. Borneman's biography on the Tennessean, so I didn't have too much information to offer up. As many people said of the dark horse candidate in 1844, "James K. Who?"

The man whose equestrian statue takes center stage a few yards away from the Polk tomb is far less obscure, both in our lifetimes and his. Nicknamed "Old Hickory," Major General Andrew Jackson rose to fame at the end of the War of 1812 as the hero of New Orleans and became the Volunteer State's favorite son. President from 1829 to 1837, he paid off the national debt and held the Union together by quelling South Carolina's secession threat that manifested during the

1832-1833 Nullification Crisis. While Jackson was hailed by many people as a champion for common Americans in Washington, the admiration wasn't unanimous. For his dramatic expansion of presidential powers, he earned another, not so complementary moniker: King Andrew the First.

Jackson was born and raised in the Carolinas, but moved to Tennessee and made his home in Nashville, where he lived at the Hermitage plantation from 1804 until his death in 1845. The mansion most associated with the 1,200-acre estate was completed between 1819 and 1821 as a Federal brick house. Renovations undertaken in 1831 and 1836 during the Jackson presidency added distinct Greek Revival elements, like its two-story façade and Corinthian columns. The interior is filled to the brim with luxuries such as marble busts and exquisite furniture, and the entrance hall is decorated with wallpaper that depicts scenes from Homer's *Odyssey*.

It all contrasts starkly from the rustic slave dwellings just a few yards north. Old Hickory was one of the many early presidents who benefited from slave labor, and the Andrew Jackson Foundation still preserves some of the quarters these enslaved people lived in. Prominent figures like Jackson and George Washington may be the prime reason many people tour well-known, early American plantations, but it is equally important for visitors to learn about enslaved populaces, whose accounts have historically been overlooked.

One Hermitage cabin my father and I examined was the residence of a man called Alfred, whose name I recognized from *Who's Buried in Grant's Tomb?* Alfred lived at the Hermitage longer than any other individual. He was born there in the early 1800s to Betty and Ned, who toiled as an enslaved cook and carpenter, respectively. When he was old enough to work, Alfred's responsibilities consisted of maintaining wagons and farm equipment and caring for the Jackson family horses. After chattel slavery was abolished in 1865 there were limited opportunities for free Black people, and Alfred was one of many freedmen who became tenant farmers. Tenant farmers rented land to work on, and much of their income went toward paying fees to landlords. Unlike sharecroppers, tenants may have possessed some of their own equipment, but sometimes they too borrowed critical supplies on credit from the landlords. It was a system with little mobility that kept an abundance of tenants, especially Black ones, dependent on white landowners. It was not a big leap from slavery to tenant farming, especially since many tenants, like Alfred, farmed on the very plantations where they had previously been enslaved.

When the Hermitage became a museum and tourist attraction in 1889, Alfred Jackson, as he was then known, continued to live on the property as a docent. Upon his death in September 1901, the Ladies' Hermitage Association hosted Alfred's funeral, fulfilling an arrangement that was made in exchange for Jackson heirlooms that Alfred had purchased at an estate sale years earlier. Alfred's body was laid out both in his living quarters and the mansion's main hall before he was interred in the garden near Andrew and Rachel Jackson, the general's wife. There is no evidence the association organized funerary services for any other individuals who were enslaved at the Hermitage.

I was uncertain how the general would feel about African Americans spending eternity buried alongside his family, as racial harmony was not one of his strong suits. During his administration, Jackson signed the congressionally-approved Indian Removal Act of 1830, which authorized the president to negotiate treaties with Indigenous tribes and relocate them west of the Mississippi River. The grim effects of Jackson's most egregious action extended beyond the end of his White House tenure in 1837. Resistance from the Cherokee Nation resulted in the forced removal of 16,000 Cherokees from their homeland in 1838. Approximately 25 percent of those Cherokees died along the Trail of Tears en route to the federally-designated Indian Territory in present-day Oklahoma.

On the home front, Jackson was a longtime enslaver who held around 300 Black men, women, and children in bondage over the course of his life. Conversely, he adopted a Creek child named Lyncoya, and his dying words were a wish that those by his deathbed "shall all meet in Heaven," enslaved people included. I was incapable of imagining what that reunion would have been like. Accepting one child into your home and offering a last-second conciliatory message before you die don't quite balance the scales when the matters being weighed include forced labor and genocide.

My father and I walked to the garden and paid our respects at Alfred's worn, shin-high headstone, with the difference in financial means just as apparent among the graves as in the different Hermitage buildings. A few feet away was Andrew and Rachel Jackson's towering Greek-style cupola. Mrs. Jackson died in December 1828, after her husband won the White House but before they were to leave for Washington. The president-elect placed blame for his wife's death on political opponents, who incessantly decried Rachel as a bigamist whose first marriage wasn't legally dissolved before she wed Andrew.

The flowery epitaph Mrs. Jackson's husband wrote in her memory encompasses the entirety of her slab on the pavilion's floor, whereas his own marker simply reads "General Andrew Jackson" – which was his preferred title – and his lifespan. The inscriptions are reproduced on a sign that abuts a fence, which inhibits visitors from reading the flush slabs with their own eyes.

Of course, that didn't fly with my father. We bided our time taking videos and photos while other tourists perused the garden, and when the coast was clear my father boosted me over the rail.

After I posed for some pictures under the dome, I rushed back down the three short steps to retrieve the camera from my dad so I could take a photo of the president's marker. Since good photography was the only intent behind my trespass, I didn't think the man under the slab would mind. Nevertheless, in case I was wrong, I was glad he wasn't around to challenge me to a duel, something the temperamental Tennessean did in response to many of the people who offended him when he was alive. A 239-year-old general versus a preteen wallflower would have been a mismatched fight.

Approaching voices soon induced me to scramble back over the fence, and my feet landed back on the other side seconds before other patrons came into view. They were none the wiser as my father and I meandered out of the garden. Given our experience at Monticello the previous summer, we knew it was possible the Hermitage visitors might not have had any issues even if they did spot us, but fortune saw to it that we didn't have to test that theory.

Jackson bumped my burial site total to 31 out of 37 presidents, a ratio which took a hit five months hence when, on the evening of December 26th, my father ascended to my bedroom to inform me of Gerald Ford's death. Eight days later the Republican was laid to rest at his presidential museum in Grand Rapids, Michigan, which I yearned to see sometime in the New Year. In actuality, it would take three years and a lot of financial wrangling to make it happen.

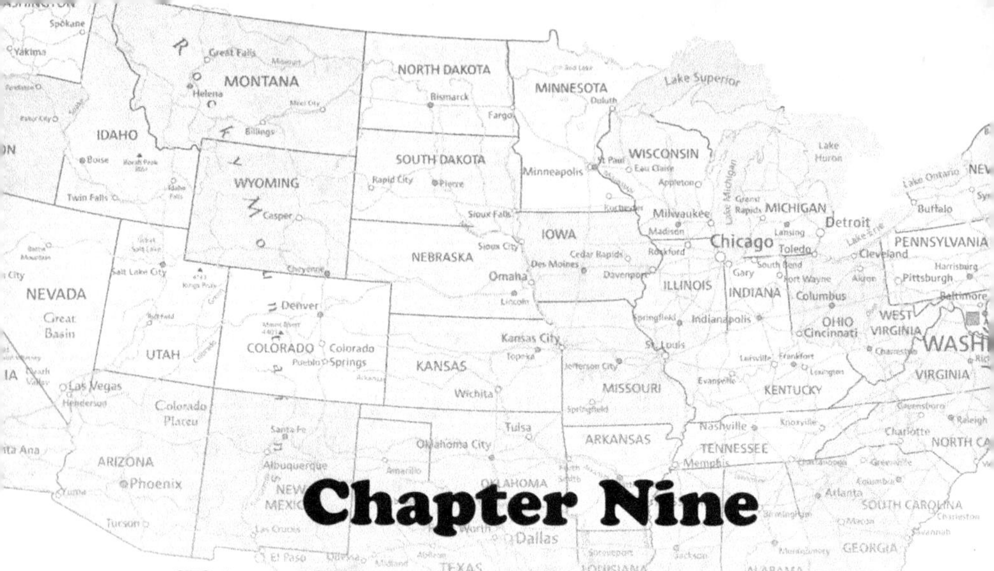

Chapter Nine
The Gipper, Tricky Dick, and the Jazzman
~ August 2008 ~

After a rough year following the closure of my father's company, 2007 looked like it would bring a financial boon to my family. Hasbro, the Rhode Island-based business that ranked as the second largest toy producer in the world, was interested in manufacturing my father's brainchild that he had been developing for two years. The name of his cartoonishly-large foam muscle arms, Pump Fakes, had a double meaning: it referenced the football move, in which the quarterback deceptively gives off the perception that he is passing the ball, and the fact that the wearer didn't really "pump iron" at the gym to get so buff. Initially, Hasbro expressed desire to adorn Pump Fakes with various athletic logo "tattoos," but in the midst of the steroid era none of the major sports leagues were willing to give licensing consent.

With Hasbro's recent acquisition of the Marvel Comics toy license, though, a Pump Fakes deal wasn't dead in the water. Many superheroes have bulging biceps, and Hasbro agreed that children would love to replicate the looks of their favorite characters of page and screen. My father's projected earnings were expected to change our lives. Scrooge McDuck wouldn't envy us, but we would be blessed with sustained financial stability and the opportunity to spend on some luxuries, like a big family trip.

California was the logical location, as I could visit two president graves – Richard Nixon and Ronald Reagan – and my mother could revisit Santa Barbara, which she had wanted to return to since my parents visited six years prior. My sister was the most eager to go. California was Olivia's dream destination. She was a die-hard fan of *Hannah Montana,* a Disney Channel show about a teenager living a double life as a musician in Malibu. Olivia earnestly believed that the fictional rock star would be holding concerts there, and wanted to go see her and the beaches. We all had a reason to want to go to California, some more realistic than others.

Three days before the scheduled contract signing, the devastating word came in: Hasbro was conducting a significant overhaul of one of the existing role-play products it inherited from Toy Biz, the previous Marvel licensee. That put the kibosh on Pump Fakes. My parents called a family meeting to break the news to me and my sister that our favorable future had suddenly turned into a halcyon that never was. The change of fortune meant money was still going to be relatively tight, and our family trip to California wasn't feasible. Olivia, sensing the sensitivity of the situation, comforted my father.

"You're a jerk!"

At least she was nine, if you want to give her a mulligan on that one.

The trip we *could* afford was to Vermont, to see Calvin Coolidge at long last. It was a bootstrap vacation. My mother had paid vacation time from work, and we stayed a few nights with her Aunt Rose at her pond-front cabin in Abbot, Maine, before heading west to the Coolidge sites. All it cost was a few gallons of gas, food, and one night's stay at the Summit Lodge in Killington. But crossing Silent Cal's long-awaited grave off my list couldn't wash the sour taste of the trip out of my mouth. Olivia was in a petulant mood the entire week, and the experience was acrimonious and plain unbearable.

The preserved village of Plymouth Notch contains the president's birthplace and the homestead where his notary public father swore him into office in the middle of night after Warren Harding's passing in 1923.[50] The Notch is bucolic, and my parents wanted to salvage the trip and enjoy the history and scenery, but it was all too much for me. My patience had run thin, and I swapped my mild-mannered persona for one of rancor and pestered them to go to the cemetery. Olivia's irascible behavior had enervated my enthusiasm. I just wanted to see the Coolidge plot and head home.

With Hasbro no longer an option, my father targeted the other toy manufacturing juggernaut: Mattel. The company was receptive and invited my father to pitch Pump Fakes at their headquarters in El Segundo, California, in August 2008.[51] I had experience helping him prepare for pitches in an NFL Super Bowl XLI commercial contest and a presentation for a different project with Topps in Manhattan, so he wanted me to accompany him to Mattel. Plus, I could cross Nixon and Reagan off my list. We still couldn't afford a full family trip, though, and my sister was mercurial. My dad felt she couldn't be trusted not to blow up in the meeting and say Pump Fakes were a horrible idea and start kicking people (not an unwarranted fear, at that point in her life). So Olivia remained home with my mother as we set out for the West Coast. The two of us hoped we were embarking on a life-altering trip.

It was, in one regard. On the second leg of our flight, from North Carolina to LAX, a passenger changed her infant's diaper on the drop-down tray, got some mess on her hands, wiped it off, but neglected to wash up before she dove into her bag of Twizzlers. My father and I agreed never to eat licorice again, a pact we have honored for 14 years and counting.

The six-hour flight was wholly unpleasant. Apart from Twizzler Baby, our travel companions included a gaggle of sick, coughing kids and a man who snored for at least three hours. Once we were on the ground, however, I had the delightful experience of meeting another

---

[50] See Figure 31.
[51] See Figure 32.

of my father's old friends, Jay. As was the case with "Puppet Master" Andy, my father met Jay through the collectibles world. Also exiled from the Island of Misfit Toy Dealers by the flatlined collectibles market, Jay worked at a warehouse and lived in a rundown apartment in North Hollywood.

I'd been told the figure most analogous to Jay was the titular character of the comic strip "Ziggy," who, despite his well-meaning and easy-going demeanor, is perpetually plagued by misfortune. Over a plate of nachos, Jay nonchalantly regaled us with a batch of absurd accounts that appeared to be his norm, like how, as "unofficial assistant block captain," he attempted to make a citizen's arrest on a sword-wielder who kicked his elderly pooch, Jazz.

In addition to an overabundance of stories, each peppered with Jay's unique phraseology, I discovered the Jazzman knew the where-abouts of, to me, one of the most iconic filming locations in television. With Jay as our guide, we traversed Griffith Park until we came upon the Bronson Caves, one of the entrances of which was ingrained in my brain as the Batcave on the 1966 ABC *Batman* show.[52] The Dynamic Duo is shown driving in and out of the cavern in the Batmobile each episode, though interior scenes were shot on a studio set. As a lifelong bat-fanatic, to be at any place connected with my favorite fictional character was fantastic. Sans modified Lincoln Futura concept car, we entered the cave in a far less stylish manner than the Caped Crusaders.

We soaked in the ambiance of the cave along with some other visitors until the dark and silent atmosphere was interrupted by a bright flash of light and an echoing cacophony of screams and laughter. Caught unaware, my companions and I hastily exited, stage left. Standing outside the cave with the benefit of the daylight, we discerned what had occurred when it happened again a short while later: two young women were deploying a Taser at the cave walls. If present, Adam West's campy Batman assuredly would have lectured about the importance of stun gun safety.

---

[52] See Figure 33.

The rest of my first day in California proceeded to get only more interesting, as a lady of the evening tried to put the moves on my father during our nighttime stroll down Hollywood Boulevard. In just a few hours, Twizzler babies, cave-tasing teens, sex workers, and canine-kicking swordsmen had already provided me with enough anecdotes for one trip.

Life resumed a more typical pattern the next day, meaning a gravesite visit. Jay accompanied us to the Reagan Library in Simi Valley, about an hour north of our hotel in El Segundo and far more scenic than Hollywood Boulevard. Coffee fiend Jay proudly held his Starbucks cup aloft in contrast to the natural beauty as he and I posed for a photo with the gorgeous backdrop.[53] My next photo buddy was a decaffeinated President Reagan, whose bronze hand I shook before entering the museum.

The statue immortalizes Reagan as the older "Great Comm-unicator," which was how I usually pictured him. After all, at the time of his death he had a greater longevity than any other commander-in-chief, and at that time he still held the record of oldest first-time president in U.S. history, at age 69. Early on, the exhibits provided a reminder of the success Reagan achieved in his much younger, pre-political days as a radio broadcaster and actor. Subsequent galleries worked their way through Reagan's years as governor and then his presidency. Mementos and gifts abounded, like a bronze-colored torch from the 1984 LA Olympics and a ten-carat gold ring given to Reagan in 1983 by Boston left fielder Carl Yastrzemski, a rare overlap in my passions of presidential places and the Red Sox.

Yet even the gravitas of Yaz's hall of fame career couldn't distract me from the magnificent 153,000 square foot Air Force One Pavilion, which houses the Air Force One 27000 used by seven presidents, from Nixon in 1973 to George W. Bush in 2001. "Alright," my awestruck father extolled, "this is one of the most dramatic scenes we've ever seen at a presidential library. Look at this!" Perched on story-high pillars, the aircraft faces a 200-foot-wide wall of glass panels overlooking the valley. "Gotta be here, folks, to appreciate this," he

---

[53] See Figure 34.

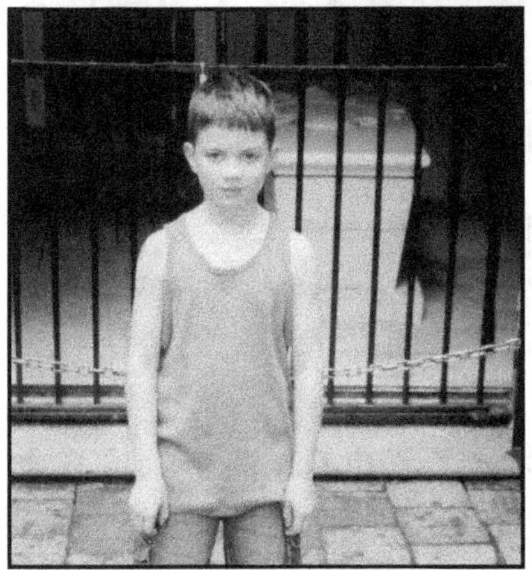

Figure 1: My mother bought me my first presidential history book, *So You Want to Be President?*, in 2002. As a tribute, in December 2022 I toted my worn copy to the grave of the book's author, Judith St. George, in Westfield, New Jersey.

Figure 2: Outside the fence at the North Lawn of the White House with my sister, Olivia, and father, Paul, in summer 2003.

Figure 3: George Washington's tomb marked my first presidential grave picture, but my fourth presidential grave. The next year, I backtracked to get photos with my first three: John Adams, John Quincy Adams, and John F. Kennedy.

Figure 4: Posing at the newly-opened World War II Memorial on June 11, 2004. It was designed by a fellow Rhode Islander, Friedrich St. Florian.

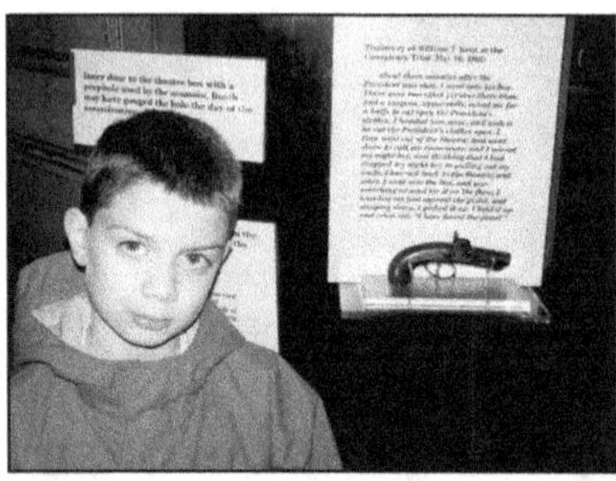

Figure 5: The derringer John Wilkes Booth used to assassinate Abraham Lincoln is displayed at Ford's Theatre.

Figure 6: With his arm in a full cast, it was not easy for my father to drive roundtrip from RI to D.C. Here we pose at the Washington National Cathedral, a day after Ronald Reagan's funeral was held there.

Figure 7: Our entire family at the Empire State Building in August 2004. By this point, my father's cast had been trimmed down (by himself).

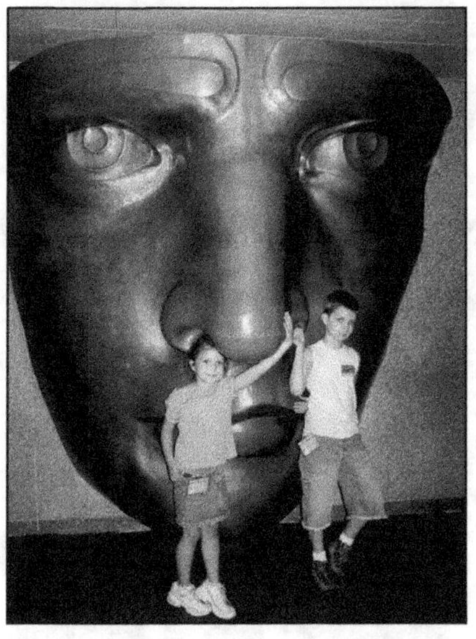

Figure 8: My sister's head fit comfortably within Lady Liberty's nostril.

Figure 9: Separated by a fence from the grave of Alexander Hamilton in Manhattan.

Figure 10: A secretive, forbidden photograph taken within the Grant's Tomb crypt in August 2004. The photo embargo has long since been lifted.

Figure 11: On my shirt, Ronald Reagan peaks around the corner to read the names upon the tombstone of Theodore and Edith Roosevelt.

Figure 12: With my sister at the graves of Franklin and Eleanor Roosevelt in Hyde Park, New York.

Figure 13: Inside the crypt at the Harrison Tomb State Memorial in North Bend, Ohio.

Figure 14: Peering through a glass pane at the locked mausoleum of Zachary and Margaret Taylor in Louisville, Kentucky.

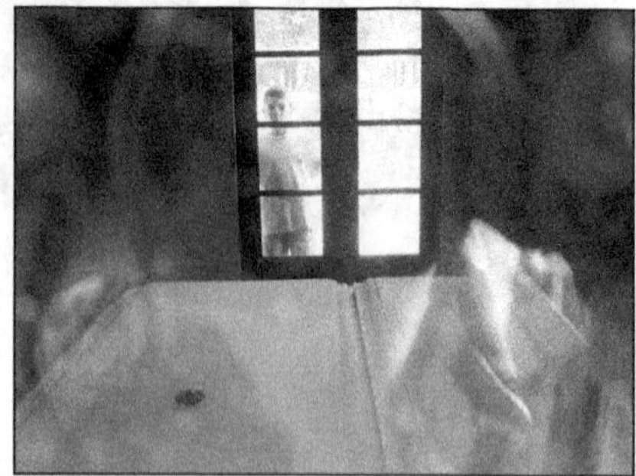

Figure 15: Reaching for the burnished bronze nose of Abraham Lincoln outside his tomb in Springfield, Illinois.

Figure 16: Abraham and Willie Lincoln's remains were temporarily contained in this receiving vault at Oak Ridge Cemetery in 1865.

Figure 17: With the subdued, hilltop final resting place of Herbert and Lou Henry Hoover in West Branch, Iowa.

Figure 18: Even with photography prohibited at this book signing, Bill Clinton was happy to pose for two pictures with me. I was ten years old at the time of his April 2005 visit to Providence.

Figure 19: Holding back shrub branches to make Millard Fillmore's headstone more visible. I skipped my last day of elementary school for this excursion to Buffalo.

Figure 20: Climbing the 108 stairs to the McKinley tomb in Canton, Ohio.

Figure 21: These gates, which once protected the White House, now surround the Rutherford B. Hayes Presidential Library in Fremont, Ohio.

Figure 22: Unremitting gratitude paved the way for me to secure a rare photograph standing immediately next to James Garfield's flag-draped casket.

<u>Figure 23</u>: Historic Site Manager Melinda Gilpin supervises as I walk beside the slabs that cover the corpses of the Hardings.

<u>Figure 24</u>: My father sitting with his friend, Andy, at Café Lombardi's in July 2005. In the background, I am at ease now that Andy's political hand puppets have been put away.

<u>Figure 25</u>: At the grave of James Buchanan, with my 1950s Louis Marx Company figurine of the 15th POTUS resting atop his monument.

Figure 26: I slipped through the fence for a better picture at the grave of Thomas Jefferson at Monticello.

Figure 27: My father crouching with the iron dog that guards the grave of young Florence Rees in Richmond, Virginia.

Figure 28: James Monroe's "birdcage" is a favorite among many presidential grave hunters.

Figure 29: A picture is worth a thousand words, so my crossed arms and scrunched face did the talking at the grave of Jefferson and Varina Davis.

Figure 30: In the daylight hours of July 19, 2006, my father and I returned to the Johnson family plot in Greeneville, Tennessee.

Figure 31: My mother and me sitting on the porch of the Coolidge homestead in Plymouth Notch, Vermont, in August 2007.

Figure 32: My father wearing his foam muscle arms invention, Pump Fakes. He sported this wrestling-inspired ensemble to our meeting with toy manufacturer Mattel in August 2008.

Figure 33: Holy Hollywood! This opening served as the entrance to the Batcave on ABC's iconic 1960s *Batman* television series.

Figure 34: Sitting with my father's friend, Jay, on a bench at the Ronald Reagan Presidential Library in Simi Valley.

Figure 35: With the graves of Pat and Richard Nixon. Both died on the East Coast, but are interred in Yorba Linda, California.

Figure 36: Preceding Kamala Harris by 92 years, Charles Curtis was the first person of color to serve as vice president. Curtis is buried in Topeka, Kansas. I visited him in 2009.

Figure 37: In Kansas City, Missouri, at my first Baseball Hall of Fame inductee grave. Satchel Paige was enshrined in Cooperstown in 1971.

Figure 38: Sitting in the same bus seat that civil rights movement figure Rosa Parks occupied during her most memorable act of resistance in December 1955. The bus is housed in Dearborn, Michigan.

Figure 39: This helicopter and staircase from the 1975 evacuation of Saigon are now in the collection of the Gerald Ford Presidential Museum in Grand Rapids, Michigan.

Figure 40: My father keeps his fingers away from animatronic Colonel Sanders's chicken at the KFC corporate headquarters in Louisville.

Figure 41: Escape from Paterson — my father arranged for us to be locked inside the barbed wire-enclosed cemetery in New Jersey where Garret Hobart is entombed.

Figure 42: The linchpin of my mission: the private final resting place of Nelson Rockefeller in Sleepy Hollow, New York. His biographer, Richard Norton Smith, later sent me a hearty "congratulations" for the rare achievement of seeing "Rocky."

Figure 43: "An act of God": my father requested I take his picture with the tree that crushed the fence that separates the Rockefeller Family Cemetery and Sleepy Hollow Cemetery.

Figure 44: Elbridge Gerry is interred at my all-time favorite burial ground: Congressional Cemetery in Washington, D.C. Here, on November 12, 2011, I sit beneath the gateway arch prior to its restoration.

Figure 45: Stormy weather made for a unique nighttime visit to the burial site of Henry A. Wallace in Des Moines, Iowa, in February 2012.

Figure 46: Lyndon Johnson's was my 38th presidential grave, and my final one when I visited on April 19, 2012. The excursion to Stonewall, Texas, was memorable for an additional, unexpected reason.

Figure 47: Crouching down close to capture the tombstone of John Nance Garner in Uvalde, Texas. He was the 36th late VP I visited, as well as my fourth House speaker.

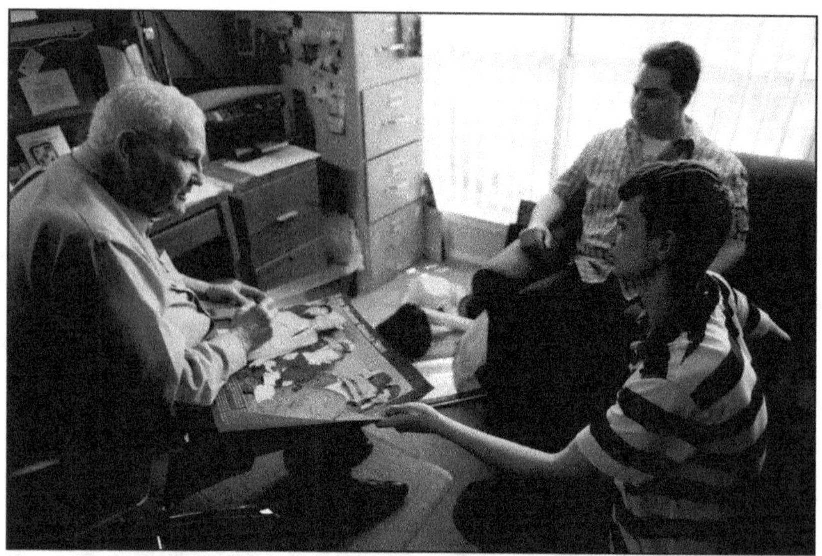

Figure 48: Pearl Harbor survivor and Kennedy assassination figure James Leavelle autographs a poster for me as we sit in his home office in Garland, Texas. (Credit: Dylan Hollingsworth)

Figure 49: "Oswald Soaked!" James Leavelle was keen to re-enact the Pulitzer Prize-winning photo of Lee Harvey Oswald's shooting for our satirical television concept. (Credit: Dylan Hollingsworth)

Figure 50: My father and I flank Jimmy and Rosalynn Carter after religious services at Maranatha Baptist Church in their hometown of Plains, Georgia. We attended on June 9, 2013.

Figure 51: My father and I dug out the snow-covered footstone of Hubert H. Humphrey in Minneapolis, Minnesota, on January 10, 2014. This brought my presidential and vice presidential gravesite quest to a temporary end.

Figure 52: Posing with C-SPAN founder and former CEO Brian Lamb in his corner office at 400 North Capitol Street NW in D.C. on July 23, 2015. (Credit: Nikhil Raval)

Figure 53: Conversing with Brian Lamb on the set of C-SPAN's *Q&A* on August 5, 2015. (Credit: C-SPAN)

Figure 54: George H.W. Bush's November 2018 death reopened a gap in my presidential and VP quests, and I reclosed it on March 12, 2019. He is buried with his wife, Barbara, and daughter, Robin, at Texas A&M University.

spoke into the camera for the benefit of a future audience. "It looks like you could just take off."

An accompanying pamphlet provided a bevy of statistics about this particular Boeing 707, like how its wingspan is over 145 feet and that it measures even longer nose to tail. Its immense size required that some of the walls not be erected until the plane was moved into the pavilion. "Look at that," my father repeated as he and I took it all in. Evident conspiracy theorist Jay, on the other hand, had already put his awe on the back burner and grilled a nearby security officer.

"Hey, man," he asked, "does this Air Force One have an escape pod like in the movie?" in reference to the 1997 Harrison Ford film. Before the guard could answer, Jay cut him off, having come to the self-realization that he was probably "sworn to secrecy." That seemed unlikely, though photography *was* prohibited on the plane. Perhaps there was concern about someone studying photos to approximate the schematics of the incumbent Air Force One used by then-President Bush. Downstairs afterward, my father resumed recording just in time to capture Jay yawning. "Unbelievable," my dad said, still in reference to the hangar's majesty and not Jay.

Soon the time arrived for my customary gravesite video commentary. Outside, I narrated about the museum's artifacts and the role of presidential libraries in the National Archives and Records Administration. My use of notes limited the number of takes needed, and I was content with my improvement upon my younger performances. My situational awareness and peripheral vision still left a lot to be desired, though. Only after reviewing the camera footage two years later did I see what tomfoolery Jay was doing behind my back.

"This library," I explained as Jay juked to either side of me, making goofy faces, "is the first presidential library that was built by the Presidential Records Act, so people can come here and look up Reagan's papers." As I began to tread backward toward the tomb the Jazzman made his exodus, keeping his cover intact.

After photographing the presidential seal emblazoned on its back, I walked to the front of the semicircular structure and looked upon the final resting place of the president whom I saw lie in state four years prior. Behind the stone with Reagan's name and lifespan, a wall displays a quote from the address he delivered at the library's opening in 1991.

I KNOW IN MY HEART THAT MAN IS GOOD

THAT WHAT IS RIGHT WILL ALWAYS

EVENTUALLY TRIUMPH

AND THERE IS PURPOSE AND WORTH TO

EACH AND EVERY LIFE

The front of the tomb is enveloped by a fence that appeared to have motion sensors, and I was beyond the age where I could get away with looking cute and hopping over barriers (curse you, puberty). All I could do was mug for pictures beside the barricade and admire the valley, unequivocally the best view held by any dead president.

My generally-idyllic perspective on presidential museums took a bit of a hit after we departed Simi Valley. To this point in my journeys, I'd been more focused on the artifacts and ambiance than historic contextualization and interpretation. A Boeing 707 is a *lot* sexier than an analysis of Reaganomics, or the racial ramifications of the War on Drugs. Growing up, I never questioned potential biases of often-laudatory historic sites, which I'd regarded as the foremost authorities on the past. I may have been smart and wise beyond my years in some regards, but I was still a kid, after all! Why should I have been skeptical of what adults put in official-looking museums?

This epiphany was spurred in part by a visit with Andy, who was also vacationing in the Los Angeles area. As my dad, Jay, and I walked up to where Andy was staying, the bombastic lawyer opened the door and greeted my Reagan shirt with some colorful language unfit for print. The Gipper was one of my favorite historical figures; he saved 77 lives as a lifeguard during his youth in Illinois, he contributed toward the dissolution of the communist Soviet Union, and his time lying in state in 2004 advanced my blooming interest in dead presidents. That there were more complicated political nuances that could make a president anathema to someone was unchartered territory for this thirteen-year-old history buff. Other than those leaders who propagated slavery or withered in the descent toward Civil War, I viewed all the presidents as equally quirky individuals who inspired vacations, and not through politically-colored glasses. But if Reagan's administration had possible downsides, as Andy was all too eager to point out, why didn't I see any of those issues mentioned in the museum?

My views on both presidential libraries and their deified namesakes were further altered at the Nixon Library. This time Jay-less, we drove 40 miles east of El Segundo to Yorba Linda, a location chosen for Tricky Dick's library because the president was born there in 1913.

Nixon's public perception was significantly impacted by the Watergate Scandal and his resignation, and it was apparent the library wanted to humanize him and boost his legacy. As such, many of the exhibits focused on the Republican's foreign policy relations. In the Structure of Peace gallery, a statue of Nixon shook hands with Zhou Enlai, who served as the premier of the People's Republic of China when Nixon helped thaw relations with the nation in 1972. In another room, an assemblage of world leaders whose time in power overlapped with Nixon's public service career stood frozen in conversation: Charles de Gaulle, Winston Churchill, Nikita Khrushchev, Leonid Brezhnev, Mao Zedong, Golda Meir, and Anwar Sadat. A Nixon blurb on the wall behind those statues opined, "They are leaders who made a difference. Not because they wished it, but because they willed it."[54]

A replica of the White House's Lincoln Sitting Room, which the facility brochure proclaimed was Nixon's favorite space in the Executive Mansion, took up valuable library real estate. Seeing a recreation of a White House room was nifty, but in my opinion it didn't

---

[54] In retrospect, it seems like a controversial quote to apply to Mao, who oversaw the murder of millions of his own people through the Great Leap Forward campaign. His hands were certainly the dirtiest, but other leaders' hands weren't totally clean: Churchill has increasingly come under scrutiny for his views on race and his contributions to the Bengali famine. De Gaulle's colonial attitudes toward Vietnam and New Caledonia are also problematic, though the leadership he and Churchill displayed in opposition to the Axis Powers during World War II will always serve to burnish their reputations to some degree, even as the legacies of "great white men" are re-evaluated.

provide a whole lot of insight about the 37th chief executive. There was one thing in particular I was itching to see, and I hoped that the replica wasn't taking away space that could be used to teach about that subject. When learning about the times of Richard Nixon, it's important to study up on his actions related to the Vietnam War, China, the Environmental Protection Agency, and other matters. But when most people think of Nixon, they think about Watergate, and I was champing at the bit to see what the museum had to say about the scandal.

For a while after the June 1972 burglary at DNC headquarters, the incident had little impact on Nixon. He handily won his re-election bid against Senator George McGovern in November, claiming victory in 49 states. After enough thread-pulling, though, things started to unravel. Soon the White House was besieged on all sides, with the Federal Bureau of Investigation, Congress, the Department of Justice, and journalists searching for clues about the level of interconnectivity between administration officials and the crime. In 1973, Special Prosecutor Archibald Cox subpoenaed audio tapes of conversations between the president and his staff. Nixon refused to comply and ordered Attorney General Elliot Richardson to fire Cox. The AG declined and resigned instead. His deputy, William Ruckelshaus, pulled the same maneuver when the decision fell to him. The third highest-ranking DOJ official, Solicitor General Robert Bork, complied with Nixon's demand. The near-simultaneous departures of Richardson, Ruckelshaus, and Cox on October 20, 1973 was dubbed "the Saturday Night Massacre."

The replacement special prosecutor who took over from Cox, Leon Jaworski, followed the same strategy as his predecessor: he wanted Nixon to relinquish 64 recorded conversations. Nixon refused, arguing the president had total executive privilege and that the special prosecutor was exceeding his authority. The battle went to the Supreme Court. In a unanimous decision handed down on July 24, 1974, the Court ruled that the president did not possess unrestricted, absolute executive privilege – he was legally obligated to release the requested tapes. On August 5th, Nixon released the recording of a damning conversation he had with Chief of Staff H.R. Haldeman. On

June 23, 1972, six days after the DNC break-in, Nixon and Haldeman discussed thwarting the FBI investigation by using the Central Intelligence Agency. The recording proved that the POTUS was, at the very least, involved in a plot to cover-up illegal activity for political gain. It became known as "the Smoking Gun Tape."

With impeachment looming in the House of Representatives, and the indication from top Republican leaders that he did not have enough support in the Senate to avoid conviction and removal, Nixon announced his resignation in a nationally-televised address on the evening of August 8th. The following day, he and First Lady Pat Nixon boarded a Sikorsky Army One helicopter on the White House's South Lawn and left Washington behind. Former President Nixon was pardoned by his successor, Gerald Ford, but dozens of other involved parties were convicted. Watergate is still regarded by many Americans as one of the most significant U.S. political scandals, and Nixon remains the sole chief executive to have resigned his office.

Taking that into account, I was growing wary as my father and I neared the end of the exhibits and there was no hint of the scandal. Eventually, the two of us came upon a room with lime green walls bereft of signs, screens, and glass cases. We located an employee to question, and she confirmed that it was the home of the Watergate gallery, which was being refurbished. The brochure maintained it was supposed to reopen in July 2008, but it was clearly behind schedule. A month past the projected rededication, the space had no more information than the infamous tape with the eighteen minutes conspicuously wiped from it. My father made a joke earlier in the trip that it would be funny if there were no mention of Watergate in the museum. His quip had proven prescient.

Joking aside, the refurbishment explanation made the Watergate omission appear innocent enough at the time of our August 2008 visit. Two years later, I was startled by a national news segment that reported the scandal was still unacknowledged at the library. At Nixon's funeral in 1994, President Bill Clinton professed his wishes for his predecessor's legacy. "May the day of judging President Nixon on anything less than his entire life and career come to a close," he pronounced. It was a fair and reasonable request, but by 2010 I was worried the Nixon Library's definition of "entire" did not factor in Watergate at all.

The gallery that was originally supposed to open in summer 2008 was finally unveiled in spring 2011, but questions about what went on in between stayed in my head for several more years. In 2016, during my final semester of undergraduate college at Bryant University, I focused my senior capstone project on the Nixon Library's history with Watergate exhibits. In my research, I learned that when the institution first opened in 1990 it was a private entity run by the Nixon Birthplace Foundation. The original Watergate exhibit was very pro-Nixon and absolved him of any wrongdoing, and also blamed his political fall on a Democratic witch hunt. The author of the script, Nixon aide Bob Bostock, ran the text by the former president, who called it "brilliant." A critic lambasted the facility and its original exhibit composition as "Nixonland."

It was only in 2007, a year before our visit, that the library was incorporated into the NARA presidential libraries system. Nixon's loyalists opposed the tactics of NARA-appointed library director Timothy Naftali, a Cold War historian who wanted to present what he said was a more balanced representation of the scandal that drew from oral history videos and extant documents. Naftali's opponents said the proposed gallery wasn't balanced, but a partisan attack. Members of the Nixon Foundation boycotted the exhibit opening in 2011, and Naftali's departure soon after did little to end the strife.

Moving on from the exhibits, my father and I stepped outside. Nixon's birth home stands at the eastern end of a reflecting pool surrounded by palm trees. Near it is his small, black granite grave marker beside that of First Lady Pat Nixon. In her capacity as first lady, Mrs. Nixon stressed the importance of helping others through volunteerism, among other causes. Her epitaph reads, "Even when people can't speak your language, they can tell if you have love in your heart." I wondered whether the president himself picked the inscription for his stone, which originated from his first inaugural address in 1969: "The greatest honor history can bestow is the title of peacemaker." It's my favorite quote, as I feel it speaks to my personal mantra and the standards I strive to hold myself to in life. Of note, however, two months after he uttered these words Nixon authorized a series of clandestine bombings in Cambodia.

A small hedge separates the Nixon burial plot from the walkway, and it would have been simple enough for me to step over it for better pictures.[55] Yet a security officer, who was dressed more like a Secret Service agent, diligently patrolled the area. I settled for standing next to the shrubbery in front of the gravesite.

Over to the birthplace 50 feet or so southeast, an elderly docent in a red blazer educated us about the president's early life in Yorba Linda. His father, Francis Nixon, built the house from a catalog around 1912, and the family lived there until 1922. At the conclusion of the tour, my dad and I checked back at the gravesite, but security was still sweeping the area. Figuring it couldn't hurt, we backtracked to the birthplace where our docent was chatting with one of her colleagues. Once we explained that Nixon's was my 34th presidential burial spot, one of them offered to keep a lookout for us. Once again, I got a ringside picture.

As for the main purpose of the trip, the following day my father lumbered into Mattel headquarters sporting the Pump Fakes and a luchador wrestling mask, highlighting how the muscle arms would complement the company's WWE license. The toy department was blown away, and the pitch couldn't have gone any better. It was a relief, especially because my father and I had both become sick and had no idea how we were going to hold up during the presentation. The consequence of sitting near those coughing kids on the flight west had reared its head. Since my dad was of more critical importance to the pitch, it was fortunate that I received the brunt of the illness. When we met up with Jay at his workplace hours later he offered up some colon cleanser that he kept out in the open on his desk, but I explained that what we contracted was just a cold. Never change, Jay.

---

[55] See Figure 35.

Illness aside, we returned to Rhode Island feeling satisfied with our grave visitations, our host of Jay stories, and Pump Fakes. The last part didn't last. When the final word came in from Mattel, it was that their toy people loved the arms but the number crunchers couldn't figure out how to make it cost-effective. We were back to square one.

Now, on the precipice of high school, I had just four unvisited president graves left, but all were located in different, distant states: Harry Truman in Missouri, Dwight Eisenhower in Kansas, Lyndon Johnson in Texas, and Gerald Ford in Michigan. Without the potential financial windfall from Pump Fakes, visiting them appeared nigh impossible.

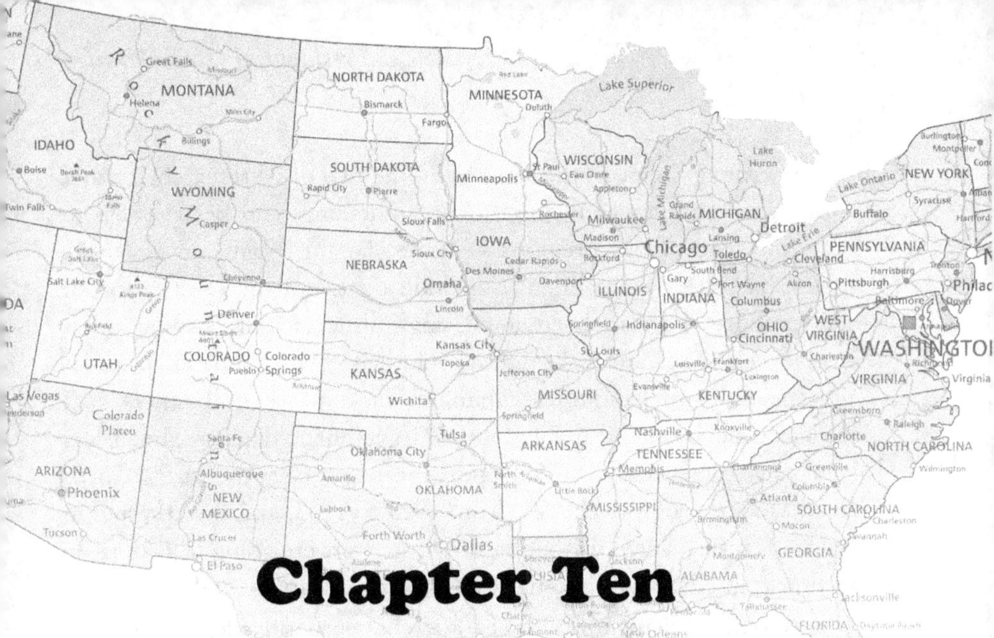

Chapter Ten
I Like Ike's Grave
~ August 2009 ~

By the time a year's worth of calendar pages turned after Mattel's crushing blow, a lot of things remained the same: high school was almost as bleak as middle school, the family funds were as low as George W. Bush's final approval ratings, and my tally of presidential gravesites remained at 34. One of the few changes was one that would be difficult to adjust to: my father's parents, in order to preserve their health, decided they would no longer summer in Rhode Island. They were moving full-time to Greenacres, Florida. Goodbye, snow and quahogs. Hello, sunshine and hanging chads!

With finances how they were, we were uncertain when – or if – we'd be able to see Grandma and Papa Joe again. For all we knew, this could be our final in-person goodbye. Our grandparents wanted to leave me and Olivia with parting gifts to remember them by, and Papa Joe floated the idea of buying me some presidential paraphernalia from Hake's Americana & Collectibles auction. Countering, my dad advised that the most memorable and lasting gift they could give me would be a trip to meet a dead president. My grandmother cut a check.

Given that Truman and Eisenhower were interred in neighboring states, my father and I knew we would get the most bang for our buck by visiting them. In the same vein, the two of us researched other historic sites and graves in the region, something we'd been remiss in doing on some of our previous ventures. By this point, my gravesite mission had already expanded to include signers of the Declaration of Independence. I'd also been increasingly interested in visiting other assorted celebrities and folk figures. The names of temperance leader Carry Nation and bandit Jesse James struck me as no-brainers as I scrolled through the invaluable Find a Grave online database, but I was given pause when my eyes fell upon the name Charles Curtis. Curtis served as Herbert Hoover's VP from 1929 to 1933, and was interred in Topeka, Kansas, which was along the route we were going to take from the airport in Kansas City to the Eisenhower Library in Abilene.

A quick calculation showed that between presidents who had also served as VPs – such as Martin Van Buren – and veeps who were buried too close to a commander-in-chief to ignore – like Thomas Hendricks – I'd already visited 14 of the 41 dead vice presidents. With another on our agenda in Harry Truman, and Lyndon Johnson and Gerald Ford destined for the future, could I justify passing by Curtis, consigned to the earth in a state I had no idea if I would get a second chance to visit should I change my mind in the future?

Nope. As the sun receded in the sky on August 11th, my father and I sped 72 miles west from Kansas City International Airport to Topeka Cemetery. Without too much effort we found the Curtis burial plot.[56] His monument was simplistic, but bore a vice presidential seal and boasted of his accomplishments as Senate majority leader, Shawnee County attorney, and his heritage as a "son of the Kanza Nation." Curtis's mother had Kaw, Osage, and Potawatomi lineage, which made her son the only vice president of verified Native American descent, although Calvin Coolidge made genealogical claims in his autobiography. Were Coolidge alive today, his assertion might put him in a dicier situation, as Senator Elizabeth Warren could attest.

The Kanza Nation, from which the state of Kansas derived its name, is represented with a statue atop the capitol dome, where we

---

[56] See Figure 36.

stopped briefly after the cemetery. The sun had descended too much by this point to take top-notch pictures, but I was able to count it as my fourth statehouse (another burgeoning quest). It was way past the time where we could tour the building, but that freed us up to devour some desperately-needed dinner.

The problem in that was Topeka's citizens seemed to subscribe to Benjamin Franklin's "early to bed, early to rise" adage. There was nary a person on the sidewalks at eight o'clock, and restaurant after restaurant was already closed for the night – even a fast food joint. When we finally were able to grab a bite, it was due to the graciousness of a bar and grille that reopened its kitchen expressly for us. If the capital city was that desolate early in the evening, what would the rest of the state be like?

A hint came as we sat at the bar. My father fielded a phone call from the motel in Abilene that we booked for the night because of its proximity to the Eisenhower Library. The clerk was checking to see if we were still coming to stay. When he hung up his cell phone, my father wisecracked that the employees were probably wondering if they could count on their dinner arriving.

The inn was not, in fact, run by cannibals, but was an unsettling environment all the same. As we walked from the rental car to our motel room, a group of utility workers gathered around their trucks stared silently and eerily in our direction. Doing nothing to assuage my uneasiness, our room's door stood a full inch apart from its frame. Once my dad secured the chain lock, he assessed the room and its two beds, one closer to the entrance than the other. I asked which one he wanted to sleep in.

"It depends," he replied. "Do you want to die in silence, or to the sound of my death scream?"

I chose the bed closer to the door, implying an immediate death and therefore silence, but was thrilled to wake up A-okay and ride down the street to President Eisenhower's grave as opposed to spending time with him in the afterlife.

The 34th president was a devoutly religious Christian: he supported the addition of the phrase "under God" to the Pledge of

Allegiance, and he signed a bill that required "In God We Trust" to be displayed on U.S. currency. He also chose to be interred in a chapel-like structure on the grounds of his presidential library.

Technically, the Place of Meditation is not a place of worship. General Eisenhower wished it to be a haven where "visitors would reflect upon the ideals that made this a great nation and pledge themselves again to continued loyalty to those ideals." The interior still contains religious overtones, but in a style that is inextricable from the decade in which it was constructed. The aesthetics just screamed "1960s" to me. Rather than depict biblical scenes, the stained glass windows are hodgepodges of colors that would be at home in a modern art museum. Stepping behind an equally modernistic decorative screen, I approached the sunken family crypt, where a three-sided travertine enclosure is supplemented with the moderate Republican's own words:

> The real fire within the builders of America was faith – faith in a Provident God whose hand supported and guided them: faith in themselves as the children of God . . . faith in their country and its principles that proclaimed man's right to freedom and justice.
>
> Abilene Homecoming, June 4, 1952

> Humility must always be the portion of any man who receives acclaim earned in blood of his followers and sacrifices of his friends.
>
> Guildhall Address, London, June 12, 1945

> Every gun made, every warship launched, every rocket fired signifies, in the final sense, a theft from those who hunger and are not fed, those who are cold and are not clothed . . . This is not a way of life at all . . . Under this cloud of threatening war, it is humanity hanging from a cross of iron.
>
> "The Chance for Peace" Address, Washington, D.C., April 16, 1953

Two stone lids cover the vault that cradles the Eisenhowers' remains. At the foot of the left-hand slab is a marker for the president. Below the slab opposite sits a plaque for First Lady Mamie Eisenhower, whose proclivity for wearing the color pink inspired a surge in its popularity among American consumers. A nameplate for their elder son, nicknamed "Icky," lies between them. The three-year-old died of scarlet fever in 1921.

As was often the case, pictures from the internet and *Who's Buried in Grant's Tomb?* prepared us for the mid-thigh fence that separated visitors from the crypt. The security camera pointed right at the graves, however, was a jolting surprise. Hopping a railing in a chapel stand-in was already pushing my limits, but surely I wasn't going to do so on closed-circuit television! I demurred, and the two of us decided to forgo any pictures for the moment.

As I built up some nerve, we explored the other major public facets of the Eisenhower Presidential Center: his childhood home and the museum. The commemorative mural in the museum foyer spanned most of Ike's life: his childhood playing baseball, farming at the homestead, his departure for the U.S. Military Academy at West Point, his marriage to Mamie, his leadership as commander of the Allied Expeditionary Force during World War II, and his presidential inauguration in 1953.

Perhaps owing to his two uncles' service in WWII, my father is totally enamored with learning about the conflict and thoroughly videotaped the wide swath of related relics on display. The goal of the military exhibition was to "illustrate the role of General Dwight D. Eisenhower, the Supreme Commander, and the men and women that served with him during the European conflict." I didn't find the historical evidence so relevant.

The collection included Ike's 1942 Cadillac staff car, a bomber jacket, and a passel of equipment that washed up on Utah Beach in 1969. Artifacts from the Axis Powers were displayed, like a Nazi officer's dagger and straw boots worn on the Eastern Front. "Totally silly and it's amazing anybody would wear them," my father guffawed, "but I guess they had to stay warm." I was not as taken with the museum as my dad. I struggled to find anything to relate to Ike about, or understand what these objects signified about his impact on the European

Theater of the war. Maybe I missed something, but the setup just felt cold and superficial. (The Eisenhower Library's museum re-opened in 2019 after undergoing its first extensive retooling since the 1970s. I hope to return someday and assess the highly-touted updates!)

The galleries eventually transitioned to the Eisenhower presidency, but the museum clearly placed significantly greater emphasis on his military career. Outside, as we worked our way back to the Place of Meditation, a statue of the general with his hands on his hips stood elevated over the words "Champion of Peace." Given context, it all made sense. The Eisenhower section of *Who's Buried in Grant's Tomb?* notes that Ike requested to be laid to rest "in an eighty-dollar standard-issue military coffin" and wearing his Army uniform. Like several other presidents with military backgrounds, reaching the White House ranked second on Ike's list of accomplishments.

Inside the sanctuary, I again faced the question of whether or not to storm the general's quarters. I took my father's picture squatting in front of the railing, and it was difficult to make out Eisenhower's vault cover between the bars. Once he scrutinized the photo, my dad shifted into overdrive pressuring me to climb into the crypt. He argued it was improbable anyone was monitoring the security camera in real time, and that it was there just to ward off wrongdoers and so the library could roll back the footage in the occurrence of vandalism. Unlike the soldiers whom the general addressed on the eve of the Normandy invasion, the eyes of the world were not, in all likelihood, upon me. Besides, he contended, according to the biography he read on the flight, Ike wasn't afraid to push authoritative boundaries. When ordered to present themselves in their dress coats before a cadet corporal at West Point, Cadet Eisenhower and a comrade showed up in *solely* their dress coats. Since I didn't intend to pose partially nude for this graveside picture, a more germane example from the book might have been that Ike repeatedly risked expulsion from the academy by "going over the wall" for nighttime sandwich and ice cream runs.

Yet even without this apropos anecdote, I was successfully swayed. I swung my legs over the rail and crouched beside the president's marker. Lest an employee or another visitor walk in on me, I opted not to cross over to Mamie's side of the pit. Once my father snapped the pictures I skedaddled back over the fence. As I reviewed his work in the shade outside, my dad fired up the camcorder.

"Hey, Kurt? Were you nervous when you jumped over the railing to get the grave shot with Eisenhower… with the security camera?" he laughed.

Disquieted, I hesitatingly smiled and returned my attention to the viewfinder. "Uh, yeah."

"Yeah," my father chuckled in agreement. "Was a little bit of an adrenaline rush. Alright, we better leave the grounds before we're arrested." He said this in jest, but I agreed all the same.

"Eventful trip," he continued. "Well, hey, say thanks to Grandma and Papa Joe," for financing the vacation.

"Thanks, Grandma and Papa Joe!"

"…for almost getting us arrested," my dad butted in.

The threat of repercussions filled my mind, but not enough to dissuade me from perusing the Eisenhower Museum store for souvenirs. We eventually started heading back east toward Missouri, with a brief second foray into Topeka to tour the capitol. As evening began to set in, we reached Kansas City's Forest Hill Cemetery, the first of two burying grounds we hoped to explore before closing time. In relatively short order I spotted the grave of Leroy "Satchel" Paige, acclaimed pitcher of the Negro Leagues who, two years after Jackie Robinson broke baseball's color barrier with the Brooklyn Dodgers, made his MLB debut with the Cleveland Indians at age 42. He played multiple seasons in the Majors with Cleveland and the St. Louis Browns, but his final appearance didn't come until September 1965, by which point Paige was an astonishing 59 years old. One side of the colorful hall of famer's monument at Forest Hill is engraved with his list of six ways to stay young.[57] "Don't look back," the hurler recommends from the dead. "Something might be gaining on you."

With a sense of urgency because of the late hour, my father and I heeded Paige's aphorism and maintained focus as we drove the

---

[57] See Figure 37.

five miles across town to Mount Moriah Cemetery. I read on Find a Grave that Mount Moriah was the final resting place of longtime CBS anchorman Walter Cronkite, who had passed away a month prior. There were no pictures submitted yet on the website, though, and thus no visual references like we used to find Paige. As we pulled onto the property we saw two suited cemetery employees, and both of us jumped out to inquire with one of them about the newscaster's where-abouts. His mouth formed a wry smile.

"Well," the man started, "he isn't here yet." Our eyes widened. It turned out that Cronkite's body was cremated in New York, where he died, and his ashes hadn't yet been brought to Missouri. So we actually beat the newsman to his own grave. And that's the way it was, to paraphrase Cronkite's newscast-ending tagline. As consolation, the employee suggested we visit the plot of Pro Football Hall of Fame defensive tackle Junious "Buck" Buchanan. My father remembered crying at age nine in 1970 when Buchanan's Kansas City Chiefs trounced his beloved Minnesota Vikings 23-7 in Super Bowl IV. It was an easy pass for him.

However, neither premature visitation nor Super Bowl sorrows could sully our day. I had my picture taken closer to President Eisenhower's tomb than any other grave hunter I was aware of, and the place we were staying at that night didn't exude a Bates Motel vibe. Our hotel in Independence, just outside Kansas City, had a pool and was neighbor to a convenience store. Best of all, the door to our room extended all the way to the frame (what a luxury!).

It was also just four miles from the Truman Library. The build-ing was nothing extraordinary architecturally; it looked similar to the plain style of the Eisenhower museum, and a galaxy apart from the abstract design I.M. Pei applied to the Kennedy Library in Boston. Yet what was inside set it apart from other presidential NARA libraries. Yes, it contained the obligatory oval office replica. Yes, it displayed interesting items like the weapons used in a failed assassination attempt by Puerto Rican nationalists, and the copy of the fallacious "DEWEY DEFEATS TRUMAN" newspaper the president hoisted jovially after the 1948 election. But the Truman Library, more so than the others of its ilk, overtly encouraged analysis and reflection.

Perhaps my experiences at the Reagan and Nixon Libraries the August prior piqued my interest in exhibit practices, or maybe, now being 14 years of age, I'd matured to the point where I was not engrossed solely by the physical artifacts, regardless of their provenance. Or perhaps the Truman Library, to a greater extent than the six other NARA presidential museums I had toured, was indeed more conversational.[58]

A pivotal and much-contested occurrence in Harry's administration was his 1945 decision to drop atomic bombs upon two Japanese cities in an attempt to end hostilities in World War II. The devastation, coupled with a Soviet invasion, prompted Japan's surrender. Fatalities, which are estimated to have exceeded 200,000, consisted primarily of civilians, many of whom survived the initial attacks but died subsequently of radiation poisoning or other effects.

Exploring the intricacies of the end result of the Manhattan Project has proven to be a precarious endeavor for museums. A planned exhibit at the Smithsonian Institution in the 1990s was assailed as "politically correct" and "anti-American" for its inclusion of the impact on the Japanese people, and it was scrapped as a result. The Truman Library presented – along with rigid facts and statistics – differing perspectives on an array of issues the Democrat faced during his presidency, including the use of atomic weapons. My father videoed as we explored a gallery titled "The Debate Continues." Its text read:

> "Few presidential acts have ignited as much controversy as President Truman's decision to use atomic weapons against Japan. Was the bombing of Hiroshima and Nagasaki necessary to bring about the surrender of Japan? Did the decision save

---

[58] My graduate studies at the University of Massachusetts Boston a decade later would emphasize the importance of shared authority. Public historians need to find a balance between relying on their expertise and enabling agency within the community and obtaining outside input. Modern public history trends endorse treating museums as facilitators of dialogue, where participants discuss their interpretation of events. In retrospect, I understand that this is what I experienced at the Truman Library in Independence.

more lives than it cost? Were there alternatives for ending the war? Half a century after the bombings, the debate continues.

"What do you think?"

A fellow museum patron vocalized his opinion. "I don't understand," he announced with incredulity. "They say, 'Oh we shouldn't have dropped the bombs.' That there is more torture."

In a gallery guestbook, I put my own thoughts on paper. "While it is unfortunate that we had to drop the bombs and take so many lives," I began, "had we not, the war could have lasted years longer, and an even larger amount of lives could have been taken. Truman made the right decision."

Today I am far less certain of the necessity of the use of the atomic weapons. My father followed up with his own entry, which concurred with my sentiments at the time. He added that, nevertheless, such destruction "should never again take place." The person who made that decision, right or wrong, was buried a few yards away, primed to become my 36th dead president visited.

A month earlier – on July 4th, appropriately – my parents purchased the domain for www.kurtshistoricsites.com, my own website akin to those of the presidential grave hunters whose online accounts had entertained me for the previous six years. The website was a more public way to showcase my photos than the small album I'd toted around since visiting the Hoover Library. I also viewed it as an opportunity to pay it forward and educate people about the facts I'd learned about the presidents in books and in my travels.

Over several weeks I added stories and pictures from past adventures, but decided I wanted a greater variety of photos than my father normally took at sites. On this trip I assumed control of the camera, except, of course, when I needed to be in the picture. My father refused to be idle, though. As we moved from the exhibits toward the gravesite, we encountered a life-size statue of Truman, which looked out a glass window, over an eternal flame, and across the courtyard to his real-life counterpart's burial site. As I snapped and evaluated photos, my dad aimed the camcorder at me.

"Why are you videotaping me taking a picture?" I queried. He was defensive. "Because it's our trip... Because I can't videotape myself!"

Entering the courtyard, we strolled along the walkway over to the graves of Harry and Bess Truman, surrounded by purple flowers. No first lady lived longer than Mrs. Truman, who reached age 97. On her gray slab, beneath her lifespan, are the achievements she must have valued most: her tenure as first lady, her marriage to Harry in 1919, and the birth of her only child five years later. Margaret Truman Daniel, in fact, was buried only a few feet away, having died 19 months before our trip.

Harry's marker also mentions the birth of his daughter, of whom he was very protective. In December 1950, he threatened a *Washington Post* critic who pilloried Margaret's singing career. "Some day I hope to meet you," the sitting president wrote to Paul Hume. "When that happens you'll need a new nose, a lot of beefsteak for black eyes, and perhaps a supporter below!"

The president was already distraught because he was mourning his longtime friend and press secretary, Charlie Ross, and perhaps he wouldn't have written such an ornery letter under different circumstances. Then again, Truman wasn't a person who shied from laying all his cards on the table. "The truth is all I want for history," says the inscription on a wall near the gravesite.

There was something just so utterly satisfying and peaceful about the courtyard, and it was difficult to peel myself away to finish up our self-guided tour of the museum. I was rewarded in the gift shop when I found a replica of Truman's "The Buck Stops Here" sign, which, like his own, was crafted by prison inmates. The display for the original sign noted it was "unclear how long it sat on his Oval Office desk," but that it "has come to symbolize Truman's decisiveness and accountability." The reproduction was an instant buy.

My dad and I forced ourselves to leave the library in order to accomplish the rest of our tasks for the day, but we were delighted to learn that the building had extended hours until 9 p.m. on Thursdays in the summer without readmission cost (and luckily it *was* a Thursday).

That put our minds at ease during our drive north to Jesse James's family homestead in Kearney. After he was shot in 1882, the notorious outlaw was buried on the property in a spot where his mother could keep a watchful eye on his grave. Despite this, souvenir hunters managed to repeatedly break off chunks of his monument. Our guide at the James Farm told us Zerelda James's solution to quell desecration: she sold the stones that covered her son's plot for 25 cents apiece. When her supply was depleted, she simply walked down to the creek with a bucket to replenish it. Later, when no one was looking, my father swiped a stone for me and deposited a quarter on the base of the memorial. He declined to account for the inflation that had accumulated over the course of 127 years, but Mrs. James's ghost did not appear and gripe.

I didn't bother to have my picture taken with the obelisk at the James Farm, for the grave no longer was occupied. Jesse James's body had been exhumed and relocated to nearby Mount Olivet Cemetery, where we stopped next. From there it was on to Plattsburg, the final resting place of a man with the dubious claim of having served as president of the United States for one day.

In 1849, the typical March 4th inauguration day fell upon a Sunday, and Zachary Taylor's swearing-in was delayed 24 hours out of deference to religious observances. Even without a ceremony, Taylor and Vice President-elect Millard Fillmore were automatically instated to their posts. Yet conjecture subsequently emerged that the reputed vacancy elevated the next person in the line of succession to chief executive, which in 1849 was the president pro tempore of the Senate. The man who held that office was David Rice Atchison, but his own term as president pro tem expired on March 4th, therefore squashing any serious historical debate. Regardless, his debunked claim to fame is included in his epitaph, and some grave hunters, such as myself and Brian Lamb, still drop in on him at Greenlawn Cemetery. Richard Norton Smith, on the other hand, quipped he had standards.

Once we wrapped up in Plattsburg and visited Carry Nation in Belton, we returned to the Truman Library, where in the nighttime the gas-lit flame created an even more serene atmosphere. I snapped photos and directed my father on precisely how I wanted him to film the flickering flame's reflection against the glass in front of Harry's statue. Nothing we captured did the scene justice. Truman's memorial wasn't the most elaborate or glamorous presidential resting place, nor did it have a view comparable to Monticello or the Reagan Library. But the poignancy and tranquility it radiated allowed it to transcend most other graves I'd seen. It was elegant, but simple enough to still jibe with Truman's principles and down-to-earth personality.[59]

On some trips, my father and I rushed around, trying to jam as many sites into our itinerary as possible for the sake of cost-effectiveness and other reasons. Yet our experience in the Truman Library courtyard proved that, sometimes, the best use of time was to slow down and appreciate the calmer moments.

---

[59] One exhibit section in the Truman Library spoke of the offers Harry received after his presidency to use his name in advertising. One proposal was the Harry S. Truman Soap Company. The bar wrappers had Independence, Missouri, printed on them, but were made in New York. "Truman would have none of it," the exhibit text read. "He adamantly refused to cheapen the office of the President with endorsements."

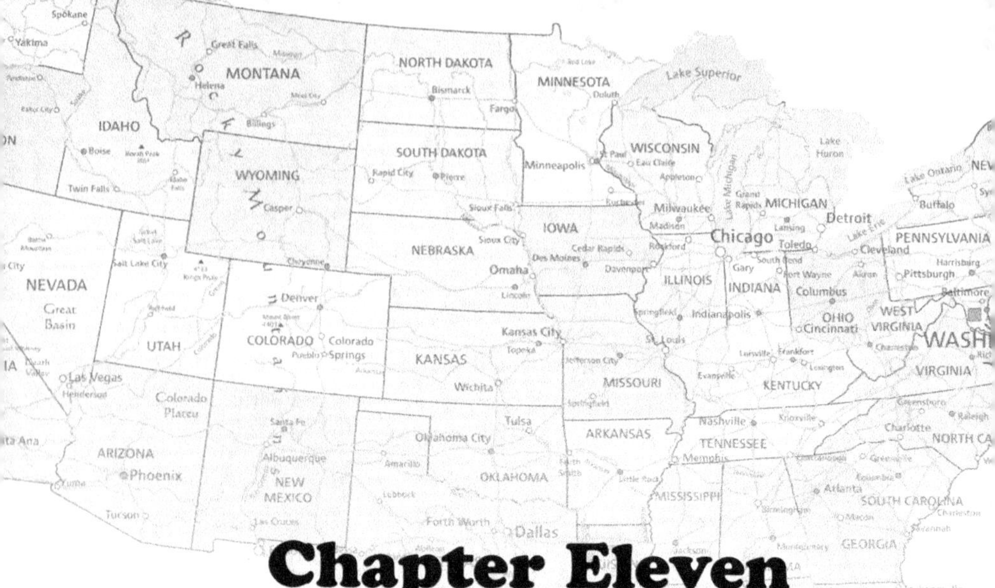

Chapter Eleven
A Gander at a Michigander
~ April 2010 ~

The Ike & Truman Trip was possible only through the charity of Grandma and Papa Joe. The United States was still dealing with ramifications from the Great Recession of 2007-2009, which exacerbated my father's job search. Meanwhile, none of his unique invention concepts reached the production stage. But it was of immense importance to him that I reach every presidential burial site before my high school graduation, and he is a very determined individual when he sets his sights on something. He and my mom would ensure my dream was realized, even if it required thinking outside the box.

That was no tall order for my father. In the spring, our family staged a yard sale and sold off the remnants of my dad's personal collections. Guilt consumed me. To help pay bills in recent years, he had parted ways with the majority of the toys and other memorabilia he accumulated over the decades. Those efforts benefited the whole family though, and this particular purge was expressly for my benefit. The most stinging departures for me were the furnishings from Collins Drugs, a defunct shop where my father bought comic books and candy as a child. When the Johnston, RI, retailer closed, my dad's business was prosperous and he swooped in to preserve that important part of his youth.

But, as he and my mother always strove to impart upon me and my sister, people are more important than things. And as much as it pained me to have my quest drive a wedge between my father and his cherished mementos, it would have bothered him more to have them stand in the way of the promise he made to his son.

The yard sale was timed so that the two of us would have the requisite funds before school's April Vacation, when we'd visit the closer of my two remaining dead presidents, Gerald Ford. Our transactions raised enough money for a few nights' motels and a rental car. Driving would allow us to see other graves and attractions on the way to Michigan and back, while renting would keep us from putting a couple thousand miles on my dad's vehicle. Furthermore, it'd enable us to visit six vice presidents (apart from Ford) and thereby save money in the long term by eliminating the need for future trips.

In another effort to possibly alleviate expenses, my dad reached out to some venues to explain my story and see if he could convince them to give us discounts or freebies. An inn outside Dearborn, Michigan, offered us a free night's stay and complimentary tickets to The Henry Ford, an awkwardly-named innovation-themed campus started by the automotive magnate. Between Gerald and Henry, it promised to be a Ford-filled week.

When we started out on Saturday the 17th, I gained a literal new perspective of our trips. Tired of chauffeuring me around, my dad announced I'd graduated from the back of the car to the front passenger seat. Aged 15, I now shared the same view out the windshield that he did as we pulled out of the driveway and commenced the voyage, our mission renewed.

It was a 265-mile haul to our first stop, and, combined with a later-than-scheduled start, it was mid-afternoon before we accomplished anything on my agenda. The first destination was the tomb of Vice President James Sherman. Sunny Jim's claim to fame is that he's the most recent VP to die in office. He succumbed to Bright's disease on October 30, 1912, six days before he and William Howard Taft were to stand for re-election. The incumbent Taft received a paltry eight electoral votes, Woodrow Wilson's 435 votes sent him to the White House, and Sherman ended up at Forest Hill Cemetery in Utica, New York. Sherman's sizable mausoleum surely cost a pretty penny, yet it wasn't the most striking grave at Forest Hill. On our way up a cemetery road, my father and I were jarred by a field full of twirling pinwheels, which we realized decorated the graves of children. These trips caused us to run the gamut of emotions, and this was one of the more heartrending moments from our travels.

Our journey through New York continued to Westernville, the burial location of Declaration of Independence signatory William Floyd, and then to Auburn. We were looking for the graves of Harriet Tubman and William Seward – secretary of state under Abraham Lincoln and Andrew Johnson. But with no map to reference, it appeared we would be striking out. Fortunately, a local pointed us in the direction of Tubman, who guided enslaved escapees north to freedom via the Underground Railroad. The stranger couldn't help in our pursuit of Seward. Fort Hill Cemetery is vast, so my father and I decided to split up. After probably 15 minutes of running around, we simultaneously stumbled upon the former presidential cabinet member.

Seward was buried at Fort Hill in 1872, but ironically might have been there sooner had it not been for a devastating carriage mishap. On April 5, 1865, Seward was seriously injured when he leapt from his fast-moving carriage in an attempt to grab the reins of its horses, who had taken off like lightning while the driver was not aboard. The bloody and bruised cabinet official was bedridden in his home with a broken jaw and dislocated shoulder. Nine days later, as part of the plot that took President Lincoln's life, the secretary was attacked by John Wilkes Booth's knife-wielding compatriot, former Confederate soldier Lewis Powell. Though Seward's face was scarred by the blade, his jugular vein was protected by a brace he wore for his broken jaw.

Seward was once Lincoln's political rival. Both men vied for the Republican Party's presidential nomination in 1860, but after his victory in the general election, Lincoln selected Seward as his right-hand man. During Lincoln's four years in office, Seward was one of Lincoln's most trusted advisors, on matters both foreign and domestic. On the issue of slavery, Lincoln's most important advisor was a person who had escaped its oppressive clutches: Frederick Douglass, whose grave was next on our itinerary.

Douglass was enslaved from his birth circa February 1818 until September 1838, when he escaped from Maryland up to New York. As a free man he dedicated himself to social causes. In 1847 he founded the *North Star* – a Rochester-based, anti-slavery newspaper – and the following year he attended the first-ever women's rights convention in Seneca Falls. There he signed the Declaration of Sentiments, a resolution which called for "immediate admission to all the rights and privileges which belong to [women] as citizens of these United States," such as suffrage and property rights. A powerful and prolific orator, one of Douglass's most memorable speeches was an 1852 address in which he expressed his view of the Fourth of July as a holiday with hollow meaning for Black Americans – both enslaved and free – deprived of "justice, liberty, prosperity and independence." During Abraham Lincoln's administration, Douglass was unafraid to publicly criticize the president for his slow pace on emancipatory action, but also eager to praise him when they aligned. Douglass continued his advocacy until his death in 1895.

I thought our late start was working against us because it was nightfall by the time we reached Rochester, but the gates to Mount Hope Cemetery were surprisingly open. We pulled in and found Douglass's plot – a straightforward task thanks to signage – and swiftly retreated toward the exit, where a most unwelcome surprise greeted us.

In the scant minutes that passed since we entered Mount Hope, a gatekeeper came by and rendered us unable to leave! We'd been locked out of a few cemeteries on our trips, but the prospect of being locked in never crossed my mind. The two of us were at a loss of what to do until we spotted a sign with a phone number to call in case of this exact situation. Our relief dissipated when the call failed because it required an area code, which wasn't listed on the sign. We had no means of looking up the code on the internet with my father's flip phone. Then I remembered, along with the cemetery addresses and reference pictures included in our elaborate itinerary, I had listed phone numbers with area codes![60] We were rescued after ten adrenaline-fueled minutes.

In the morning, we continued west toward a city we already visited during one of our previous presidential journeys: Buffalo. In 1901, the Nickel City hosted the Pan-American Exposition, and President William McKinley was mortally wounded while glad-handing visitors in the extravaganza's Temple of Music. The expo's structures weren't intended to be permanent, and the temple was torn down after its conclusion. The site eventually transformed into a residential neighborhood, where we parked across from a rock-mounted memorial plaque in a road median. There was no comparison to the museums at Ford's Theatre and the former Texas School Book Depository, but it was a lot better than the nothingness that hitherto existed at James Garfield's assassination site.

A more substantial reminder of McKinley's death resides in the Buffalo History Museum's collection: the .32 caliber revolver Leon Czolgosz greeted the president with. When my father and I arrived at the museum, though, we were informed that the weapon is housed off-site in a building opened only by appointment. The two of us were told we could try our luck and see if anyone was there, but we got no answer at the facility and were forced to continue our sojourn toward Michigan.[61]

The quickest and easiest route to the Wolverine State from Buffalo was through Canada, but, to provide some extra drama, my father misplaced his license-size passport card as we were in line to cross the border. It was in his hand one moment, and the next it was nowhere to be found. Despite our lack of documentation, we were

---

[60] I had the foresight to list area codes, but sadly forgot to include suffragist Susan B. Anthony on the itinerary. She is interred at Mount Hope Cemetery in Rochester as well.

[61] Along with my friend, Kelvis, my father and I returned to Buffalo to see the weapon and other McKinley assassination artifacts in January 2016.

allowed to pass through after a brief delay. Thank goodness, because we were still trying to fit in two final resting places that day: Henry Ford and civil rights icon Rosa Parks in Detroit.[62] If we had to cut through Pennsylvania and Ohio we definitely would've missed out on their graves, and possibly our complimentary room in Dearborn as well.

Once we re-entered the U.S. at Detroit, we headed straight for the small cemetery at St. Martha's Episcopal Church where Ford and his wife Clara rest. The Fords are interred beneath slabs covered by a mortsafe, which is a protective cage. Perhaps the industrialist was concerned his antisemitic views would spur some grave desecration? Or perhaps that an aggrieved assembly line worker would seek retribution? No matter the reason, the mortsafe made it difficult to photograph me and capture the Fords' inscribed names at the same time. In typical fashion, my father found a solution by climbing up a nearby tree to take an "aerial" photograph.

Elsewhere in Detroit, we had less success with Rosa Parks. The two of us searched a gigantic mausoleum in Woodlawn Cemetery for her and came up short, only to later discover the smaller, locked Rosa L. Parks Freedom Chapel. The Woodlawn office was also closed, which effectively ended our day.

Although the frustrations were mounting, at least we had our free room at the inn, and the following day we used our comped tickets at The Henry Ford. Its namesake established the complex in 1929 ostensibly to showcase the history of American innovation, but its contents had branched out in genre. Mixed in with giant machines and an R. Buckminster Fuller concept house were items like George Washington's wartime cot and the chair Abraham Lincoln sat in during his fateful viewing of *Our American Cousin*. Honest Abe's rocker seemed out of place from a technological standpoint, but it fit the theme of Lincoln death seats. The 1961 Lincoln Continental convertible that John F. Kennedy rode in while in Dallas was parked in the hall, part of the museum's collection of presidential vehicles.

---

[62] Parks, who is most often associated with Montgomery, Alabama, relocated to Detroit in 1957 and lived there until her death in 2005.

I was unsettled, but more so because the contraption where JFK spent his last moments of consciousness was positioned facing an Oscar Mayer Wienermobile. The limousine no longer appeared how it did on that nightmarish November day. Rather than retire it, a committee saw that the limo was retooled to better protect subsequent presidents. When it was reintroduced into the presidential fleet in June 1964, it had a permanent non-removable roof, new armor and trim, and a different, darker paint color, among other internal mechanical modifications. Additional alterations were made in 1967. The car remained in use until early 1977, and, taking that into account, I reasoned perhaps it was best it didn't look at all like it did during the Kennedy administration. If I were Presidents Johnson, Nixon, Ford, or Carter, my stomach would have churned every time I sat in that back seat.

The Kennedy limo's facelift may have dulled my reaction to seeing it in person, but I *was* jostled in the civil rights display, where I came face-to-face with a mannequin in full Ku Klux Klan regalia. The hooded figure cast a menacing presence over the gallery and its "Whites Only" drinking fountain. I couldn't even begin to imagine the emotions racial minorities must have felt when they were confronted with such overt vitriol.

The exhibit became more uplifting as we progressed. Narration about Jackie Robinson breaking baseball's color barrier, and audio of Lyndon Johnson's 1965 speech on the Voting Rights Bill played from a speaker system as my dad and I approached the gallery's centerpiece: the Cleveland Avenue bus from Montgomery, Alabama. On December 1, 1955, seamstress Rosa Parks rode that segregated city bus home from work. She was seated in the first row of the "colored section" that occupied the rear half of the bus, but when the white section at the front of the vehicle became full, driver James F. Blake ordered Parks and three other Black people to move farther back. Parks, who was the secretary for the Montgomery chapter of the National Association for the Advancement of Colored People, took a stand by remaining seated. Parks was not the first person of color to challenge Montgomery's racist transportation accommodations. She was preceded by people like

15-year-old Claudette Colvin, who was brought into custody nine months before Parks for the same type of civil disobedience. But Parks's arrest was the final straw for oppressed locals, who were galvanized to launch the Montgomery bus boycott in the ensuing days. A year later, the financial and legal campaign to integrate Montgomery's buses was won.

The Henry Ford actually allows visitors to enter the refurbished Parks bus, and we followed a school group tour onto the historic vehicle.[63] "When you hear Rosa Parks's voice," an employee announced, "the seat that she was sitting in, this light on top will shine brighter." My father and I stood in the back of the dimly lit bus as a recorded narrator described what life was like for African Americans in the South in the mid-1900s. He then instructed us to "Listen to Rosa Parks tell us what happened on *this* bus that day."

"The driver said that if I refused to leave the seat," the disembodied Parks began, "he would have to call the police, and I told him just call the police, which he did and when they came, they placed me under arrest." As the audio ran, a light suddenly shone on a green leather seat on the right side of the bus, where a young Black girl sat. She and her friends stirred with excitement. "The time had just come," the seamstress continued, "when I had been pushed as far as I could stand to be pushed, I suppose. I had decided that I would have to know, once and for all, what rights I had as a human being and a citizen, even in Montgomery, Alabama." The tape ended with a recording of the song "This Little Light of Mine," which prompted all the children to start clapping to the rhythm in unison. "That was *awesome*," one of them exclaimed.

To complete the Rosa Parks history tour, my father and I ducked out in the early afternoon to return to Woodlawn Cemetery, and we found an employee to unlock the chapel where she was interred. The two of us then returned to The Henry Ford, where our attention shifted from the indoor museum to the picturesque Greenfield Village, stocked with Model Ts, trains, and uprooted buildings like the Wright Brothers' bicycle shop. It was as if we'd stepped through a time mach-

---

[63] See Figure 38.

ine. It would have been fortuitous if my father and I actually found such a device in Thomas Edison's recreated Menlo Park laboratory so that we could've prolonged the day. We hadn't even begun to scratch the surface of the hamlet by the end of operating hours.

The next day, in Grand Rapids, we visited a different Ford museum that was much more condensed in its scope — the life and presidency of Gerald Ford. I was careful not to use the term presidential library in front of the camcorder because the archive with Ford's papers is located in Ann Arbor. He's the only president whose NARA library and museum are housed in different communities.

One narrative the museum tried to convey was that Jerry Ford was a man of the people. A placard noted that, as a candidate in the Republican primary for Michigan's 5th Congressional District, Ford promised a farmer that he would milk his cows if he won. The day after his victory, Ford showed up at 4:30 a.m. and told the astonished farmer, "I'm not going to break my campaign promises." It was that kind of integrity that propelled Ford to House minority leader, vice president, and president.

Ford's ascension to the latter office was made possible by the Watergate Scandal. Unlike the Nixon Library, which had no mention of the president's political downfall when we visited in 2008, Watergate was a crucial focus of the Ford Museum. A glass case enclosed the tools burglars used to break into Democratic National Committee headquarters, and one of Nixon's Oval Office tape recorders was displayed as well. Elsewhere, we read the contrite resignation letter Nixon wrote to Secretary of State Henry Kissinger, and envisioned Ford grasping the pen he used to authorize his predecessor's pardon in September 1974. Ford received criticism for what some inferred was a crooked deal — the presidency for a pardon — but in truth, there was no unscrupulous arrangement with Nixon. The new chief magistrate felt America must get past its "long national nightmare" and move forward. He needed to be able to govern without the sword of Damocles hanging over his head.

Things weren't easy for Ford. In September 1975, he survived two separate assassination attempts. Museum patrons huddled around the Colt .45 wielded by Lynette "Squeaky" Fromme as the president approached the California State Capitol. The year 1975 was fraught with peril for Ford and his administration. In the spring, communist forces surged through U.S.-backed South Vietnam, promising a bitter end to the two-decade-long quagmire that was the Vietnam War. The People's Army of Vietnam advanced toward the Southern capital of Saigon with rapidity, and the U.S. commenced Operation Frequent Wind to evacuate fearful South Vietnamese civilians. On April 29th, the day before the city was taken and South Vietnam ceased to exist, CIA Air America helicopters picked up desperate soon-to-be-refugees atop Saigon buildings. The most recognizable photograph from the mission, captured by Dutch photojournalist Hubert van Es, shows evacuees ascending a crowded staircase toward a chopper. The building in van Es's picture was mistakenly reported as being the U.S. Embassy, when it was really an apartment building. The helicopter, the staircase, and all they symbolized were now on full display in Grand Rapids.[64]

For me, of course, the main attraction was Ford's grave. The former president was entombed in an oval-shaped, concrete memorial just north of the museum. Metal letters affixed to the upright slabs that comprise the memorial spell out that he and his wife, First Lady Betty Ford, led "Lives Committed to God, Country and Love." Underneath are their names and their lifespans, though Mrs. Ford was still among the living at the time of our visit – she passed away 15 months later on July 8, 2011.

I thought the tomb to be uninspired and drab, especially compared to the grandiose sepulchers of some of his nineteenth-century predecessors. In the midst of my video commentary, a tractor trailer transiting Highway 131 right behind the park blared its horn. When Bill Clinton visited the grave of his easy-going, Midwestern-reared predecessor years prior, he voiced his approval. "This is so Jerry Ford. This is perfect Jerry Ford."

With my penultimate presidential resting place secured, we worked our way down to South Bend, Indiana, to see our second vice

---

[64] See Figure 39.

president grave of the day: Schuyler Colfax. At City Cemetery, I instructed my father to take an immediate left inside the gate, and we drove around a loop fruitlessly searching for Colfax. Eventually we ended back at the entrance, and there he was, right at the front. Sometimes I didn't live up to my title of grave hunter.

Our trek continued down to Kentucky, where we planned to visit two more VPs, a presidential candidate, and a fried chicken restaurateur – if you thought my father forgot his failure to see Colonel Sanders's grave in 2004, then I've done a poor job of describing him in this book. Beyond that, my dad discovered that the KFC Corporate Headquarters in Louisville hosted a small museum about the colonel's life and career. He barely contained his excitement as we drove to HQ, which resembled a southern plantation. Out front, a bird was perched on a bust of Sanders, and my father whipped out the video camera.

"You're only brave enough to do that, bird, because you're not a chicken," my father quipped. "So the story goes here at the corporate headquarters of KFC. Kentucky Fried Chicken. *Or is it? You be the judge!*" He zoomed in dramatically on the unsuspecting creature. "You're strange," I deadpanned.

In the midst of the clowning, a security guard pulled up in a cart beside us. "Sorry sir, video *only inside*," was his warning. My father wanted to get this straight: recording was prohibited *outside* the building, which anyone could find a picture of on the internet – but it was permissible to take videos *inside*, where the secret recipe with the eleven herbs and spices might be held?

"That's correct," the officer verified. Bemused and amused, we entered the headquarters and found, standing next to a giant KFC bucket, none other than the founder himself! Or perhaps it was just an animatronic Sanders, but it was *very* realistic.[65] "Welcome," the figure greeted. "My name is Colonel Harland Sanders, and this museum is all about my life, don't you see?"

My father engaged in a slew of shenanigans with the faux colonel, and the lunacy continued at Cave Hill Cemetery, which by then we

---

[65] See Figure 40.

knew to be the real Sanders's resting place. His grave was such a popular attraction that a line was painted on the cemetery roads leading up to it so pilgrims wouldn't constantly ask the office employees for its location. At the columned monument, my father subjected me to what I hoped was the last of his antics for the day. I filmed as he stood next to the memorial, which included yet another likeness of the chicken man.

"Paul Deion, *gravy* hunter here at the original gravesite of Colonel Sanders. We couldn't find the extra crispy one."

Ugh.

"Anyway," he continued, "it's been rumored that the colonel *isn't* dead because of the MSGs and other chemicals that were in the eleven secret herbs and spices, that he actually cannot die, and that if we were to go to his secluded mansion, his plantation in Southern Kentucky, we might actually see what's really happening."[66] My father's plan was to edit the footage to make it seem as if we uncovered the real-life Colonel Sanders welcoming visitors to his museum. I don't know if I should be glad he never followed through and finished the video, or upset that I had to endure the embarrassment for nothing.

The colonel and his chickens were then mercifully put on the back burner. We drove an hour east to Frankfort, site of the graves of pioneer Daniel Boone and Richard Mentor Johnson, Martin Van Buren's vice president.[67] Both men's monuments in Frankfort Cemetery display marble bas-reliefs that depict scenes a person would expect to see only in the absurdly distasteful murals that decorate the walls of Pawnee Town Hall on the sitcom *Parks and Recreation*. In keeping with Boone's distorted, posthumous reputation as a ruthless "Indian fighter," one of the four panels on his monument shows him in mortal combat with an Indigenous man. The native threatens Boone with a knife and a tomahawk, while the frontiersman – with a rifle and

---

[66] Louisville is actually located in Northern Kentucky and borders Indiana.

[67] Some historians have argued that Boone's body is still interred in its original grave in Missouri, and that the corpse of a different man was mistakenly exhumed and reburied in Frankfort in 1845.

his own blade in hand – stands upon the body of a tribesman, ready to vanquish another foe.

As for Richard M. Johnson, he served as a militia colonel during the War of 1812, while he was a member of the House of Representatives. At the Battle of Thames in October 1813, the lawmaker is alleged to have killed William Henry Harrison's rival, Shawnee leader Tecumseh, who was allied with Great Britain against the U.S. The veracity of Johnson's status as Tecumseh's killer is difficult to determine, but it proved effective in his subsequent political campaigns. The claim has also followed the ninth vice president to his grave; on the monument's southern face, a marble figure of Johnson sits atop a steed, warm pistol in hand. Due to what appears to be natural wear incurred over a century and a half as opposed to vandalism, Johnson's head is missing, the stone worn away. Tecumseh crouches on one knee, grasping at his throat, having just been dealt a fatal blow by the Headless Congressman. Johnson's and Boone's graves are an interesting snapshot of the perspectives held by white Kentuckians in the nineteenth century, and a dramatic contrast to what would be deemed appropriate on a gravestone in modern times.

As is the case with the grave of the second veep with the Johnson surname, Andrew Johnson, Richard M. Johnson's memorial includes a column that culminates with an eagle at its top, talons resting on a flag. The bird clutches a wreath in its beak. Vertically-aimed cannons are carved into the four corners of the marker's base, each side of which bears five stars. Johnson's was the most ornate grave my father and I viewed that day, but not necessarily the most spectacular, at least from my 15-year-old point of view. That title I awarded to Henry Clay, legislator and perennial presidential candidate. Loser of presidential elections in 1824, 1832, and 1844, Clay was speaker of the House in 1820 and played a key role in the passage of the Missouri Compromise, which temporarily held the Union together by papering over sectional differences.

The statesman is entombed in Lexington in a marble sarcophagus in the chamber of a 120-foot monument, which sports a statue of Clay atop its shaft. My father had to lie down on the ground with the camera in order to fit me and the entire structure in frame together. The tomb couldn't contrast any more with our main quarry at Lexington Cemetery, Vice President John C. Breckinridge, whose final resting place is marked with a barely legible headstone.

With sites in Ohio remaining on the day's agenda, time was of the essence as we drove for the exit. It was just before the five o'clock closing time, but the gates were already sealed shut! For the second time on the trip, we were locked in a cemetery. Just like in Rochester, there was a phone number to call on the gate, but the sign was as unreadable as Breckinridge's headstone. The number I had in our itinerary served only to put us in contact with an answering machine. My father then phoned the local police station, and the representative said if we reversed direction and banged every right turn in the cemetery we'd reach the maintenance building. Someone there could aid us. We did as we were told, but there were no employees at the maintenance building. Across the way was a house we assumed to be the caretaker's home, and my father rapped on the door. When a man answered, my dad asked whether or not he was the caretaker and if he had the key to let us out.

Not only was he *not* the caretaker, to our great shock he revealed that his wife, who wasn't home, had the lone key. This couple randomly lived in a house inside a gated cemetery, and they had just *one* key between them to get in and out. I know visiting graves on vacation is my version of fun, but that's a creepy line even I wouldn't cross.

The Prisoner of Lexington Cemetery said a security guard was likely patrolling the grounds and that if we drove around we would find him. We chose to head back to the main gate, and sure enough the officer was letting out another trapped car, which we followed. In our nearly seven years of grave hunting, my father and I had never before been locked in a cemetery, but in the first five days of this trip it happened to us twice. It wouldn't be the last time.

With dusk closing in fast, we reached Dayton, Ohio, hometown of Orville and Wilbur Wright, who in 1903 engineered the first sustained flight of a heavier-than-air aircraft. Woodland Cemetery's gate was already closed, but it appeared to me that there was an access point where the perimeter wall ended. My father, for whom these trips could be like a *Mission: Impossible* adventure, insisted that I was mistaken and ushered me *over* the wall instead. When we landed on the other side, we found ourselves in the company of a woman and her canine. My baffled father inquired how they got in, and she replied they simply walked around.

My dad didn't wait for my "I told you so," and immediately asked if the woman knew where the Wright Brothers were buried. The dog-walker directed us up the main road, and we amscrayed to take advantage of what little daylight remained. As we ran, I saw a sign pointing to the burial site of Erma Bombeck. I had no idea who she was, but my father explained she was a famous newspaper columnist and that we should go back for her grave after we located the aviation pioneers.

Successful in that venture, we retraced our steps to the sign for Bombeck's grave and followed the arrow. Oddly enough, she evaded us. We saw a memorial bench for the Wright Brothers and a gigantic boulder, but couldn't spot the humorist's stone anywhere. Was it flush with the ground? Was it removed? After we scoured the area around the rock for a good ten-fifteen minutes, my father had an epiphany: the giant boulder *was* Bombeck's grave. In a final attempt at humor in death, the woman who made her career through words had none in-scribed on her monument.

By the time of this realization, it was completely dark out, so I made due with flash photography. We recovered from being duped and set out for Columbus, where I wanted to stay overnight so we could see the Ohio Statehouse in the morning. But my father wanted to make more headway east, and I had to live with a nighttime photo in which the capitol was nearly indistinguishable in the background. We pushed onward, a decision we grew to regret in the coming hours.

My father steered us all the way through Ohio and into West Virginia before he was ready to call it a night and look for somewhere to sleep. Around 2:00 a.m., after striking out at a few fully-occupied locales, we arrived at a well-known motel brand in Western Pennsyl-vania. If we needed a sign portending this wasn't going to be a great stay, the actual sign out front would have done. In place of a fabricated corporate logo was a display with the letters comprising the company name inserted into individual slots, beneath an arrow of lights. So basically the same kind of sign a corn maze or low-end road-side drive-in movie theater might use. I stayed secure in the car while my father talked with the front desk clerk, who sported a wife-beater t-shirt. The Memphis Peabody, this wasn't.

Entering our room, my dad checked its big front window and discovered it unlocked. After remedying that would-be crisis, he examined the door and observed that it'd been marked up by a knife, likely by someone who tried to break in. I could only wonder whether or not they were successful. His response was to barricade the door with some furniture and our suitcases. Substituting for the star system, my father described this as a "two-chair" motel.

In the bathroom, a small window with no lock effortlessly slid open. Although our room was on the second floor, there was an elevated street and a fence just feet away from the window which would enable someone to climb in. "MacGyver" is a verb in my father's vocabulary, and he removed the two racks from the mini fridge and wedged them against the window to hold it shut. He also bent a microwavable tray and stuck it in there for good measure. As we drifted to sleep, our thoughts rested with the painting that hung on the wall between our beds: what would the artist think if they knew where their work was hanging?

We woke up safe and sound after our stay at the murder motel, eager to get on the road and make the most of our good fortune. Over the next two days in Pennsylvania, Maryland, and New Jersey, we toured two state capitols and an assortment of graves: nine signers of the Declaration of Independence and Constitution, one Pro Football Hall of Famer, and two vice presidents, one being Spiro Agnew in Timonium.

The other, Garret Hobart, died in 1899 during William McKinley's first term and was replaced on the re-election ticket with Theodore Roosevelt. Had Hobart not succumbed to heart failure, he would have become president rather than TR when McKinley was assassinated in 1901. Though he may be obscure to most modern-day Americans, Hobart cemented his place in our memories that April afternoon.

When we pulled up to the gate of Cedar Lawn Cemetery in Paterson, New Jersey, the last scheduled stop of our entire trip, an employee was ushering out a car. One of the jettisoned people vented to us that his family was visiting from Colorado, and they were none too happy to be the victims of cemetery hours. The two of us approached the cantankerous employee, who roared that her boss instructed her to close up shop. My father used his salesman skills to attempt to wheedle her into keeping the gate open a few minutes more, but to no avail. In my mind, New Jersey wasn't too far from home and we could return another time. But my father thought differently and, without consulting me, he made a proposition.

"What if," he suggested to her, "you locked us in the cemetery?"

And no, he wasn't kidding.

He explained we would leave our vehicle parked outside and enter on foot. That way, the employee could lock the gate and not get chastised by her boss. "Don't worry about us," my father reassured when she asked how we'd get out. Mind you, Cedar Lawn is surrounded by a seven-foot wall topped with barbed wire. But she acquiesced, and we moved the sedan so it was parked half in the break-down lane and half on the lawn. We asked the worker for the location of Hobart's imposing mausoleum, but she had no idea who or where he was. My father didn't want to risk the rental car being towed, so we took off running so we could make our escape as soon as possible. Our movements startled a family of deer that darted ahead of us. Their presence, my father postulated, indicated that there was another way in and out of the cemetery. Or they could've actually lived in the cemetery, as I figured, but my father filed his thoughts in his back pocket while we looked for the VP.

Like we did to find William Seward a few days earlier, we acted like Scooby-Doo's gang and split up. I was the one to find Hobart's mausoleum, which was even more colossal than I thought it appeared in internet pictures. After I flagged down my partner in crime for photos, we began to search for an exit. As we scouted the perimeter, my dad instructed me to look for the weakest link in the chain, be it figurative or literal. Eventually we came upon a point where the big concrete wall ended and the barrier continued on as a chain-link fence. The barbed wire remained, though. Unsure if this was the most favorable location, we resumed our hunt until we found a spot where the barbed wire sagged – conveniently right beside a tree. Figuring this was our best shot, we started climbing. I scaled the tree, latched onto a branch, and swung myself over to the other side unscathed. Thirty-four years older and a lot heavier, my father didn't clear the barbed wire as gracefully. With some new cuts to remember Paterson by, he lagged behind as I raced to check on the rental car, which was right where we left it.

The lengths we'd gone to in order to see Garret Hobart's mausoleum made the accomplishment all the more satisfying.[68] Yet, for my father in particular, there was another vice president's final resting place that promised to provide even more gratification – *if* we could manage to visit it. Seeing Nelson Rockefeller's elusive memorial, located on the private family estate, was going to be the most difficult task of our grave hunting lives.

---

[68] See Figure 41.

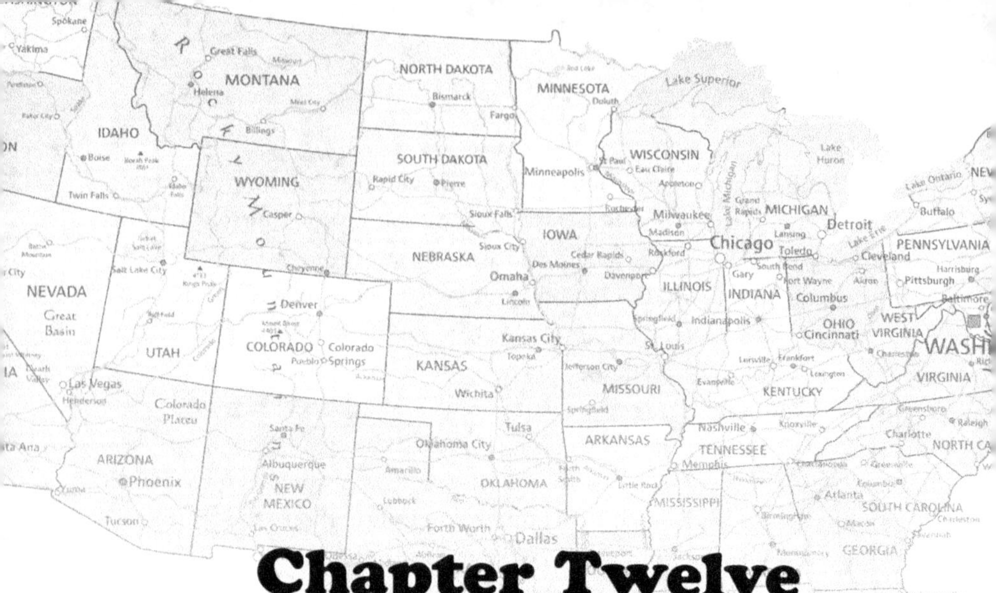

Chapter Twelve
Rocky Road
~ May 2010 ~

Among grave hunters, part of the appeal of U.S. presidents is that all of them can be visited. The number is very manageable compared to some groups, and all are publicly accessible.[69] Some, yet not all of us, have expanded to include the vice presidency, but one member of this less celebrated group has been an impediment for everyone as far as I can ascertain. Our white whale is the unadorned, unremarkable headstone of Gerald Ford's second-in-command, Nelson Rockefeller.

After his tabloidesque demise in 1979 – which involved a mistress, a delayed call to emergency services, and conflicting reports of the place of death – the liberal Republican's family declined to have an autopsy conducted. His remains were swiftly cremated and his ashes deposited in the family's private cemetery in Sleepy Hollow, New York. The Rockefeller mansion, Kykuit, is open for public tours, while the cemetery a mile away remains off limits to visitors – adding another layer of mystique. My father first became aware of Nelson's

---

[69] In 2019 I was told of an ambitious grave hunter who is on a quixotic mission to pay his respects at the burial sites of every dead Major League Baseball player, a number which is in the thousands and ever rising.

status as forbidden fruit from the same National Press Club discussion about *Who's Buried in Grant's Tomb?* that triggered this entire journey. Even C-SPAN CEO Brian Lamb's esteem and influence couldn't sway former Second Lady Happy Rockefeller to indulge his request to pay homage to her late husband.

Nowhere on the internet could we find any account of a successful visitation. Mike Reed, a grave hunter who operated a website titled The Cemetery Project, approached the Rockefeller Family Cemetery gate on Route 9, but was forced to move along by a law enforcement officer. Our research yielded just one solitary photograph of Nelson Rockefeller's burial site on the web, uploaded to Find a Grave. Black and white and grainy, it was apparently lifted from a decades-old edition of *Newsday*.

As a 15-year-old with a generally reserved personality, I was willing to let this grave go. If even Brian Lamb couldn't get Rockefeller, I didn't think anyone would fault us for falling short. The same could not be said for my father. The level of difficulty was an impetus for him, and it became his primary focus grave-wise. He sought permission in a phone call to the office of U.S. Senator Jay Rockefeller, the vice president's nephew, but was turfed over to a family representative at Rockefeller Center in Manhattan. My father explained the situation, but was met with a firm no. "I hope you understand," the spokesperson imparted. Once the call ended and there was no one to hear him, my father issued his rebuttal.

"I hope *you* understand," he asserted over the dead phone line, "we're going to get it anyway."

Some time passed until May, when my father traveled to bordering Connecticut to pay his respects at a wake for a relative's relative. Afterward, since he was roughly halfway there, he proceeded farther west to New York, where he planned to conduct reconnaissance on the vice president's grave. The Rockefeller Family Cemetery is adjacent to the public Sleepy Hollow Cemetery, where notables such as writer Washington Irving and steel magnate Andrew Carnegie are interred. A fellow graver remarked on his website that, according to the book *Great Graves of Upstate New York,* the Rockefeller headstones could be seen behind the mausoleum of automotive bigwig Walter Chrysler. When the graver visited Sleepy Hollow Cemetery, he walked behind Chrysler's mausoleum and saw the properties were separated by two tall fences – one chain-link, one wooden. He came prepared to scale the barriers, but in person he realized the eight-foot wooden fence, which was flat with no backer rails on the Rockefeller side, would make it difficult to get out. He chose to err on the side of caution and merely stuck his video camera over the fence, though he remained unable to see any markers amidst the snow and trees.

Armed with insight from our comrade's website and accompanying YouTube video, my father drove to Sleepy Hollow Cemetery and honed in on the Chrysler Mausoleum. He was not alone. A group of workers with machinery was dug in close by, which nullified my dad's plans to evaluate the scene. Instead, he chose to walk alongside the fence and look for another potential point of access. Partway through his jaunt, the wooden wall ended and just the chain-link fence remained. Unsatisfied, he continued to scout the perimeter until, in the back corner of the cemetery, he came upon an unexpected Achilles heel: a fallen behemoth of a tree.

Mother Nature saw to the demise of this great giant, and its fall was fortuitous enough to occur on top of the fence, which was squashed beneath its immense weight. In his suit and tie, my dad stepped over the crumpled barrier and into the woods. He emerged minutes later with photographic proof of his endeavor, which he presented to me on the family desktop in the evening. My father then began to calculate our next move. The Rockefellers, he projected, had the funds to remove the fallen tree and repair the fence expeditiously. If I were to see the grave it had to be soon. The next weekend would be most prudent.

Per usual, I chose to abide by my dad's decision, despite my reservations about disobeying the Rockefeller family. After a three-hour car ride during which I experienced serious cognitive dissonance, my father steered the car through the entrance of Sleepy Hollow Cemetery. Clad in green shirts for camouflage, we parked and walked to the Chrysler tomb. I was equipped with the digital camera and my father with the camcorder, which he turned on to document the feat. "That's right, provide the prosecutors with video evidence for our trial," I silently worried. My dad narrated briefly as we skulked along the outskirts of the grounds, but soon indicated that we should switch to non-verbal communication. Our trek continued until, suddenly, the fallen tree came into view. Sure enough, workers had already begun to remove its limbs, just as my dad predicted. Regardless, it was still massive and still atop the flattened fence.

We strode around the tree and entered into the forbidden zone from the right side. My father paused to signal some instructions to me before we ventured farther in. Not far onto the property we encountered a maintenance shed, but no one was there and we continued onward. The two of us scurried along cobblestone and pavement, all the while exposed from the road, before we reached the lush garden. Unseen, we advanced onto the grass as I looked around at the pathways and the identical tombstones scattered throughout. The only difference was the information carved into them. As I followed my father, I read some of the names: Mary French Rockefeller, Laurance Spelman Rockefeller...

Then, on my right, set back deep among the greenery, I saw the white whale:

Nelson

Aldrich

Rockefeller

Born + Bar Harbor

Maine

July 8th 1908

Died + New York

New York

January 26th 1979

Ahead of me, my father cleared stray leaves and plants that obscured the marker. I started to photograph the plot as soon as he was done. The camera had a delay of several seconds between shots, though it felt like eons as I rushed to finish. I haphazardly passed the camera off to my father, who took several photos of me beside Nelson's tombstone.[70] I started to get up when he concluded, but was ordered to remain while he switched back to the camcorder. As the camera zoomed in I raised my eyebrows in urgency and motioned for him to pick up the pace. With permission granted, I practically leapt back to the still camera and resumed taking photos.

Meanwhile, my dad walked deeper onto the grounds, recording the graves of more Rockefellers. On his left, over the plants and the fences, he saw the Chrysler mausoleum. As he pressed the zoom button to take a closer look, he heard it. We both did.

SLAM

At the sound of the closing car door, we bolted. With no idea where the vehicle was, we made a beeline for the crushed section of fencing. I scanned the vicinity for any people eager to catch trespassers as I approached the circular pavement. With none in sight, I broke into a sprint. Mid-stride, I glanced back at my father with a face that could be interpreted only as, "I'm checking to see if you're back there, but I'm not coming back for you if you're caught." The whole operation was his doing, anyway.

After a heart-stopping 74 seconds, we were both off the premises and back at the tree. We assessed the situation and determined the door slam came from within Sleepy Hollow Cemetery and not the Rockefeller property, so there was actually no danger. With the harrowing ordeal over, I took snapshots of the tree and fence, including one with my father next to them for posterity and a sense of scale.[71]

Hours later, I checked off two more vice presidents, fellow New Yorkers Levi P. Morton and George Clinton. Then in July, we tracked down Vice President Hannibal Hamlin in Bangor, Maine, and VP William Wheeler, who was tucked away in the upstate New York town of Malone. Wheeler elevated my vice presidential burial site total to 29. My father sat just below me at 28, having not accompanied me and my mother to Henry Wilson's grave in Natick, Massachusetts, the previous September. It wasn't a purposeful omission at the time, but after visit-

---

[70] See Figure 42.
[71] See Figure 43.

ing Rockefeller, he saw an opportunity: if I managed to wrap up my remaining VPs – with Lyndon Johnson pulling double duty as POTUS – perhaps I could become the sole individual to visit all 66 collective presidents and vice presidents.

Bold? Sure. Plausible? We thought so. Pathological, as Richard Norton Smith might say? Unquestionably.

Chapter Thirteen
The Lone (Star) President Left
~ April 2012 ~

I would have preferred to break through that finish line tape with the speed of the hare as opposed to that of the tortoise, but my last remaining president grave presented a couple of problems. The first was that, though the ranch where LBJ was buried was open to the public, the cemetery itself was private. Every photo from the internet showed visitors outside the wall, with the inscription on the distant headstone illegible. Usually my father's philosophy is, "the worst people can do is say no," but I surmise being rebuffed by the Rockefeller family dissuaded him from attempting to contact presidential offspring Lynda Bird Johnson Robb and Luci Baines Johnson Turpin. If I wanted to get the best possible pictures and stand right next to the graves of Lyndon and his wife Lady Bird, I was going to have to trespass. Again.

The second issue was the recurrent dilemma of funding. The Johnsons were buried nearly 2,000 miles away in Texas, which required plane tickets and, therefore, a good deal of money. The yard sale held to finance our passage to the Gerald Ford Museum effectively depleted my father's collection of all items of substantial monetary value, so he brainstormed alternative solutions. The best one that came to mind was sponsorship. Would someone be interested enough in my story to help pay for this last presidential journey?

The answer was no. I reached out to folks at AAA, since travel was within their purview, but that was a non-starter. The agency asked me to write a 500-word article, though, for its August 2010 issue of *Horizons*, AAA's Southern New England publication. That netted me $150, which, while nice, hardly put a dent in our expenses. My father felt the next logical angle was to contact Brian Lamb at C-SPAN. I called the network office and reached a representative, to whom I explained how Mr. Lamb had inspired me when I was in the fourth grade, that my father had watched the *Grant's Tomb* book talk on C-SPAN, and that, at 15 years old, I had just one president's grave remaining. She was quick with her response.

"And?"

The disinterest in the voice on the other end of the line was palpable. I composed myself to the best of my ability and further explained Mr. Lamb's influence on me. "And?" she rebuffed again.

Before I could even broach the subject of financial sponsorship, she had enough of our one-sided conversation and provided me with an e-mail address to contact. I read the address back to her to make sure I'd copied it down correctly, and after she affirmed as much she hung up the phone. Later, my father and I crafted a missive titled, "How Brian Lamb has impacted my life," which immediately bounced back. It appeared that the e-mail account I was given was non-existent.

The two of us were ardent believers that Brian Lamb would be interested in my story if we could just bypass his gatekeepers one day. In the meantime, I had to sit tight. 2011 passed by – the first year since I assumed my quest that I didn't cross a "new" presidential gravesite off my list. I picked up two more vice presidents, Daniel D. Tompkins in Manhattan and Elbridge Gerry in D.C., but Lyndon Johnson eluded me.[72] Salvation seemed to arrive in February 2012 in the form of another Pump Fakes deal, but a bizarre turn of events dashed our hopes once again. The lone saving grace of the business trip, which brought

---

[72] See Figure 44.

my father and me to the Midwest, was that it provided ample opportunity to visit Vice Presidents Charles Dawes in Chicago, Henry Wallace during an intense midnight snowstorm in Des Moines, Iowa, and Adlai Stevenson I in Bloomington, Illinois.[73] Progressive politician Robert La Follette and *Saturday Night Live* alum Chris Farley were welcome additions as well.

Despite the devastation of yet another Pump Fakes disappointment, enough time had passed since the April 2010 Michigan Trip that my parents were able to save up just enough money to make a Texas tour viable. The vacation was to be an early graduation present, scheduled two months ahead of my father's self-imposed deadline to bring me to each president's final resting place before I completed high school. It was going to be an occasion for the whole family. Even though my mother hadn't accompanied me on every presidential outing as my father had, she played an equally important role in facilitating my dreams. So, of course, she wanted to be present during my moment of triumph at the LBJ Ranch.

Fate intervened.

✛ ✛ ✛

On a late March morning, just three weeks before we were set to leave for Texas, I came downstairs from my room and found my father with a look of consternation on his face. My mother was sick in bed, but it didn't seem like a traditional illness. Apart from the intense nausea, she had no sense of equilibrium and she couldn't hear out of her right ear. Most startling of all, there was a painful burning sensation throughout the entirety of her body. Every muscle was in pain.

As a medical professional, my mother has invariably said, "When in doubt, call a rescue." My father put her longstanding advice to practice that day. Olivia and I watched with fright from upstairs as the paramedics wheeled our mom out the front door and into the ambulance. A whirlwind of thoughts and emotions bombarded me at

---

[73] See Figure 45.

once. "How did this happen? She was fine yesterday! Is it contagious?" and, most importantly, "Is Momma going to be okay?"

Mercifully, the answer to that last question was yes, relatively. My mom was discharged from Miriam Hospital a few days later. I stood by the front door as my dad guided her up the front walkway. The nausea had subsided, but it would be some time before her sense of balance readjusted. The constant burning sensation was here to stay, and the hearing loss was permanent too.

Clearly, my mother would be unable to fly to Texas in just a few weeks' time, and the status of the entire trip was uncertain. Though she was still adjusting to her "new normal," she eventually reached a point where she and my father felt comfortable enough to leave her at home with Olivia. I was torn about reaching my milestone without her there to share the experience, but she wanted us to carry on. With heavy hearts, my dad and I landed in Austin on April 18th, as planned.

We had seven days to jam in as many Texas sites as possible, so as soon as we checked out the rental car we rushed to our first stop. There was no wading into the shallow end on this vacation; we just jumped right in with the trespassing. But not to get Lyndon and Lady Bird Johnson – yet.

The list of famous Texas burials I compiled before the trip included Baseball Hall of Fame inductee Rogers Hornsby, interred in a family cemetery on the outskirts of Austin, where there were no skyscrapers in sight – just trees, roads, and more trees. My father parked on a dirt patch near the cemetery entrance, where a green guide sign let us know we were in the right place. The two "No Trespassing, Keep Out" signs by the closed gate were less welcoming. With no people around, though, and a gap between the gate and the fence, we began to mosey our way down the unpaved road.

I specifically emphasize there were no *people* around, because we soon became aware of two chained Dobermans staring at us from the yard of the neighboring house. We knew there was a risk of getting caught climbing the wall at the Johnson Family Cemetery, but would Rogers Hornsby's grave be our Waterloo instead? Getting jailed before I could see LBJ's stone was not an enticing scenario.

The guard dogs never strayed in their menacing gaze, but they didn't make a sound, either. Our continued movements down the road elicited no reaction, so we proceeded uninterrupted on our trek. After a third of a mile we reached Hornsby Bend Cemetery, enclosed by a chain-link fence with an unlocked gate. We caught all the breaks. Even the second baseman's grave was easy to find – it was covered in baseballs. Were they left by family members, or did some St. Louis Cardinals fans also disregard the warnings? I didn't dwell on that question long, heaven forbid the delay lead to the discovery of our rental car. Once I was satisfied with the pictures, the two of us hurried back up toward the main road. As we passed the dogs this time they began to sound the alarm, but the deed was done.

The rest of the Austin stops included a hall of famer from another sport – Dick "Night Train" Lane, who as a rookie set the NFL single-season interceptions record of 14 (in a twelve game season, it must be noted). We then went to the Texas State Cemetery for the graves of Stephen F. Austin – the Father of Texas – and Governor John and Nellie Connally, who were in the Kennedy limousine during its doomed drive through Dealey Plaza. The governor was injured in the attack as well, but survived. I also checked off my eighteenth state capitol and briefly explored the LBJ Library. Though there wasn't much to see due to renovations, the Johnson artifacts that were displayed brought to the forefront the thought I had largely suppressed during the day's adventures: in less than 24 hours, I was going to complete my quest.

Strategically, my father booked a night's stay in Johnson City, just 15 minutes down Route 290 from the president's ranch. Johnson City was also where LBJ's family lived during his childhood, after they left his birth home in Stonewall. When we woke up in the morning, our plan was to explore the boyhood home and then go to the ranch. But then an employee at the visitor center nonchalantly mentioned that the ranch would be incredibly busy later in the day when the droves of tour buses arrived. My father and I turned to each other in horror. Large gatherings of people would make a surreptitious expedition over the cemetery wall near impossible. We realized we had to go *right then* to head them off.

The LBJ Ranch grew to encompass 2,700 acres during the Johnson administration, and its size was still vast in its modern incarnation as a National Park Service site. Guests explored the land by vehicle, and we picked up our driving permit, a map, and an audio tour CD at the ranch visitor center. Our car crossed over the Pedernales River, and I started down the literal final stretch of my presidential journey. We passed the Junction School and had just driven by Lyndon's birthplace when the cemetery came into view on our left. My father parked in the small lot nearby and we walked over to the low wall, where a lone tourist stood looking at the Johnsons' granite graves. We engaged him in some brief small talk, but I soon took advantage of the auspicious conditions and climbed over the barrier.

A park ranger cruised by in a pick-up truck not long before I entered the cemetery, so I crouched down as I captured up-close shots of the reddish-brown stones. LBJ's was emblazoned with the presidential seal, and Lady Bird's sported an etching of a flower, like those planted across the country as part of her beautification campaign. When I was finished taking photos, I gestured to my father and he joined me over the wall. He hurriedly snapped my picture as I squatted half-hidden behind the president's monument, my eight-and-a-half-year mission accomplished.

Before I had the chance to pose at Lady Bird's grave, my father beckoned toward me and we climbed back over the wall. There was a man on a riding mower in an adjacent field, and he appeared none too pleased about our excursion into the cemetery. My dad suspected he may have radioed in a call about us on his walkie-talkie, and intimated it was best to go explore the rest of the ranch. That should give "Mower Guy" time to finish up in that area, and then – if there were still few tourists around – we could return and get some additional photos inside the cemetery.

We reversed course and drove back toward the park's anterior, where the Junction School stands. LBJ attended the one-room schoolhouse for only a short while, in 1912, but brought it into the spotlight when he used it as the signing location of the Elementary and Secondary Education Act in 1965. His first teacher, Kathryn Deadrich Loney, sat beside the president during the event. Johnson was no stranger to theatrics, be they policy-related or just for kicks. LBJ used to take visitors on rides around his ranch and, with his car speeding toward the river, he shouted that the brakes weren't working. He didn't tell his panicked guests that they were sitting in an amphibious vehicle. I was amused when I read about the raucous river hijinks, but only because I was not in danger of being one of LBJ's hapless victims. The Amphicar was displayed alongside some of the president's other rides in a glass enclosure.

The ranch was littered with all sorts of features that highlighted different points on the timeline of LBJ's life. The Texas White House – the home where LBJ died just four years after he left Washington – was within spitting distance of the structure where he took his first breaths. The "birth home" was actually a reconstructed replica built during his presidency in 1964. According to the NPS website, he "delighted in showing guests his version of the birthplace" and "found great pleasure in escorting visitors from room to room." The audio tour showcased LBJ's personal tastes as well, and played his favorite song, "Raindrops Keep Fallin' on My Head," while we drove past descendants of his Hereford cattle. Johnson's aura was omnipresent.

After we made the rounds, we returned to the cemetery, which I had all to myself. This time my father stayed on the outside, and I ventured in alone. Emboldened by the absence of tourists and lawnmower sounds, I stood behind Lady Bird's gravestone as my father zoomed in with the camera. I then switched back to LBJ's marker, as I figured standing photos would come out much better than the previous ones in which I squatted.[74]

My innocuous photo session was truncated when something suddenly emerged from behind my father. Mower Guy had turned off his blades and was riding toward the cemetery! He'd gone into stealth mode!

---

[74] See Figure 46.

I fled to my right and clambered over the side wall of the cemetery before I dashed at breakneck speed around the rectangular perimeter to the back wall. If Mower Guy tried to approach me from either direction, I could maneuver the opposite way. I had no desire for confrontation. This left my father to experience the wrath of our nemesis alone. He knew it wasn't good when I started sprinting, and he turned to come face-to-face with the angry landscaper.

"That's the second time your boy's been in there," he castigated in his heavy southern drawl. He pledged to alert the park rangers unless we vacated immediately. My dad has a proclivity for recalcitrance toward authority, but he decided it was best not to mess with Texas, where the rangers might be armed.

"You're absolutely right, sir. We're leaving immediately."

For once, he had no witty rejoinder.

He grabbed the camera bag and started for the car, where I joined him once I judged Mower Guy was a comfortable distance away. We were booking it out of there, but just before we drove back over the Pedernales River we realized my sunglasses were left by the cemetery gate. Now, reason would argue that we should've continued on our path to the ranch exit, but someone had other ideas. I had a bad track record with sunglasses, which were often broken or lost, and my father was tired of paying for replacements. My objections were summarily rebuked as he whipped the car around.

My dad parked a distance away from the cemetery and ushered me out, possibly feeding me to the wolves. Mower Guy hadn't ventured far, and I had no plans to spur a walkie-talkie conversation between him and the rangers. As such, I opted to stage an overdramatic performance that made it abundantly clear I had no intentions of re-entering the cemetery.

"I think my sunglasses are over here!" I shouted, ostensibly to my father. Mower Guy eyed me as I sashayed back toward the cemetery entrance, and as I dramatically leaned toward the glasses to pick them up. "Here they are!" I yelled as I held up the shades to punctuate my point. Satisfied no authorities would be called, I scurried back to the vehicle.

Although *we* were in the wrong – *not* Mower Guy – getting evicted from my final president grave put a damper on what was supposed to be a glorious moment – the culmination of a journey that started in the fourth grade. Over the next few days we made various stops around Texas, including the San Antonio River Walk, Dwight Eisenhower's birthplace in Denison, and a bunch of graves. Among the dead we visited were Lee Harvey Oswald, Bonnie & Clyde, and John Nance Garner, my 36th VP.[75] In one Dallas cemetery alone, we visited sports legends Lamar Hunt, Tom Landry, and Mickey Mantle, along with actress Greer Garson and Sarah T. Hughes, the federal judge who administered the oath of office to LBJ aboard Air Force One after the Kennedy assassination. Yet only one historical figure had the ability to save our trip, and we couldn't visit his grave.

He was still alive.

---

[75] See Figure 47.

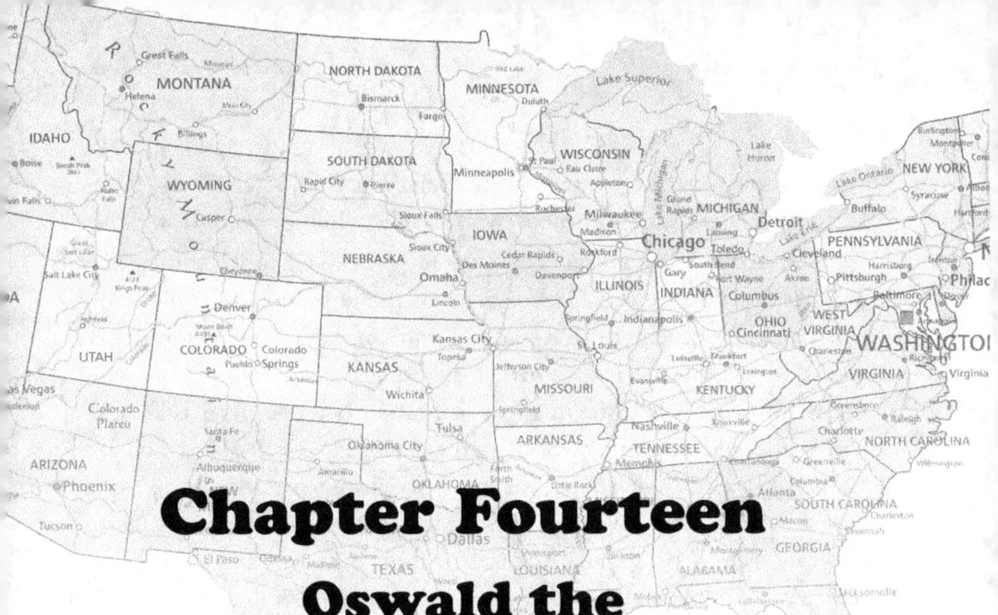

Chapter Fourteen
Oswald the Unlucky Assassin
~ April 2012 ~

In my teen years, my favorite area of presidential history to study was undeniably the assassination of John F. Kennedy. I spent countless hours reading about his death and watched numerous documentaries and scientific programs on the subject. Viewing one such program in March 2012 put me in the position to have an extraordinary experience.

It was titled *JFK: The Ruby Connection* and aired on the Discovery Channel. During the show, Lee Harvey Oswald's murder at the hands of Jack Ruby was recreated for analytical purposes with the help of James Leavelle. Many people don't know Mr. Leavelle by name, and prior to that TV re-airing, I didn't either. Anyone who has seen Robert Jackson's Pulitzer Prize-winning picture of the Oswald shooting, however, is familiar with the man in the light-colored suit and hat handcuffed to the accused assassin. That was Mr. Leavelle.

To be honest, I was surprised that Mr. Leavelle was still alive. In the famous photograph he was only 43 years of age, but he had struck me as older. It was equally astonishing to learn that he was stationed at the Pearl Harbor Naval Base when it was attacked on December 7, 1941, which precipitated direct U.S. involvement in World War II.

Around this time my family was planning our trip to Texas, and I knew I had to do my utmost to meet Mr. Leavelle while we were down there.

Based on his presence in the Discovery Channel show, which had Mr. Leavelle return to the scene of the crime in the Dallas Municipal Building basement, I assumed the former detective still resided in Texas. My assumption was correct, as a quick internet search proved. I found an address for Mr. Leavelle located in Garland, near Dallas, that fan mail could be sent to. Soon after, I crafted a letter in which I explained I was a high school senior who visited president graves, and that I would love to meet him and interview him for my history-focused website in April. My father took care of the pre-addressed return envelope – stamp included – and mailed the letter on March 5th.

To my shock, three days later there was a message in my e-mail inbox from the 91-year-old former homicide detective.

> "Kurt, you have a very ambitious project cut out for yourself. Hope you are able to complete the last two [items on your agenda]. I would be happy for you to drop by for a visit. I have appointments every ay [*sic*] starting on the 16th. through the 20th. If you can arrange your time on the other days we can make contact.
>
> "You can call me when you get here."

Elation isn't a strong enough word to adequately describe what I felt as I read Mr. Leavelle's phone number, but it gets the point across. Through subsequent e-mails we arranged to meet on Monday, April 23rd, which I eagerly awaited.

Sometime after we finalized our plans, my father's Philly friend Big Mike told him about a YouTube video he viewed concerning a recent development in Florida. The Republican National Convention was to be held in Tampa a few months hence, and for security purposes the mayor wanted to temporarily prohibit concealed firearms in the surrounding area. The state's gun laws prevented this from happening, and instead a ban was being placed on Super Soakers. In addition to Pump Fakes, my father and I were developing a reality TV show concept, *Scofflaws* – or *Scofflawz* – which satirized laws, rules, and regulations that we viewed as asinine. The premise: with me tagging along as the voice of reason and counterbalance, my father and his crackpot friends would traverse the country on a mission to violate these blue laws in the most madcap, over-the-top, inane ways possible.

With this in mind, my father hatched the idea to recreate Jackson's Pulitzer Prize-winning picture of Oswald's shooting with Mr. Leavelle, except with a Super Soaker. True to form, I was not supportive of the plan, as I didn't want to risk alienating the former detective and cause him to turn us away. My dad rebutted that it would be an incredible publicity picture for the show and insisted we would ask Mr. Leavelle to participate *after* the interview, when he had already warmed up to us. Per the norm, I reluctantly acquiesced.

The plan was for me to portray Oswald, my father play his assailant, Ruby, and Mr. Leavelle would obviously be himself. We did need someone else to take the picture though, and my mother and sister were no longer accompanying us due to my mom's ailments. A photographer friend of ours, Troy, was already booked for a paid event and was unavailable. My father requested some referrals from him, and we made an arrangement with a photographer Troy knew in Texas. The photographer said that if we could convince Mr. Leavelle to sit for a portrait he wouldn't charge us, although my father promised to give him some gas money. With that taken care of, my father and I went out and bought toy handcuffs and facsimile attire so the murder scene could be properly recreated. We went as far as to obtain the same model Stetson Ruby wore. If you're going to act crazy, be committed.

Now, here we were on Saturday, April 21st, two days out from our interview date. My dad called Mr. Leavelle to confirm our Monday plans. Unfortunately, the retired lawman had a heart-related health scare just that morning and was rushed to the hospital. He'd returned home, but now had an important medical appointment scheduled on Monday. The nonagenarian inquired if we could move up our visit and go over the very next day, Sunday. We had no choice but to accept. The change nearly ruined our arrangement with our photographer, who had a family event Sunday afternoon, but we worked it out that he would join us for just a short while, before the party. That meant, though, we couldn't interview Mr. Leavelle, allow time for him to warm up to us, and *then* ask if he'd take part in our satirical picture. We needed to make our outlandish request first.

Late the next morning my father and I set out on the half-hour drive to the assisted living facility where the Leavelles resided. We arrived a few minutes early and gathered together our belongings. My dad reasoned we should bring the items for the photograph recreation inside with us, as Mr. Leavelle would be less likely to turn us down if we'd already taken the clothing and props in. Around this time, the photographer, Dylan, showed up, and after we became acquainted the three of us approached the door. We were greeted by a facility employee, who was just leaving, and then by Mr. and Mrs. Leavelle, who were seated in the living room. We introduced ourselves and I presented Taimi Leavelle with a bouquet of flowers we'd purchased. The former detective insisted the day before that we didn't need to bring any food or gifts along, but my father explained that, as part Italians, that would go against our credo.

Momentarily, Mr. Leavelle led us into his office. Once we were situated, due to Dylan's time constraints, my father had to delve right into the photo recreation pitch. He laid out that, separate from my website, we were working on a reality TV concept that provided satirical social commentary on bizarre laws and rules. He also conveyed that our photograph idea did not intend to poke fun of the Oswald killing, but rather the silly Super Soaker ban in Tampa. Mr. Leavelle took it all in while he perused a portfolio my father handed him related to a different, abandoned television concept (my dad's creative noggin was full of endless TV show and product ideas). All the while Dylan snapped pictures of the exchange, which captured my father's animated gesticulations and the trepidation on my face.

Even though he was not a proponent of increased gun control measures – in fact he believed more people should be armed – Mr.

Leavelle readily saw the absurdity of the prohibition of Super Soakers. Therefore, he agreed to replicate the photograph with us!

Before we got ready for our photo shoot, I asked the former detective if he would autograph a poster of the famous picture to me. He inquired whether I wanted him to sign it "James Leavelle" or "Jim Leavelle," noting he typically signed as the latter for his friends. In near unison my father and I said he could sign with whichever name he was comfortable. Already greatly relieved that he was willing to be in our Super Soaker picture, I was happier than Bill Clinton eating McDonald's when I watched him sign as "Jim Leavelle."[76]

Readying for the recreation, I changed into a collared shirt and sweater like Oswald wore, while my father donned a suit jacket and the Stetson. The Leavelles' residence had a brick exterior, which we determined provided the best backdrop for the photo. On the off chance Mr. Leavelle didn't have a hat, we bought one that was similar in color to the headgear he wore during the shooting, though it didn't otherwise resemble his famous Resistol. Mr. Leavelle saw our "just-in-case" hat and promptly marched back inside to retrieve some better-looking headwear. He soon returned with a much more suitable hat, and I handcuffed myself to the same man Oswald was handcuffed to 49 years earlier (albeit with fake cuffs this go-around).

Using my just-signed poster as a reference, Dylan directed the three of us so we were positioned as our counterparts were in 1963.[77] He snapped several dozen pictures in black and white. When we were done outside, we headed back into Mr. Leavelle's office and changed out of our costumes. We chatted some more with the legendary lawman while Dylan continued photographing. He was so pleased with what he took that when he left he waved off my father's attempt to give him money for his gas tank.

After Dylan's departure, we set up for the interview. I had some pre-written questions on a notepad that I tried practicing on the ride to the assisted living community, but I was nervous and fumbled a bit during the test run. I decided practicing wasn't worth the stress and I

---

[76] See Figure 48.
[77] See Figure 49.

would just wing it when the time came. To start off, I joked that since the two violent events Mr. Leavelle witnessed occurred on a Sunday, the same day of the week as our meeting, I prayed we weren't in any danger. "I hope not," the former detective chuckled. We were off to a good start.

I first asked him about his time on the USS *Whitney*, the destroyer tender he was assigned to at Pearl Harbor. "I was a storekeeper, and we kept accounting of all of the supplies and so forth," Leavelle recalled. As he put it, a destroyer tender provided a destroyer with everything "from toilet paper to torpedoes." On the date which Franklin Roosevelt declared would "live in infamy," Leavelle had just finished breakfast and walked onto the deck of the *Whitney* when he saw Japanese aircraft approaching. At first he and a boatswain's mate thought they were target planes used in drills, but then one of them dropped its payload on Ford Island. Everybody rushed to their battle stations. For SK3 Leavelle, that was "an eight-inch gun on the bow," he said, "but I didn't fire a shot that day." The weapon had a capacity to shoot 30 or 35 miles, and with the planes only half a mile away he feared he would kill civilians in Honolulu. Though Leavelle and his fellow *Whitney* crew members were unharmed, others at the base and in the surrounding area were not as fortunate. No fewer than 2,335 American service members perished, as did 68 civilians – some of whom were killed by "friendly fire," as Leavelle had feared.

It goes without saying that personal communication capabilities in 1941 were not as advanced as they are today. There was no texting, nor e-mailing, or anything so immediate. I asked Mr. Leavelle how long it took after the Pearl Harbor raid for him to contact his family and friends in Texas and let them know he had survived the attack that was dominating the front pages of newspapers and radio airwaves. "It was over a month," he divulged. I leaned back in my seat, aghast. "All of our mail went by ship from Pearl to the coast, and vice versa." And given the circumstances, expediting postal deliveries was not a top priority for the powers that be.

"They were more anxious, interested in the defense – getting set up for the war – than they was communications."

With their offensive, the Japanese managed to sink or substantially damage 19 U.S. Navy vessels. Because its fleet was diminished at such a crucial time, Mr. Leavelle explained, the Navy took over the mail-carrying ships and repurposed them to carry troops. Meanwhile, his relatives were worried sick until he was able to get word to them all those weeks later. It must have been excruciating for the stateside families of all Pearl Harbor survivors.

Leavelle continued to serve aboard the *Whitney* as U.S. engagement in World War II ramped up, but his tenure ended after he sustained a significant non-combat injury. He was sent to recuperate at a convalescent hospital in Southern California, where he had the good fortune of meeting the future Mrs. Leavelle, a nurse. After his medical discharge, Leavelle accepted a civilian position as a storekeeper at an Air Force base – an easy decision since the work was similar to his duties on the *Whitney*, but for more than four times the pay.

Leavelle joined the Dallas Police Department in early 1950, and around five years later he was promoted to detective. At first he was a member of the burglary division, but his subsequent transfer to the homicide division put him on a collision course with other unforgettable events. We discussed those events, the Kennedy assassination and Oswald's murder, at length.

Other than President Kennedy and Governor Connally, there was a third person whom Oswald shot on November 22, 1963. Approximately 45 minutes after the gruesome Dealey Plaza scene unfolded, Officer J.D. Tippit was driving through Dallas's Oak Cliff neighborhood when he spotted Oswald, who matched the description of an assassination suspect. The suspect had been seen holding a rifle out a window on the sixth floor of the Texas School Book Depository – Oswald's place of work – though Tippit was unaware of that connection. As he disembarked from his patrol car to accost Oswald, the 24-year-old Marine used a pistol to end the officer's life. Within the hour Oswald was arrested inside a nearby theater, where he had snuck in without paying admission.

Once Oswald was in custody, the first law enforcement member to interrogate him was Detective Leavelle, but only in relation to

Officer Tippit's murder. It never crossed the detective's mind in those first few moments that Oswald could be connected with the presidential assassination. When Leavelle confronted him about killing Tippit, though, Oswald provided a broad answer that extended beyond the policeman: "I didn't shoot anybody." Later, Leavelle realized that Oswald was denying shooting Kennedy and Connally before he was even officially implicated in that attack.

Leavelle interrogated Oswald for 25 minutes at most. By then, outside of the interrogation room at police headquarters, the puzzle pieces were starting to come together. Officials had found a 6.5 mm Carcano rifle hidden among boxes on the School Book Depository's sixth floor. Oswald's supervisor, Roy Truly, had also reported him missing from work. Armed with this information, after the police captain confirmed the identity of the man held in the interrogation room, he was taken off Leavelle's hands. However, since Oswald was still technically Leavelle's prisoner, he was tasked with accompanying him during the doomed transfer to the county jail two days later.

When the news spread that Oswald was going to be sent to a different facility, a cornucopia of threats came the accused murderer's way. One person forewarned that a mob would wrestle him away from authorities during the procedure. As a preventative measure, Detective Leavelle handcuffed his left wrist with Oswald's right before they walked out into the basement. If a crowd was going to take Oswald, they were going to have to carry Leavelle off too.

That strategy, in my interview subject's mind, inadvertently lowered Oswald's chances of surviving the assault that was really coming. As Leavelle and the rest of the transfer contingent walked toward the awaiting vehicle, they passed by a horde of media members who had been given permission to gather in the basement and cover the hottest news story in the country. The television flood lights blinded Leavelle temporarily, but in his peripheral vision he could make out a figure with a handgun lunging toward the captive. The detective had mere milliseconds to react, and yanked Oswald back by his waistline. But, because he was handcuffed to Oswald, they were standing too close for Leavelle to have any real leverage. "If he had been out here at arm's length," Leavelle gestured to me, "I coulda jerked him plum off his feet." Instead he managed only to slightly turn Oswald, who was then shot in the abdomen. He vividly described the path the bullet took through Oswald's body, which I've elected to spare potentially squeamish readers from. The gunman, local nightclub owner Jack Ruby, was immediately swarmed and apprehended. Leavelle accompanied Oswald to Parkland Hospital, where he died almost two hours after the shooting.

Leavelle, who complimented me on my knowledge of the subject, remembered facts in exquisite detail. The things he said that I already knew matched up, and I was very impressed with his sharp memory. He also filled in many gaps in my education, such as how Ruby snuck into the city jail's garage. The exit ramp on Commerce Street – where Oswald was set to leave – was carefully guarded by five or six officers, but I asked why the Main Street entrance that Ruby accessed was unattended. Mr. Leavelle corrected that there *was* one policeman posted at the Main Street entrance, but he stepped away to stop traffic while Lieutenant Rio Pierce backed his vehicle into the street. Pierce was unable to pull forward out the Commerce Street exit because it was blocked by an armored car. While the officer positioned at the entrance was distracted by Pierce, Ruby slipped in and gunned down Oswald.

Why did Ruby do it? "I just wanted to be a hero," he confided to Mr. Leavelle, who transferred him the day after the shooting. "Looks like I messed things up good."

As is the case with most JFK assassination-related conversations, the topic of conspiracy theories arose. I started to say how my research showed Leavelle personally did not believe in the theories, but as I was mid-sentence the Texan interjected. He retorted that he *knew better* than to believe in them, which prompted a laugh from me. The retired detective recounted various instances when people asserted to him they possessed evidence of a conspiracy, with some of the stories bordering upon absurd. One that stuck out to him was when someone tried to convince him the president was shot by his limo driver, Secret Service Agent Bill Greer. Skilled at his job, Leavelle often caught these people in lies, after which they admitted to making up their tales. Even a priest confessed to lying to him!

Mr. Leavelle himself was not immune from speculation about being a nefarious participant in the deaths of Kennedy and Oswald. "As crazy as this sounds," I braced him, "I actually have a teacher that was suggesting to me that *you* and Ruby might have been in cahoots." In reality, she had been quite firm in her assertion, but I chose to be more delicate in broaching that subject. "Oh, well I've been accused of that too," our host noted. He'd received numerous anonymous and accusatory letters since Oswald's death, some of which he had kept. "I think one of them says, 'How much did the Mafia pay you to get in and shoot...', Oh yeah, I went through all that too." Dealing with allegations like that must have gotten tiring decades before I met him, but Leavelle handled everything with aplomb.

With my last question, I queried if his involvement in Pearl Harbor's attack and Oswald's killing had any effect on how he lived his life subsequently. Mr. Leavelle chose to use a recent incident to illustrate his answer, and revealed that the previous year he fell at his daughter's home and sustained an injury that required the removal of his left eye. I previously read on the internet that he had fallen, but I didn't know the extent of the damage. He moved around with such ease that my father and I would never have suspected he had a glass eye. "I don't let what happened interfere with my regular life or my family's life any," he remarked. Between his wit, recollection of facts, and fortitude in the face of adversity, it was very easy to be in awe of the 91-year-old.

The insightful interview lasted just under an hour. After it wrapped up, we spent some more time in Mr. Leavelle's office. He pointed out different mementos in the room, like a picture of him with Gerald Ford, who recognized and approached the lawman when he encountered him at an airport. Awards that spanned many years adorned the shelves and walls, reflective of a career of service that was so much more than those few moments with Oswald that the public saw.

After three hours, as much as we would have liked to stay longer, it was getting to be time to leave. Before we did, though, my dad had a final request for our new friend, Jim. Big Mike, who alerted us to the RNC ban, told my dad there was no possibility he could convince Mr. Leavelle to participate in the Super Soaker reenactment. Was he willing to be in another, brief video to rub it in Mike's face?

We didn't have to ask twice. My dad started off as I rolled the camera.

"Mr. Leavelle, my friend, Mike Paquin, said I could never get this shot," he averred as he raised the squirt gun toward him.

"You mean Paquin from Philly?" the former detective questioned, as prompted.

"Yeah!"

"Oh, he's an ass… you can't trust anything he sells ya," Mr. Leavelle ruled, with a little improvisation at the end.

Everyone laughed. "I'll say," my dad responded as I ended the video.

We picked up our possessions and Mr. Leavelle bid us goodbye, ending one of the most incredible experiences of our lives.

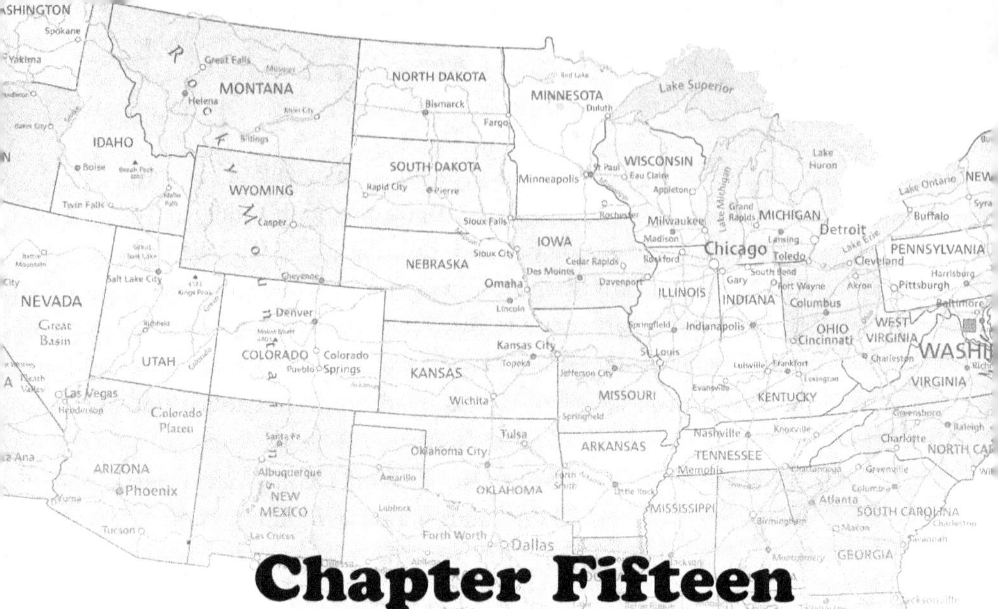

Chapter Fifteen
Schooled by Jimmy Carter
~ June 2013 ~

There was something surreal about our flight from Texas back to New England. For the first time in my life, I was returning home from a presidential trip with no follow-up sojourn to arrange. My 3,043-day quest was over. I'd spent close to half of my 17 years on earth on a mission to get my picture taken with every late chief executive's burial site – and now this driving force had dissipated with the click of a camera. It was no wonder why several other presidential grave hunters expanded their quest to encompass vice presidents – without other tombs to visit, I'd go mad!

Fortunately I'd really begun to diversify my grave hunting portfolio, so an endless stream of entertainers, activists, criminals, and other assorted departed folks were sure to keep me occupied long after I crossed my last vice president off my list. For the moment, though, I had five VPs to keep my engine revving. Of course, to make it all the more difficult logistically and financially, they were dispersed among five states, with the shortest distance between any two of them being over 400 miles.

I figured I'd be able to winnow down my list of outstanding vice presidents to four soon enough – my mother's parents offered to accompany me on a vacation to a location of my choosing as their high school graduation gift. I selected South Carolina, interment site of John C. Calhoun. But then, like every president has done at one time or another, I made a blunder.

While naturally I excelled in history in school, math was a constant thorn in my side – much like Calhoun was to the second president he served under, Andrew Jackson. I'd been a year behind in math since sophomore year at Cranston High School West, and while Bryant University had accepted me into their undergraduate history program, it was a prerequisite that I take a summer course to catch up before the Fall 2012 semester. I lagged behind in the unstructured, largely self-taught algebra class at the Community College of Rhode Island and had to plead for an extension to finish the course – an extension that conflicted with my South Carolina trip. It pained me to call it off, but not anywhere near as painful as it would have been to have my acceptance and much-needed scholarship withdrawn by Bryant. Calhoun was pushed aside, an experience many little-consulted VPs would have found relatable.

By the time I clawed my way through a tumultuous first year at Bryant, I was raring to step back into my role as a grave hunter. In addition to my delayed South Carolina vacation, set for the first week of June 2013, my father and I were formulating a plan of attack to get two other distant veeps: Alben Barkley in Kentucky and William Rufus DeVane King in Alabama. As I laid out our itinerary and racked my brain for other southern sites to visit, I had an epiphany: one of the cities we'd tour in Alabama was less than two hours from Plains, Georgia, the hometown of former President Jimmy Carter and First Lady Rosalynn Carter. I previously read that Jimmy sometimes taught Sunday School at the Maranatha Baptist Church and that visitors were welcome to take a picture with him and Rosalynn after the services concluded. That definitely would be a step up from having to sneak in a disposable camera, à la Bill Clinton.

By going to Georgia, we could visit my father's Uncle Georgie and Aunt Virginia as well, both in their nineties and in failing health. Also, though the former president and first lady were in relatively fine health, they were edging toward their tenth decade themselves. And, after all, part of the point of trekking to cemeteries was that I didn't have a chance to meet their occupants in life. Just like I realized when I discovered that Mr. Leavelle was still alive, traveling to Plains was not an opportunity we could even *consider* passing up. My dad and I conferred with Jimmy Carter's Sunday School schedule – posted online – and set a departure date for our trip.

When June arrived, I found myself on a whirlwind tour of the South. My grandparents and I returned from visiting Calhoun in Charleston on the 6th, and on the 8th I was on a plane headed back down to Atlanta, two and a half hours from Plains by car. We stayed just outside Plains on Saturday night and awoke from our slumber at dawn to dress for church. Sunday School was not set to begin until 10 a.m., but prior attendees recommended arriving rather early so as to get good seats – and we did *not* want to be relegated to watching the ex-president on an overflow room television.

The drizzly drive from our hotel in Americus to Plains was ten miles of trees and fields, with a few houses and telephone poles intermittently scattered along the route. As we passed over Plains's town line, the structures were more clustered – a water tower jutted out from a grouping of silos and storage buildings. Farther down the stretch, parallel with train tracks, was the downtown district, where a line of mom and pop shops sat side by side. The Main Street USA look was completed by a prodigious red, white, and blue sign mounted to the façade of one such business. "PLAINS, GEORGIA," it shouted in all caps, "HOME OF JIMMY CARTER, OUR 39TH PRESIDENT." Before we turned off Route 280, I spotted a dinged-up pole topped with a Phillips 66 logo, which manned the front of the gas station museum once operated by Jimmy's beer-hawking younger brother, Billy.

The two of us cruised by the turnoff for the former Plains High School – now the visitor center for the Jimmy Carter National Historic

Site, which seemed to have subsumed the entire town and its 700-plus residents.[78] If the circularly-shaped community *had* any corners, none of them would have been safe from Cartermania. After the road split, we passed by a tall Styrofoam statue of a peanut that harkened back to Jimmy's pre-presidential days as a farmer there in Sumter County. The anthropomorphic legume's lips were pulled back in an everlasting smile, mimicking a grin rivaled only by Theodore and Franklin Roosevelt's in its political iconography. The whimsical and indispensable Roadside Presidents mobile travel app, launched in February 2012 to my irrepressible delight, commented that this 13-foot sculpture dated back to Carter's election year of 1976 and "could be the world's second largest peanut." The proprietors of the convenience store it was planted at estimated the effigy was Plains's most frequently photographed site.[79]

In total, the RoadsideAmerica.com team counted nine Carter-themed attractions worthy of our attention in Plains, which was just one mile in diameter. Yet none of these historic sites and oddities were as good of a tourist magnet as Maranatha Baptist Church, where the Carters had worshipped since their return from the White House in 1981. As we made the slow right turn into the church driveway, I was half-surprised by the long line of visitors already stretching out the door. They must have been privy to the same salient advice to arrive exceptionally early, and they too weren't letting a few raindrops deter them. Once the bomb-sniffing dogs approved our rental car, we parked and entered the queue.

At the front of the building the Secret Service searched us. One agent gave my companion's *Scofflawz* necktie a thorough analysis, and since he had no knowledge of our reality TV concept he probably kept a watchful eye on my dad throughout the morning. The two of us were

---

[78] As of the 2010 Federal Census, taken three years prior to our visit, Plains recorded 776 residents.

[79] Apparently, none of the sculpture's adulation is generated from its subject. According to a tip published on the Roadside Presidents app the month after our visit, "Jimmy passes by [the peanut] every Sunday on his way to church but looks at the house across the street because he hates the thing. He's asked the owner several times to take it down."

assigned a pew toward the rear of the center section. As I took my seat I noticed the giant wooden cross behind the pulpit, one of several items in the house of worship crafted by the multi-talented – and prolific – former president.

Around nine o'clock, a middle-aged woman at the front of the sanctuary gripping a microphone began to address the crowd of visitors. Though I'd never met her, my research about the parish made me all too familiar with this emcee. Known popularly as "Miss Jan," Jan Williams was a member of the congregation who had several roles and responsibilities, including instructing guests on the proper protocol for interacting with the Carters. Miss Jan, through no fault of her own, had a reputation that preceded her for being rather strict and no-nonsense about these Carter-approved by-laws. Perhaps it was the former teacher in her – decades earlier she educated presidential offspring Amy Carter.[80]

Miss Jan acknowledged her notoriety, but also imparted hope that she would not be as intimidating as rumors suggested. She attempted to keep the atmosphere light by getting things rolling with a quiz, which seemed elementary at first. "What is Mrs. Carter's first name?" she softballed. In near unison, the crowd shouted "Rozz-a-lynn," as we heard it stated all those years. Not so, Miss Jan corrected! The first lady was named after two people, Rosa and Lynn, and her name was pronounced as such – most of the world had been mispro-nouncing her name for the past four decades! If we couldn't get even *this* right, it was going to be a long morning.

Next question: where do the Carters intend to be buried? A lot of people, including myself, posited they'd be interred at the Carter Presidential Library and Museum in Atlanta, following in the foot-steps of many of their fellow twentieth-century first couples (such as the Hoovers, Roosevelts, Trumans, Eisenhowers, Nixons, Fords, and Reagans). That too was untrue. They'd chosen to be interred right there in little ol' Plains – and not even in Lebanon Cemetery, where

---

[80] For another Carter connection, albeit an unrelated one, Miss Jan's mother once dated Jimmy Carter sometime before he and Rosalynn Smith were married in 1946.

their parents and siblings were laid to rest. Miss Jan unveiled Jimmy and Rosalynn were going to spend eternity in their front yard on Woodland Drive! It came off as an unusual choice, especially with Plains being so far from the beaten path, but I soon learned the Carters played by their own rules.

Miss Jan was a nice woman with a good sense of humor, but the hour-long instructional period that followed her quiz was anxiety-inducing. There was a laundry list of do's and do not's: do not refer to Jimmy as "ex-President Carter"; answer his questions *only* if he directs his attention to your specific section of pews; don't attempt to start a conversation with the first couple during the photo session; keep your hands at your sides at all times, and so on and so on. I'd say the amount of structure was unexpected, but this was the same Jimmy Carter who personally reviewed every request to use the White House tennis courts for the first six months of his term – he'd never really been laissez-faire. We spent considerable time practicing the various procedures, and whenever there was a mistake, Miss Jan was quick to correct – *very* assertively. Abruptly, a poor sap in the right pew section spoke out of turn while Miss Jan was testing the center pew people. May God have mercy on his soul.

Tensions were high as ten o'clock drew near, but overall Miss Jan was pleased with us. With the regular churchgoers having already filed in, orientation ended. We were instructed to close our eyes and bow our heads in prayer, and when our eyelids snapped open a minute later, there at the front of the room stood Jimmy Carter, sporting a bolo tie and flashing his aforementioned toothy grin.

"Good morning, Mr. Jimmy," Miss Jan said as she yielded the floor. "Morning, Jan. How's the class... What kinda class we got?" the former prez amiably grilled. "I think I have a gifted class this morning, Mr. Jimmy," she reported as Rosalynn Carter entered from the left-hand door and grabbed a pew. "I really do. They've done well."

Pleased, the featured speaker returned his attention to his guests. "Nice folks to come out in the rain," he complimented. "It's raining pretty hard now, which is okay for farmers. This is an area that plants cotton, corn, soybeans, peanuts, and grows pine trees," the former peanut farmer cheerfully stated as cameras flashed all around him. "That's our main crops, and the rain is good for all of them.... Tourists don't like the rain, and maybe merchants might not like the rain 'cause it keeps customers away.... I'm always smiling when it rains," he chuckled. "So that's one reason I'm smiling this morning. Also because we've got a very good crowd for this bad weather. I always like to know where you're from," he disclosed before he proceeded to poll us on place of origin.

It was an eclectic list: Alabama, Florida, Tennessee, Kentucky, Indiana, California, Georgia, and China were represented in the first two sections alone. Pilgrims had come from far and wide to have this possibly once-in-a-lifetime experience. While Carter's gaze was focused on the center section, I shouted, "Rhode Island," which he repeated in acknowledgement.

Once all the represented states and nations were reported and Carter selected a visiting Lutheran minister to conduct the invocation, the former president used the presence of his Chinese guests to segue into the top U.S. news story that week: President Barack Obama's informal meetings with President Xi Jinping. Their summit partly focused on cyber security and global economics. Xi assumed office as the seventh president of the People's Republic of China three months prior, in March.

"This is the first time that President Obama has met with Xi since he's been president of China. I have met with him four times, as a matter of fact," the 88-year-old informed us. "I go to China every year, and I've been meeting with Xi Jinping now for four different years as he prepared to become president." Carter's administration was a significant period in U.S.-China relations. In December 1978, he announced the United States would formally recognize the People's Republic of China, which it had refrained from doing since Mao Zedong's communist revolution in 1949. The former president maintained a relationship with Beijing in his post-White House years.

The 39th president continued on about some of the Asian and Middle Eastern projects of the Carter Center and its endeavors to achieve a peaceful, disease-free world. In due course, our Nobel Peace

Prize-winning Sunday School teacher waded into the week's exercise, titled, "Reading the Bible." The lesson started off in a straightforward manner.

"What has been your relationship with books? Anybody?"

Silence encapsulated the sanctuary – even crickets were too intimidated to chime in. Carter used his wit to attempt to put us at ease. "How many of you have never read or seen a book? Raise your hand," he asked, eliciting boisterous laughs from throughout the chamber. A few brave visitors felt comfortable enough to start opening up. I expended most of my energy concentrating on staying quiet and not embarrassing myself by somehow incorrectly responding to even the easiest of the former president's queries. My father confessed later in the day that if Carter asked "Who other than Adam was expelled from the Garden of Eden?" or a question with a comparably easy answer, he was intent on keeping his mouth shut as well.

Carter's own relationship with books was extensive – and unlike us mere mortals, he knew exactly how many linear feet of book shelving he and his wife dedicated to specific subjects: nine feet for books on how to craft furniture, more than six feet for books about bird-watching, and twelve feet for fly fishing publications. "I'm making a confession to you," he remarked amid laughter. "I also do some work, by the way."

That was an understatement. President Carter was always working, always learning. He revealed that he and Mrs. Carter read passages from the New Testament each night – in *Spanish*. I was inspired to recall a 1974 episode of the war dramedy *M*A*S*H*, in which commanding officer Henry Blake tells the industrious and overly-fastidious Major Frank Burns, "you are the only man I know who makes George Washington seem like a slacker." Frank had nothing on Jimmy Carter.

The crux of the hour was spent encouraging the assemblage to read the scripture, drawing almost entirely from the book of Nehemiah. President Carter delivered the closing prayer, and then invited us to stay for Reverend Jeffery Summers's service and the photo op afterward. "And Jan, as you can well imagine, will give you adequate instructions," he assured us. We chortled, having already been briefed on the various steps.

Well before the trip, my dad and I strategized how we would handle the photography: I would stand between Jimmy and Rosalynn, with my dad rapidly taking multiple pictures with one of our smartphones. The instructions, as referenced by President Carter, wiped out all of our planning.

The inflexible process went as follows: when Miss Jan signaled your row, you stood up and waited in line. Each party was allowed one picture, so if you came to the service as a group of 20 people, your picture with the Carters was taken as a group of 20 people – there was no splitting it up into multiple shots. When it was your turn, you'd pass your camera to one of the parishioners, then walk up and pose with the Carters with your hands by your sides. After the singular photograph was taken, your camera would be relayed to another church regular, and once you stepped away from the former first couple you'd be handed back your device to review the picture. If it looked poor, a retake might be allowed.

It came off as a tad stringent at first blush, but I also understood why the aging couple didn't want to spend an exorbitant amount of time standing with hundreds of guests individually.

Following the conclusion of the reverend's sermon, the church regulars vamoosed for lunch and the visitors remained. We patiently waited in our pew until Miss Jan motioned for us to stand up. As we established ourselves in line, I readied the camera feature on my cell phone. When the people in front of us moved on, I passed my phone over to the designated congregation photographer. The Carters both smiled at us as we strode over, with President Carter asking how we were doing. My father responded that he was well, while I blurted out, "A bit tired," which is *always* how you want to introduce yourself to the former leader of the Free World.

I stepped over to the former president's side, and my father stood over by the former first lady. The Carters held hands during these photo ops and were sure not to be separated. Additionally, if you were the lone church guest in your party, you were required to stand on Mrs. Carter's side during the photo op, not the former president's. Had my father not joined me for the picture, I actually would not have been allowed to stand next to Jimmy Carter. But since he *was* there, Mrs. Carter put her left arm around my father's right, and President Carter placed his hand on my lower back.[81]

Just like my presidential grave quest, my interaction with this living commander-in-chief was over in the blink of an eye. Once the picture was taken, our approximately seven-second interaction with the former first couple was finito. We shuffled aside and retrieved my phone, then reviewed our picture. It was an unflattering image, with my father and me both looking stiff and awkward, but we decided it'd suffice and headed outside after signing the church guestbook. Before we departed, the Carters emerged from a side exit and Jimmy waved to those of us still lingering. He and Rosalynn climbed into their Lincoln Town Car and rode off to their residence three streets over.

There were several sites in Plains that I wanted to visit, so my dad and I planned on staying in town for a few hours. Before we did anything else, though, we had to address our appetites and replenish the calories we nervously sweated out during basic training with Miss Jan. Commensurate with its shortage of residents, Plains had a paucity of dining options. We selected one of the town's two restaurants, the since-closed Cafeteria, and after a few minutes of standing in line, two married churchgoers struck up a conversation with us. They graciously invited us to sit at their table when we were finished ordering, and we accepted.

My dad and I carried our southern-style meal over to the pair's table, which they shared with other members of the community. The couple introduced us to one of Rosalynn Carter's childhood school-mates, as well as a woman named Mildred, whose Secret Service agent husband protected both Harry Truman and Mr. Carter in their post-presidencies. We ate up their stories about life in Plains, and everyone was equally enraptured by our accounts of meeting Bill Clinton and visiting president graves. About an hour was spent going back and forth from one tale to another. The locals could sense how passionate I

---

[81] See Figure 50.

was about presidential history, and I was able to further ascertain how Jimmy and Rosalynn had touched the lives of the people of Plains.

As we parted ways after lunch, the couple extended us another invitation — that time, to stay at their house on the next occasion we were in Plains. My father sheepishly admitted that we were likely to come down again only after the Carters passed away so we could visit their graves. Unfazed, the husband kept the offer on the table. "Well when that happens, just give us a ring!" He and his wife were very understanding of our circumstances.

Making the most of our *current* stay, we spent the next three hours soaking in Plains's atmosphere and checking off all the Carter attractions on the Roadside Presidents mobile app. Beside the train tracks that ran parallel to the main drag, the two of us stepped into the defunct railroad depot that served as Carter's campaign headquarters as he sought to make the leap from state politics to the national stage. The shed didn't appear to have changed much at all in the past 40 years, barring a few interpretive signs. A banner that proclaimed, "This Is Carter Country," hung near a frame that held 50 different campaign buttons from the '76 election. One boasted, "Jimmy Carter lusts… for me!" It referred to the notorious *Playboy* interview in which the Democratic candidate admitted he had "looked on a lot of women with lust. I've committed adultery in my heart many times." The confession was a paraphrase of the biblical passages Matthew 5:27-28.

I couldn't imagine either he or Mrs. Carter felt comfortable with the suggestive button being manufactured or showcased in this hometown display, but anything and everything Carter-related seemed to have been deemed worthy of protection and preservation. For posterity, the president's boyhood home lacked electricity — just like it did when he grew up there in the 1920s and 30s. One of the classrooms in the shuttered high school was decorated to resemble its appearance from when Jimmy and Rosalynn were students. In a small general store, I stocked up on Carter trinkets destined to join my presidential memorabilia shelves back home. (I also procured a souvenir for my friend, Brianna, who had recently spent her spring break volunteering with Habitat for Humanity — an act of service I attributed equally to her kind heart and to her affinity for a certain former president long-affiliated with the charity). There was no shortage of Carter knick-knacks: magnets, stickers, buttons, bobble heads, and more. Peanuts were still a major export in Plains, but the town's current bestseller was clear.

What else was evident was that Plains loved – and needed – Jimmy and Rosalynn Carter. With the former first couple undoubtedly among its eldest residents, there might not have been any locals who could remember a Plains without the Carters. They had known them their whole lives as neighbors, parishioners, and friends. There is undoubtedly baggage that comes with claiming an ex-president and first lady as residents, but Plains had apparently wholeheartedly embraced the Carters and the outsider traffic they brought. Local commerce assuredly benefited – the pair turned the remote town into a tourist hotspot. And even after they'd passed on, I realized, the Carters could continue to draw thousands of visitors from around the world annually.

Plains was certainly one of the smallest and quaintest communities my father and I had been to on our presidential trips, but it was also one of the most accommodating. It's small wonder why President and Mrs. Carter chose to stay there for nearly all of their lives – and why, the afterlife notwithstanding, they wanted to remain in Plains in death. If my hometown were anything like Plains, I'd want to be buried in my front yard too.

In the days that followed our visit to Plains, my father and I tracked down three of my four remaining vice presidential resting places: William Rufus DeVane King's mausoleum in Selma, Alabama; Alben Barkley's insipid stone in Paducah, Kentucky; and George Mifflin Dallas's slab in Philadelphia, Pennsylvania. That left me with just Hubert Humphrey, which I supposed was appropriate since his running mate – LBJ – was my final presidential burial site. On January 10, 2014, during the winter break of my sophomore year of college, my father and I flew to Minneapolis, where we dug out Humphrey's snow-laden grave, marking the end of my vice presidential journey.

At 19 years and 123 days old, I had become, to the best of my knowledge, the lone person to visit all 66 collective presidential and vice presidential gravesites.[82]

---

[82] See Figure 51.

Epilogue

Among the most profound struggles I faced in writing this book was determining which experiences to elaborate upon extensively, which ones to award a cursory mention, and which to omit for the sake of brevity. Thus some historic sites and graves visited during these travels have been left out entirely, as have the accounts of how I fielded a phone call from the office of George H.W. Bush and the time my father fell from a frozen waterfall. Ditto for how, during our stay in Independence, Missouri, an armed teenager was pursued by a nun on a three-wheeled tractor, and our museum tour where singer Brad Paisley's first grade teacher guilt-tripped me into holding a mechanical chicken. I've also chosen to leave out how I damaged my cellphone while photographing the parking space memorial where Abraham Lincoln's father married his step-mother, but that stems more from embarrassment than a desire to be concise.

Likewise, it was a quandary to select which story to conclude this memoir with. Lyndon Johnson's grave, being my 38th and final presidential resting place, might have been a natural ending point, but that would have necessitated that I exclude the extraordinary afternoon my father and I spent with Mr. Leavelle and our Sunday School lesson from President Carter. And I chose not to end with my encounter with 2012 vice presidential candidate Paul Ryan, or the time I caused former Secretary of State Hillary Clinton to gasp in front of news cameras. In truth, there's only one way to satisfyingly conclude this account.

As a rising senior in summer 2015, I took advantage of Bryant University's relationship with the Washington Center for Internships and Academic Seminars and procured an internship with the U.S. Capitol Historical Society in D.C. My two and a half months in Washington allowed me to further my academic and professional career, as well as visit a host of graves and historic sites. I also wanted to use the opportunity to possibly meet Richard Norton Smith, who had been living and working in the area. A year earlier, my father had sent his representative at The George Washington University my picture at the grave of Nelson Rockefeller, whose pending biography the historian was putting his finishing touches on. I acquired Mr. Smith's e-mail address when he signed the guestbook on my webpage.

> "Congratulations on Rocky! I know [better] than anyone just what an achievement it is. Likewise on your interest in presidential history. You're lucky to have a father who encouraged you - remember that when [your] six (or seven, or eight, or twelve) year old clamours for - ? I hope our paths cross one day. In the meantime, thanks for your kind words. And best wishes for the years ahead. RNS."

With my upcoming internship in D.C., it appeared to be the prime time to cross paths with Mr. Smith, as he had written. When I reached out to him on May 14th, two weeks before my arrival, I was dispirited to learn he had just relocated up to Grand Rapids in preparation for a comprehensive biography of Gerald Ford. "[I]f you haven't already," he alternatively suggested, "you might want to drop a note to Brian Lamb… I'm sure he would enjoy meeting you."

On the internet I found Brian Lamb's e-mail, which I didn't have at my disposal during my initial outreach in 2010. I now attempted to contact the C-SPAN founder directly. My first message to Mr. Lamb went unanswered, but as summer marched on and the clock wound down on my internship, my father successfully goaded me to inquire again. On July 20th, I was ecstatic when I opened my inbox on my phone and saw a reply. The Presidential Medal of Freedom recipient expressed that he was excited to hear from me and extended an invitation to "come over to [the C-SPAN] office for a chat."

Two days later, I took the morning off from my internship and walked the mile from my apartment in the NoMa neighborhood to C-SPAN headquarters on Capitol Hill. I received my visitor pass from security on the first floor and rode the elevator up, fully prepared to have to explain why I, a 20-year-old, had even heard of the Cable-Satellite Public Affairs Network. I hadn't even passed over the threshold to the station's suite before the receptionist greeted me.

"Good morning, Kurt, and welcome to C-SPAN." I was floored. Not only had I arrived at the network offices, but I had *arrived*.

She called down to Mr. Lamb's personal office. He didn't answer, and she said that he often walked around the suite and was probably planning on swinging by to pick me up for our nine o'clock appointment. A few moments later, the person who inspired me to visit all those graves strode through the inner glass doors. We both grinned ear-to-ear as we shook hands, and I proudly showcased my ragged copy of *Who's Buried in Grant's Tomb?*, stitched together with scotch tape.

In his office, we exchanged gifts before we got down to business. "How did you get Rockefeller?' Mr. Lamb inquired. I knew the question was coming, but I expressed my reluctance to recount the story, admitting that it wasn't conducted in the most ethical manner. But, especially in light of Mrs. Rockefeller's passing two months prior, Lamb suggested that my story wasn't going to harm anybody and pressed me to tell. I opened the photos application on my phone and showed him the picture I took of my dad leaning against the tree that felled the fence.

Mr. Lamb delighted in the few anecdotes I related to him before he dialed his desk phone and asked one of his producers to walk down to his office. I peeked at the clock on my cell and saw it was 9:07, just seven minutes into our meeting. Once he hung up, Mr. Lamb informed me that he didn't want to talk about my exploits or website any more that day – that instead he wanted to interview me on TV! The producer, Nik Raval, entered and Mr. Lamb introduced us. Nik professed he thought he had already heard of me and questioned if I had contacted C-SPAN before. I confirmed I had, five years prior, but that I was rebuffed. The pair were appalled and asked if I could remember whom I spoke with. I couldn't, but I wouldn't have thrown the employee under the bus even if I did. I handed Nik my business card and he conveyed that he would be in contact soon about scheduling my network appearance.[83]

----

[83] See Figure 52.

I left the C-SPAN office so exuberant and frazzled that I traipsed back to my apartment and started inundating my contact list with calls, forgetting that my residence was in the opposite direction from my internship site, near the Supreme Court Building. Realizing I was too distracted to work, I walked back down to the USCHS suite at the Veterans of Foreign Wars Memorial Building, only to report that I was going to take the whole day off.

When I conducted reconnaissance on the C-SPAN website later, I ascertained that I was going to be appearing on the program *Q&A*, on which Mr. Lamb had interviewed not only historians like Richard Norton Smith and Doris Kearns Goodwin, but President George W. Bush, civil rights movement legend John Lewis, and former Supreme Court Justice John Paul Stevens. How could I, at 20 years old, possibly have as interesting a story to tell as these public figures? All past episodes of the show seemed to be available to watch online, and I viewed two interviews. The programs were pre-recorded, but I recognized that there were no breaks. It would be a straight hour of me talking with Mr. Lamb, with no advanced preparation.

Through a series of e-mails, Nik and I set up a time for the interview on Wednesday, August 5th. On such short notice my mother was unable to take time off from work to travel to Washington, but my father drove the 400 miles south so he could watch and help me mentally prepare. Between high school and college I had taken two public speaking courses, but in light of the elevated circumstances, I appreciated my father's coaching on stopping my incessant fidgeting and stimming habits. Then he settled into the control room. Nik previously asked if my dad was willing to appear in a ten minute introductory segment at the start of the episode, but my dad declined the offer. He didn't want to detract from what he insisted was *my* moment. The sentiment was appreciated, but the achievement wouldn't have been possible without both of my parents, so I was sure to give them their due during the recording.[84]

By the time the episode aired on August 23rd, I had completed my internship and returned home to Rhode Island, where I held a

---

[84] See Figure 53.

viewing party with my friends and family. They weren't the only ones watching, however. Before the end credits even started to roll, scores of laudatory e-mails and website guestbook comments poured in. Growing up, I was often ostracized by my classmates for our dissimilar interests, none more so than grave hunting. Now people from all over the United States were writing to tell me how much they enjoyed the interview and the Kurt's Historic Sites website. But even without the validation of others, I had long overcome any self-doubt engendered by financial woes and bullying to realize that pursuing my dream was worth it because it was important to *me*.

My interview with Brian Lamb is the perfect valediction for *Presidential Grave Hunter*, as it truly brought my mission of seeing every presidential and vice presidential interment site full circle. Yet I feel obligated to mention the obvious, which is that the characterization of this quest as completed belies the reality of its impermanence. Certain groups, such as Declaration of Independence signers or The Three Stooges, are a finite collective whose place in time is fixed, and for them there can never be any more graves in existence than there are at present. On the other hand, as long as the U.S. Constitution is in effect, there will continue to be presidents and vice presidents who, like all of us, will one day shuffle off this mortal coil.

After Gerald Ford's death in 2006, no other president or vice president died before I managed to complete my quest, a reprieve that lasted nearly twelve years. The inevitable occurred on November 30, 2018, when George H.W. Bush passed away. His death was not wholly unexpected. In his last years he suffered a series of medical episodes that stemmed from vascular parkinsonism. He was age 94, longer-lived than any other chief executive to that point.

Since he served as both president and VP, Bush's death reopened both of the main goals that comprise my gravesite quest. Although my father advised me that I likely would have more money to spend on a trip to College Station, Texas, once I completed graduate school in May, it was difficult to argue with the significantly cheaper mid-January plane tickets. Yet my intentions were foiled by the unprecedentedly-long partial government shutdown, which resulted in the closure of the presidential libraries reliant on federal funds. The gravesite was actually still open to the public, but I wanted to enjoy the full experience and tour Bush's museum, the first unvisited presidential library I was going to see since I began my master's degree program at the University of Massachusetts Boston. The undergraduate capstone project I completed on the development of the Nixon Library's Watergate exhibit steered me toward UMass Boston's public history program, and I wanted to apply my education in the analysis and evaluation of the Bush Library's galleries. The shutdown's impact on air traffic controllers and aviation-safety inspectors – who were denied pay and furloughed, respectively – further cemented that it would be best not to add to the strain placed upon American airports.

The government shutdown temporarily halted on January 25th, and another such disruption was averted with the signing of a long-term deal three weeks later. This reassurance allowed my father and me to reschedule our trip to mid-March, during spring break. Yet even as I stood at the gate to George and Barbara Bush's burial plot, I knew my appetite for history-based travel would not die there, just as it didn't at Hubert Humphrey's grave in Minnesota.[85] My expedition to explore America's cemeteries, museums, and miscellaneous sites is a lifelong journey of learning. There's always going to be a yet-unvisited site I want to explore, another adventure to be had, and another opp-ortunity to grow as a historian and bond with travel companions. I cannot possibly see every single place that in the research process has garnered my interest, so something will always be left undone – but that doesn't mean I won't try.

Beyond that, although I believe paying my respects to former President Bush restored my self-postulated unique achievement, it's entirely possible that one day I may have to permanently relinquish any claim I have to being the lone person to have visited the graves of each U.S. president and vice president. I am acutely aware that there may come a point when a president or VP opts not to have a gravesite.

---

[85] See Figure 54.

Prepared for his demise during a health crisis in 2010, Dick Cheney instructed that – if he didn't survive his scheduled emergency heart surgery – his body was to be cremated and the ashes returned to his adoptive home state, Wyoming. There was no public clarification on whether his desire was for his cremains to be deposited in a niche or burial plot like Nelson Rockefeller or Walter Mondale (whose clay urn, as of this writing, awaits interment in Minneapolis). Cheney – or any other VP or chief magistrate – could shake precedent and forgo burial by having their ashes privately retained or scattered.

Even if the tradition of presidential and vice presidential interment is upheld, perchance some future intrepid grave hunter will also access Rockefeller's gravesite – or maybe someone already has! In August 2019, I met Frank J. Scaturro, president of the Grant Monument Association, who subsequently e-mailed me George A. Christensen's 2008 article, "Here Lies the Supreme Court: Revisited," published in the *Journal of Supreme Court History*. On the piece's second page, Christensen asserts he has "managed to visit the graves of all U.S. Presidents (except the relatively recent interments of Ronald Reagan and Gerald R. Ford), [and] all U.S. Vice Presidents." Of course, Ford was also a VP, which contradicts the author's claim later in the sentence to have been to the graves of *all* vice presidents. As far as Rockefeller's plot, because of its exclusivity, maybe he omitted him entirely from his count, as I have found many grave hunters do. Or perhaps Christensen indeed persevered and managed to pay his respects to the New Yorker years before I did.[86] Even so, it's possible the Rockefeller family will change its tune and open the burial grounds to the public one day a year, as Chief Justice John Jay's descendants do annually on Memorial Day, thereby allowing numerous pilgrims to join our ranks. And I suppose a Rockefeller family member also could take up such a quest, visit their relative no problem, and then track down the remaining dead VPs. There's a lot of what-if scenarios.

------

[86] In October 2023, five months after this book was first published, I successfully contacted Mr. Christensen, following prior failed attempts. He remembered "telephoning some Rockefeller estate office" and making an appointment to visit the vice president's burial site circa 1994. In February 2024, *Grave Trippers* co-author Vincent Gardino informed me of another Rockefeller gravesite account in Carll Tucker's 2008 book, *The Bear Went Over the Mountain*.

No matter what, I can say this: in a testament to my parents' adoration of their son and my passion for presidential history, I was able to one-up my inspiration, Brian Lamb, who one-upped his own inspiration, Richard Norton Smith, and proudly held this uncontested and possibly unique claim to quasi-fame for nearly five years, if not more. Title or no title, my memories of these formative trips are everlasting, as will be my desire to contribute to the field of public history and traverse the country for my own education and edification. I hope you will follow suit. If – or when – the day arrives that I myself am somehow one-upped by another taphophile, the history community may benefit. It might mean that someone's love of history and historical travel surpasses my own, and that's not a bad thing. The world is better off with people who are knowledgeable and passionate about history, be it through teaching, curating, archiving, writing, researching, patronizing, or any other methodology.

Given that you have picked up this book, I assume that presidential and vice presidential history is of interest to you, though you may be fond of additional historical subjects as well. As I've grown as a historian, I've come to understand how people of power and influence, such as politicians, have possessed the means and allies to have their record preserved. Individuals without such resources are often neglected or forgotten by subsequent generations. Yet this doesn't mean that their stories don't matter, or that they are less deserving of your attention than leaders like presidents.

While my path as a public historian has taken me the presidential route, I've learned through my travels and my academic studies that it's all interrelated. In his famous address in November 1863, Abraham Lincoln iterated the Union soldiers who perished on the bloody fields of Gettysburg, Pennsylvania, did so for the preservation of "government of the people, by the people, for the people…." The needs, the votes, and the will of the people of the United States dictate who is elected to office, and their stories can be just as enlightening about a historical period as those they designate to serve them.

So no matter if you are interested in history as it relates to the presidents, or military history, or LGBTQIA activism, or something rooted in the fabric of your local community, I encourage you to pursue your passion. That may bring you to the classroom, or plunge you waist deep in a sea of archival materials. All are admirable avenues. Yet, owing to my own background, I can endorse no field more fervently than public history. I've been fortunate to have the opportunity to experience public history from multiple sides: as a visitor to museums and historic sites, as a graduate student studying methodologies, and as an intern putting what I've learned and observed into practice by designing scripts for partially self-guided tours at historic homes. Each aspect, I believe, is fundamental to historical learning. Museums and national parks are not infallible monoliths, as I learned progressively in my travels, because they are filtered interpretations disseminated by human beings. Many are excellent establishments run by intelligent, passionate professionals and volunteers who consistently work to improve their institutions with modern public history practices. Yet even ones that need updating can immerse visitors in the past and help promote discussions and debates.

Burial sites – although closer in nature to commemorative monuments if lacking historical interpretation – are, like a museum or historic site, a tangible location connected to individuals of the past. Secrets lie buried beneath the surface, and not just in the form of the decomposing dead. Questions persist of who will remember us – and how will they remember us – after we have departed. The final disposition of our remains is personal, and can be telling about an individual's personality and desire for recognition among future generations. Graves can also hold the stories of those who are not buried there – like the enslaved people who helped construct the Washington Tomb at Mount Vernon.

Each burial site has its own unique story, and each cemetery visit can be its own memorable adventure. So next time you see a graveyard, stop in and tell them Kurt sent you. Just don't be surprised if the departed answer you, because dead men tell many tales.

Acknowledgments

I extend my sincere thanks to the following people for their help with the creation of this book in various capacities: Phyllis J. Beckman, Stephen R. Beckman, Patrice Charnley, Cameron Coyle of The Zachary Taylor Project, Lynne Deion, Olivia Deion, Paul Deion, William C. diGiacomantonio, Rebecca Farias, Stephanie K. Gagnon, Angela Giaquinto, Kathleen Jailene Gonzalez, Samantha Grabelle, Chris Hall, Kelvis Fabian Hernandez, Susan Krupp of SusansArt@99D, Andrew J. Levison, Bradford Martin, Marcy McGuire, Louis L. Picone, Jayne Siegel, Steve Stewart, Donald M. Stinson, and Alex Terreault.

My appreciation goes out to Phyllis J. Beckman, Stephen R. Beckman, the late Catherine M. Deion, the late Joseph E. Deion, Angelo James Pagano, Lisa Pagano, Louis J. Pagano, and my friends at RoadsideAmerica.com, whose financial contributions made some of the travels in this book possible.

I am also grateful for my late dog, Lily, who kept me company during the early years of writing and refining these pages. All the while, she never uttered a discouraging word.

And to Momma and Daddow – I love you to the end of the numbers.

Notes

Prologue

xiv	"I have long believed": Richard Norton Smith, forward to *Who's Buried in Grant's Tomb?: A Tour of Presidential Gravesites*, by Brian Lamb and the C-SPAN staff (New York: PublicAffairs, 2000; repr., New York: PublicAffairs, 2003), xviii.

xv	"could hold four average-sized men": "A Large Bath Tub," *Engineering Review,* February 1909.

xv	"being lowered into": Judith St. George, *So You Want to Be President?* (New York: Scholastic Inc., 2000), 17.

xv	"beauty contest": Ibid., 20-21.

xvi	"'The President has lots of homework'": Ibid., 10.

xvi	"Do you have pesky brothers": Ibid., 22.

xviii	"stipulated in his last will and testament": George W. Thompson, *The Law of Wills and the Manner of their Drafting, Execution, Probate and Contest Together with Testamentary Forms* (Indianapolis: The Bobbs-Merrill Company, 1916), 920.

xviii	"'perfect tranquility'": "The Resolution to Bury President George Washington at the U.S. Capitol," United States House of Representatives: History, Art & Archives, accessed May 22, 2020, https://history.house.gov/Historical-Highlights/1700s/The-resolution-to-bury-President-George-Washington-at-the-U-S--Capitol/.

Chapter One: Before the Beginning

3	"every denomination of Christians": Mass. Const. pt. I, art. IV.

6	"only one to serve in the lower chamber": "The House of Representatives Elected John Quincy Adams as President," United States House of Representatives: History, Art & Archives, accessed January 18, 2019, https://history.house.gov/Historical-Highlights/1800-1850/The-House-of-Representatives-elected-John-Quincy-Adams-as-President/.

7	"quarried from his beloved Cape Cod": "Kennedy Grave Reopens, With New Marker," *New York Times,* October 8, 1994, https://www.nytimes.com/1994/10/08/us/kennedy-grave-reopens-with-new-marker.html.

7   "remarked he could stay forever": "Sen. Kennedy Joins Brothers at Arlington," *CBS News*, August 29, 2009, https://www.cbsnews.com/news/sen-kennedy-joins-brothers-at-arlington/.

8   "standards befitting": "Mansion," George Washington's Mount Vernon, accessed May 22, 2020, https://www.mountvernon.org/the-estate-gardens/the-mansion/.

8   "bloodletting and enemas": Dr. Howard Markel, "Dec. 14, 1799: The excruciating final hours of President George Washington," PBS.org, December 14, 2014, https://www.pbs.org/newshour/health/dec-14-1799-excruciating-final-hours-president-george-washington.

8   "mixed in the paint": "Adventure Map of Mount Vernon," The Founders, Washington Committee for Historic Mount Vernon (ca. 2003): Puzzle 5.

9   "One puzzle said… 'freed his slaves'": Ibid., Puzzle 2.

9   "'insuperable difficulties'": Thompson, *The Law of Wills*, 913.

10   "larger in scale": Ibid., 920.

11   "'lifelong habit of dragging'": "Who's Buried in Grant's Tomb," C-SPAN video, 1:26:15, Filmed [March 21, 2000], https://www.c-span.org/video/?156140-1/whos-buried-grants-tomb.

11   "'pathological'": Ibid.

11   "'I tried… picture of the gate'": Ibid.

Chapter Two: R.I.P. the Gipper

14   "raise \$10,000": *Magazine of Western History* vol. x, May-October 1889: 348, https://books.google.com/books? https://books.google.com/books?id=smwKAQAAMAAJ&pg=PA348&_ga=2.25742397.1263268777.1672668940-454742272.1672668940#v=onepage&q&f=false.

15   "Nixon's family eschewed… Tricky Dick made himself": Lamb et al., *Who's Buried in Grant's Tomb?*, 168.

16   "radio malfunction": "Capitol evacuated before Reagan procession," CNN, June 9, 2004, http://www.cnn.com/2004/ALLPOLITICS/06/09/capitol.evacuation/.

17   "104,682 other mourners": Chief Terrance W. Gainer, "Lying In State for former President Reagan," USCP.gov, June 11, 2004, https://www.uscp.gov/media-center/press-releases/lying-state-former-president-reagan.

18   "reddish Stony Creek granite": "President William Howard Taft Memorial Grave," Arlington National Cemetery, accessed September 3, 2022, https://www.arlingtoncemetery.mil/Explore/Monuments-and-Memorials/President-William-H-Taft-Gravesite.

19   "Congress allocated $9,740,000": Jeffrey B. Morris, "What Heaven Must Be Like: William Howard Taft as Chief Justice, 1921-30." *Yearbook 1983*. Washington, D.C.: Supreme Court Historical Society, (1983): 95.

19   "showed Lincoln's personal attendant": James L. Swanson, *Manhunt: The 12-Day Chase for Lincoln's Killer* (New York: Harper Perennial, 2007), 38-39.

20   "bed was auctioned off": "The Passing of a President," Chicago History, accessed August 25, 2022, https://www.chicagohistory.org/the-passing-of-a-president/.

21   "resting a coffee mug": "July 1991 Washington DC / Richmond Dave's Circle Tour," Travelin-Tigers.com, accessed September 3, 2018, http://www.travelin-tigers.com/ztravel/prez9107.htm.

21   "where as university president": Kenneth O'Reilly, "The Jim Crow Policies of Woodrow Wilson," *The Journal of Blacks in Higher Education* 17, (1997): 117.

21   "'a social blunder of the worst kind'": Harvard Sitkoff, *New Deal for Blacks — The Emergence of Civil Rights as a National Issue: The Depression Decade*, 30th anniversary ed. (New York: Oxford University Press, 2009), 16.

21   "'singing silly ditties'": St. George, *So You Want to Be President?*, 29.

22   "inability to compromise": Judith L. Weaver, "Edith Bolling Wilson as First Lady: A Study in the Power of Personality, 1919-1920," *Presidential Studies Quarterly* 15, no. 1 (1985): 66.

22   "January 1893... McKinley administration": "The 1897 Petition Against the Annexation of Hawaii," National Archives, accessed May 8, 2020, https://www.archives.gov/education/lessons/hawaii-petition.

23   "a dangerous man": Ron Chernow, *Alexander Hamilton,* (New York: The Penguin Press, 2004), 680.

24   "'to *reserve*… pause and reflect'": Ibid., 694.

24   "The projectile… paralyzed": Ibid., 704.

24   "angered and unsettled": "Aaron Burr, 3rd Vice President (1801-1805),"
       United States Senate, accessed June 8, 2020, https://www.senate.gov/
       about/officers-staff/vice-president/VP_Aaron_Burr.htm.

Chapter Three: I ♥ NY Gravesites

28   "Hamilton rented a pew": "Alexander Hamilton's Church
       Attendance | Ask Trinity Archives," Trinity Church Wall
       Street, October 2, 2020, https://trinitywallstreet.org/videos/
       alexander-hamiltons-church-attendance-ask-trinity-archives.

28   "where his office was": Chernow, *Alexander Hamilton*, 288.

28   "Five of his eight children": "Alexander Hamilton and
       Trinity: A Third Century and Counting," Trinity Church Wall
       Street, May 15, 2020, https://trinitywallstreet.org/videos/
       alexander-hamilton-and-trinity-third-century-and-counting.

28   "Financially hampered": Lamb et al., *Who's Buried in Grant's Tomb?*,
       20-21.

28   "exhumed and transported:" Ibid., 21.

29   "Grant listed New York": Ibid., 76.

29   "largest mausoleum": "Overview," grantstomb.org, accessed June 26,
       2019, https://grantstomb.org/overview/.

29   "used federal troops… in the South": *Reconstruction: America After the
       Civil War*, Part 1, directed by Rob Rapley and Cyndee Readdean (New
       York: McGee Media, 2019).

31   "Algonquin term": *The Roosevelts: An Intimate History*, "Get Action,"
       directed by Ken Burns (Walpole, NH: Florentine Films, 2014).

31   "where he took joy": Edmund Morris, *Colonel Roosevelt* (New York:
       Random House, 2010), 557.

32   "'sudden, massive heart attack… Youngs Memorial Cemetery.'":
       jlouis, "Obituary: Nick LaBella, Dies at Age 77 Lived
       for the Presidents," *Oyster Bay Enterprise-Pilot*, September
       30, 2011, https://oysterbayenterprisepilot.com/2011/09/
       obituary-nick-labella-dies-at-age-77-lived-for-the-presidents/.

34   "first time in history": "The British Royal Visit," fdrlibrary,org,
       accessed September 3, 2022, https://www.fdrlibrary.org/royal-visit.

35   "formulate her policy recommendations": "Eleanor Roosevelt National Historic Site," NPS.gov, accessed March 23, 2019, https://www.nps. gov/nr/travel/presidents/eleanor_roosevelt_valkill.html.

35   "fear of being buried alive": United Press International, "Eleanor Asked For Slit Wrist After Death Fear Of Being Buried Alive," *Sandusky Register*, September 21, 1977, https://newspaperarchive.com/ sandusky-register-sep-21-1977-p-14/.

36   "less than one percent": Will Weissert, "Nixon papers moving to Yorba Linda," *Orange County Register*, April 23, 2010, http://www.ocregister. com/articles/nixon-245379-library-presidential.html.

36   "millions of veterans": "GI Bill History," Veterans Education Success, accessed February 12, 2019, https://veteranseducationsuccess.org/ gi-bill-history/.

Chapter Four: Land of Lincoln

38   "an apparent cold": Lamb et al., *Who's Buried in Grant's Tomb?*, 36.

39   "all that remains": "Harrison Tomb State Memorial," Columbus: Ohio Historical Society, 2001.

39   "a 1924 addition": Marjorie Byrnside Burress, *Wm. Henry Harrison, Ninth President of the United States – Tomb Rededication* (Cleves, OH: George C. Dreyer, Harrison-Symmes Memorial Foundation, May 26, 1997), 3.

40   "one-time $25,000 payment": "First Lady Biography: Anna Harrison," National First Ladies' Library, accessed June 9, 2020, http://www.first-ladies.org/biographies/firstladies.aspx?biography=9.

41   "professor Clara Rising:" Michael McLeod, "Clara Rising, Ex-UF Prof Who Got Zachary Taylor Exhumed," *Orlando Sentinel*, July 25, 1993, https://www.orlandosentinel.com/news/os-xpm-1993-07-25-9307230997-story.html.

41   "Samples such as fingernails": Michel Marriott, "Zachary Taylor's Remains Are Removed for Tests," *New York Times*, June 18, 1991, https://www.nytimes.com/1991/06/18/us/zachary-tay-lor-s-remains-are-removed-for-tests.html?mtrref=www.google. com&gwh=FC5F0923AD05088163F2773141AD7918&gwt=pay.

42   "cyanide or a deadly mushroom": McLeod, "Clara Rising, Ex-UF Prof Who Got Zachary Taylor Exhumed," *Orlando Sentinel*, July 25, 1993.

42   "in October 1850": Louis L. Picone, *The President is Dead!: The Extraordinary Stories of Presidential Deaths, Final Days, Burials, and Beyond* (New York: Skyhorse Publishing, 2020), 148.

42   "On November 1st": Ibid., 148.

42   "700-acre farm": "Zachary Taylor House," Historic Louisville Guide, accessed June 9, 2020, http://historiclouisville.com/zachary-taylor-house/.

42   "Aquia Creek sandstone": Kymberly Mattern, "The Public Vault," Congressional Cemetery, July 25, 2018, https://congressionalcemetery.org/2018/07/25/the-public-vault/.

43   "April 25th attack": Walter R. Borneman, *Polk: The Man Who Transformed the Presidency and America* (New York: Random House, 2008), 201.

43   "two weeks later": Ibid., 204.

45   "*thoroughly* despise": Charles W. Calhoun, *Benjamin Harrison* (New York: Times Books, 2013), 174-176.

45   "disinheriting his offspring": Cormac O'Brien, *Secret Lives of the U.S. Presidents* (Philadelphia: Quirk Books, 2004), 134.

47   "vault of concrete and steel": Lamb et al., *Who's Buried in Grant's Tomb?*, 69. For further reading, see Thomas J. Craughwell, *Stealing Lincoln's Body* (Cambridge, MA: Belknap Press of Harvard University Press, 2007).

47   "One previous nose-rubber": "1980 Campaign," Ronald Reagan Presidential Library and Museum, accessed June 10, 2020, https://www.reaganlibrary.gov/content/10493.

50   "disassembled and reconstructed": *A History of the Demolition and Reconstruction of the Old Illinois State Capitol* (Springfield, IL: Illinois State Register, 1968), 4.

50   "purchased it for $1,500": Lincoln Home National Historic Site, "Lincoln Home Official Visitor Guide," National Park Service, U.S. Department of the Interior, 2003.

52   "Nobody is actually starving": Nick Taylor, *American-Made — The Enduring Legacy of the WPA: When FDR Put the Nation to Work* (New York: Bantam Dell, 2008), 31.

52   "to shore up weak banks": Ibid., 69.

52   "It is not the function": Ibid., 69.

53　"Lou was disinterred": hooverarchivist, "On the Passing of Lou Henry Hoover," National Archives Hoover Heads blog, January 10, 2018, https://hoover.blogs.archives.gov/2018/01/10/on-the-passing-of-lou-henry-hoover/.

Chapter Five: Bill & Kurt's Excellent Adventure

54　"inappropriate relationship": James Barber, *Presidents* (New York: DK Publishing, Inc., 2000), 61.

56　"first ten waiting": Norman Boucher, "Clinton Comes to Campus," *Brown Alumni Magazine*, July/August 2005, https://www.brownalumni-magazine.com/articles/2007-04-28/clinton-comes-to-campus.

56　"'I'm slipping quickly'": Jack Perry, "Fans don't mind waiting for Clinton," projo.com, April 30, 2005.

Chapter Six: The Ohio Gang

61　"urged Congress to pass": Lyndon Johnson, "November 27, 1963: Address to Joint Session of Congress," Miller Center, https://millercenter.org/the-presidency/presidential-speeches/november-27-1963-address-joint-session-congress.

63　"John and Elizabeth… January 1884.": Douglas Keister, *Stories in Stone in New York: A Field Guide to New York City Area Cemeteries & Their Residents* (Layton, UT: Gibbs Smith, 2011), 234.

65　"exhumed from West Lawn": Lamb et al., *Who's Buried in Grant's Tomb?*, 109.

67　"built by his uncle": "Rutherford B. Hayes Presidential Center," Columbus: Ohio Historical Society, 2005.

67　"president who banned the substance": "Lucy - Wife, Mother, and Advocate," Rutherford B. Hayes Presidential Library & Museums, accessed June 11, 2020, https://www.rbhayes.org/hayes/lucy-webb-hayes/.

67　"disinterred from… farm in Dummerston, Vermont": Lamb et al., *Who's Buried in Grant's Tomb?*, 81-82.

68　"Since 1928, the estate": "White House Gates," Rutherford B. Hayes Presidential Library & Museums, accessed September 3, 2022, https://www.rbhayes.org/whitehousegates/.

68   "Boston's 10-9 victory": "Boston Red Sox at Cleveland Indians Box Score, June 20, 2005," Baseball Reference, accessed January 22, 2019, https://www.baseball-reference.com/boxes/CLE/CLE200506200. shtml.

69   "coated with dark residue": Mary Kilpatrick, "What the heck is happening to the Garfield monument in Cleveland's Lake View Cemetery?," cleveland.com, February 6, 2020, https://www.cleveland. com/metro/2020/02/what-the-heck-is-happening-to-the-garfield-mon- ument-in-clevelands-lake-view-cemetery.html.

69   "Italian marble statue": *The James A. Garfield Monument at Lake View Cemetery*, (Cleveland: Lake View Cemetery Association, ca. 2005).

69   "poor medical practices": For more information, watch the American Experience episode, "Murder of a President," directed by Rob Rapley, 2016.

70   "memorial of Georgia marble": *Warren Harding Home and Tomb?*, (Columbus: Ohio Historical Society, July 2004).

71   "ran the paper's Circulation Department": "Florence Kling Harding," whitehouse.gov, accessed May 22, 2020, https://www.whitehouse.gov/ about-the-white-house/first-ladies/florence-kling-harding/.

71   "mingling with the Fourth Estate": "Florence Harding Biography, National First Ladies' Library, accessed May 22, 2020, http://www. firstladies.org/biographies/firstladies.aspx?biography=30.

71   "'Well, Warren Harding'": Carl A. Sferrazza, "First Ladies Day of Destiny on Inaugurations," *Washington Post*, January 20, 1985, https://www.washingtonpost.com/archive/life- style/1985/01/20/first-ladies-day-of-destiny-on-inaugurations/ b82f14eb-1378-4c55-9d0a-b916ee14cf68/.

71   "his own driving force": John W. Dean, *Warren G. Harding* (New York: Time Books, 2004), 56.

71   "donated by 200,000 school children.": Lamb et al., *Who's Buried in Grant's Tomb?*, xiv.

Chapter Seven: Virginia is for (Cemetery) lovers

73   "faults and imperfections": *John Adams to Abigail Smith, May 7, 1764*, in *Adams Family Correspondence* I, ed. L. H. Butterfield (Cambridge, MA: Belknap Press of Harvard University Press, 1963), 45.

73   "'You lose.'" William Bushong, "The Life and Presidency of Calvin
      Coolidge," White House Historical Association, 2015, https://www.
      whitehousehistory.org/the-life-and-presidency-of-calvin-coolidge.

74   "he purchased in 1848": William G. Clotworthy, *Homes and Libraries
      of the Presidents*, 2nd ed. (Blacksburg, VA: McDonald & Woodward
      Publishing Company, 2003), 109.

76   "the same quarry": Jessiekratz, "The other FDR Memorial,"
      National Archives, April 10, 2015, https://prologue.blogs.archives.
      gov/2015/04/10/the-other-fdr-memorial/.

76   "'and placed in the center'": Ibid.

76   "became public knowledge": Lawrence Meyers, "President Taped Talks,
      Phone Calls; Lawyer Ties Ehrlichman to Payments," *Washington Post*,
      July 17, 1973, https://www.washingtonpost.com/wp-srv/national/
      longterm/watergate/articles/071773-1.htm.

77   "uncharacteristically brief notes": US National Archives, "Watergate:
      The 18 ½ Minute Gap and Haldeman's Notes," YouTube video, 04:27,
      posted [June 2011], https://www.youtube.com/watch?v=IJDX7AFujYs.

78   "It was such… save his life.": Liam Stack, "Jerry Parr, Secret Service
      Agent Who Helped Save Reagan, Dies at 85," *New York Times*, October
      10, 2015, https://www.nytimes.com/2015/10/10/us/jerry-parr-secret-
      service-agent-who-helped-save-reagan-dies-at-85.html.

78   *The Dick Cavett Show*. "Gov. Ronald Reagan/Bob Newhart/James Wong
      Howe." Aired December 17, 1971, on ABC.

78   "A metal star": Steven, "The Unmarked Site of the July 2, 1881
      Assassination of President Garfield," civilwarwashingtondc1861-1865.
      blogspot.com, July 1, 2012, http://civilwarwashingtondc1861-1865.
      blogspot.com/2012/07/unmarked-site-of-july-2-1881.html.

79   "president's paternal grandfather": *Restoring the Home of James and Dolley
      Madison*, (Montpelier Station, VA: Montpelier Foundation, 2003).

80   "periwinkles planted by": C-SPAN, "American Artifacts
      Preview: Madison & Slave Cemeteries at Montpelier," YouTube
      video, 04:48, posted [March 2012], https://www.youtube.com/
      watch?v=wUzZsjB9-bY.

81   "'[O]pposed in death'": "Alexander Hamilton Bust (Sculpture)":
      Monticello.org, accessed September 3, 2022, https://www.monti-
      cello.org/research-education/thomas-jefferson-encyclopedia/
      alexander-hamilton-bust-sculpture/#fn-1.

81   "'Thomas Jefferson survives'": Lamb et al., *Who's Buried in Grant's
      Tomb?*, 8.

81   "'Help me[,] child, help me.'": Susanna Boylston Adams Clark
      Treadway, *Susanna Boylston Adams Clark Treadway to Abigail Louisa Smith
      Adams Johnson, July 9, 1826*, letter, from National Archives, *Founders
      Online*, accessed December 30, 2021, https://founders.archives.gov/
      documents/Adams/99-03-02-4665.

83   "not officially recognized": Lamb et al., *Who's Buried in Grant's Tomb?*, 41.

83   "unmarked until 1899": Picone, *The President is Dead!*, 161.

84   "Héloïse d'Argenteuil and Peter Abelard": Ibid., 71.

84   "some newly-purchased": Scott H. Harris and Jarod Kearney, "Articles
      of the Best Kind," White House Historical Association, 2014, https://
      www.whitehousehistory.org/articles-of-the-best-kind.

85   "618 cast iron pieces": "Monroe Tomb Returned to its Original
      Appearance in Time for Birthday Observance," *James Monroe Museum
      Newsletter*, May 2017, 3-4, http://jamesmonroemuseum.umw.edu/
      wp-content/blogs.dir/351/files/2011/08/May-2017-E-Newsletter.pdf.

85   "paint analysis": "Restoration of Monroe's Beloved 'Birdcage'
      Complete," *Friends of Hollywood 7*, no. 1 (Spring 2017), http://files.
      constantcontact.com/98dc66ec001/2942e764-f9c2-4d92-a504-
      59ca24b82f9e.pdf.

85   "reunited in 1903": "Elizabeth Monroe Biography," National First
      Ladies' Library, accessed May 24, 2020, http://www.firstladies.org/
      biographies/firstladies.aspx?biography=5.

Chapter Eight: King of Rock 'n' Roll

91   "declared it unconstitutional": "The Impeachment of Andrew
      Johnson," National Park Service, updated March 2, 2017, https://www.
      nps.gov/anjo/learn/historyculture/impeachment.htm.

93   "placed beneath his head": Lamb, et al., *Who's Buried in Grant's Tomb?*,
      73.

94 "birds were first placed:" "The Peabody Memphis Ducks," Peabody Memphis, accessed January 24, 2019, https://www.peabodymemphis.com/ducks-en.html.

95 "POTUS was initially buried": Lamb, et al., *Who's Buried in Grant's Tomb?*, 45.

96 "maintaining wagons": "Andrew Jackson's Enslaved Laborers," Andrew Jackson's Hermitage, accessed May 20, 2020, https://thehermitage.com/learn/mansion-grounds/slavery/.

97 "Ladies' Hermitage Association… mansion's main hall": "Burials and Bereavement: Funeral Customs at The Hermitage," Andrew Jackson's Hermitage, accessed May 20, 2020, https://thehermitage.com/funeral-customs-at-the-hermitage/.

97 "authorized the president": "Indian Treaties and the Removal Act of 1830," Office of the Historian, Department of State, accessed May 21, 2020, https://history.state.gov/milestones/1830-1860/indian-treaties.

97 "16,000 Cherokees… present-day Oklahoma": John Meacham, *American Lion: Andrew Jackson in the White House* (New York: Random House, 2008).

97 "held around 300": "Andrew Jackson's Enslaved Laborers," Andrew Jackson's Hermitage, accessed May 20, 2020, https://thehermitage.com/learn/mansion-grounds/slavery/.

97 "'shall all meet in Heaven'": Lamb et al., *Who's Buried in Grant's Tomb?*, 28.

98 "first marriage wasn't legally dissolved": "Rachel," Andrew Jackson's Hermitage, accessed February 28, 2019, https://thehermitage.com/learn/andrew-jackson/family/rachel/.

Chapter Nine: The Gipper, Tricky Dick, and the Jazzman

105 "wingspan is over 145 feet": *Ronald Reagan Presidential Library and Museum*, (Simi Valley: Ronald Reagan Presidential Foundation, ca. 2008).

105 "walls not be erected": *WELCOME ABOARD Air Force One 27000!* (Simi Valley: Ronald Reagan Presidential Library and Museum, ca. 2008).

106   "address he delivered": "Ronald Reagan remarks at his 1991
        Presidential Library Dedication," C-SPAN, 19:59, filmed
        [November 4, 1991], https://www.c-span.org/video/?c4551159/
        ronald-reagan-remarks-1991-presidential-library-dedication.

107   "Nixon's favorite space": *Visitor Guide*, (Yorba Linda: Richard Nixon
        Library & Birthplace Foundation, 2008).

107   "Mao, who oversaw": Ilya Somin, "Remembering the biggest mass
        murder in the history of the world," *Washington Post*, August 3,
        2016, https://www.washingtonpost.com/news/volokh-conspiracy/
        wp/2016/08/03/giving-historys-greatest-mass-murderer-his-due/?nore-
        direct=on&utm_term=.e1358c6ecc9d.

108   "president did not possess": "United States v. Nixon," Oyez, accessed
        June 12, 2020, https://www.oyez.org/cases/1973/73-1766.

109   "Nixon and Haldeman discussed": "User Clip: Smoking Gun Tape,"
        C-SPAN video, 05:15, Created [September 27, 2019], https://www.c-
        span.org/video/?c4819680/user-clip-smoking-gun-tape.

109   "May the day": "President Nixon Funeral," C-SPAN video, 1:37:50,
        Filmed [April 27, 1994], https://www.c-span.org/video/?56426-1/
        president-nixon-funeral.

110   "aide Bob Bostock": Christopher Goffard, "A new take on Watergate
        at Nixon Library," *Los Angeles Times*, April 1, 2011, https://www.
        latimes.com/politics/la-xpm-2011-apr-01-la-me-0401-watergate-nixon-
        20110401-story.html.

110   "'Nixonland'": Scott Martelle, "Talk of Moving Nixon Archives Raises
        Concern," *Los Angeles Times*, April 9, 1997, http://articles.latimes.
        com/1997-04-09/local/me-47009_1_nixon-library.

111   "clandestine bombings": "Nixon Again Deplores Leak on Bombing
        Cambodia," *New York Times*, March 11, 1976, https://www.nytimes.
        com/1976/03/11/archives/nixon-again-deplores-leak-on-bombing-cam-
        bodia.html.

Chapter Ten: I Like Ike's Grave

114   "Kaw, Osage, and Potawatomi": "Charles Curtis, 31st Vice President
        (1929-1933)," United States Senate, accessed May 12, 2020, https://
        www.senate.gov/about/officers-staff/vice-president/VP_Charles_
        Curtis.htm.

114   "made genealogical claims": Calvin Coolidge, *The Autobiography of Calvin Coolidge* (New York: Cosmopolitan Book Corporation, 1929), reprinted (Chatsworth, CA: National Notary Association, 2006), 16.

116   "'In God We Trust'": "The Legislation Placing 'In God We Trust' on National Currency," United States House of Representatives: History, Art & Archives, accessed January 25, 2019, https://history.house.gov/Historical-Highlights/1951-2000/The-legislation-placing-%E2%80%9CIn-God-We-Trust%E2%80%9D-on-national-currency/.

116   "'visitors would reflect upon'": "Place of Meditation," Eisenhower Foundation, accessed December 10, 2019, https://www.dwightdeisenhower.com/265/Place-of-Meditation.

118   "first extensive retooling": Heather Hollingsworth, "Newly renovated Eisenhower museum reopens in Kansas," Military Times, July 29, 2019, https://www.militarytimes.com/off-duty/military-culture/2019/07/30/newly-renovated-eisenhower-museum-reopens-in-kansas/.

118   "'in an eighty-dollar'": Lamb et al., *Who's Buried in Grant's Tomb?*, 152.

118   "*solely* their dress coats": Michael Korda, *Ike: An American Hero* (New York: Harper Perennial, 2008), 92.

118   "'going over the wall'": Ibid., 92.

121   "coupled with a Soviet invasion": Gregg Herken, "Five myths about the atomic bomb," *Washington Post*, July 31, 2015, https://www.washingtonpost.com/opinions/five-myths-about-the-atomic-bomb/2015/07/31/32dbc15c-3620-11e5-b673-1df005a0fb28_story.html?utm_term=.725ae1eed71a.

121   "estimated to have exceeded": "Survivors of Hiroshima and Nagasaki," Atomic Heritage Foundation, July 27, 2017, https://www.atomicheritage.org/history/survivors-hiroshima-and-nagasaki.

121   "'politically correct'": *History Wars: The Enola Gay and Other Battles for the American Past*, edited by Edward T. Linenthal and Tom Engelhardt (New York: Henry Holt and Company, 1996), 11.

123   "'Some day I hope'": David McCullough, *Truman* (New York: Simon & Schuster Paperbacks, 1992), 829.

124   "but his own term": Senate Historical Office, "David Rice Atchison: (Not) President for a Day," senate.gov, November 13, 2020, https://www.senate.gov/artandhistory/senate-stories/no-david-rice-atchison-was-not-president-for-a-day.htm.

124 "quipped he had standards": "National Press Club book talk," C-SPAN video.

Chapter Eleven: A Gander at a Michigander

128 "his jugular vein was protected": Joel Achenbach, "Abraham Lincoln's assassination: Great joy, then a gunshot," *Washington Post*, March 27, 2015, https://www.washingtonpost.com/ lifestyle/style/abraham-lincolns-assassination-great-joy-then-a-gun- shot/2015/03/27/3e93b202-cbe0-11e4-a2a7-9517a3a70506_story. html?noredirect=on&utm_term=.e86654b5c4a6.

129 "justice, liberty… independence." Frederick Douglass, "The Meaning of July Fourth for the Negro," July 5, 1852, https://www.pbs.org/ wgbh/aia/part4/4h2927t.html.

131 "antisemitic views": "Ford's Anti-Semitism," PBS, accessed December 1, 2018, https://www.pbs.org/wgbh/americanexperience/features/ henryford-antisemitism/.

132 "it was reintroduced… early 1977": "Kennedy Presidential Limousine," The Henry Ford, accessed January 27, 2019, https://www.thehenry- ford.org/collections-and-research/digital-resources/popular-topics/ kennedy-limo/.

135 "'This is so Jerry Ford.'": "Marvin DeWinter," Gerald R. Ford Oral History Project, Gerald R. Ford Presidential Foundation, accessed January 27, 2019, https://geraldrfordfoundation.org/centennial/ oralhistory/marvin-dewinter/.

137 "corpse of a different man": "The Body in Daniel Boone's Grave may not be his, *New York Times*, July 21, 1983, https://www.nytimes. com/1983/07/21/garden/the-body-in-daniel-boone-s-grave-may-not- be-his.html.

Chapter Twelve: Rocky Road

144 "swiftly cremated": Richard Norton Smith, *On His Own Terms: A Life of Nelson Rockefeller* (New York: Random House, 2014), 710.

145 "influence couldn't sway": "Who's Buried in Grant's Tomb," C-SPAN video.

Chapter Thirteen: The Lone (Star) Grave Left

155   "2,700 acres": "Ranching the LBJ Way," National Park Service, updated August 19, 2010, https://www.nps.gov/lyjo/planyourvisit/lbjranching.htm.

156   "sat beside the president": *Junction School,* National Park Service, U.S. Department of the Interior, ca. 2012.

156   "speeding toward the river": O'Brien, *Secret Lives of the U.S. Presidents,* 219.

156   "'delighted in showing'": "Reconstructed Birthplace," National Park Service, updated March 31, 2012, https://www.nps.gov/lyjo/planyourvisit/reconstructedbirthplace.htm.

Chapter Fourteen: Oswald the Unlucky Assassin

160   "instead a ban": The Young Turks, "RNC Protesters Can Carry Guns But Not 'Super Soakers'," YouTube video, 04:25, posted [April 2012], https://www.youtube.com/watch?v=UZaNlz0Zxs4.

164   "2,335 American service members": "How Many Pearl Harbor Deaths Were There?," Pearl Harbor Visitors Bureau, accessed May 29, 2020, https://visitpearlharbor.org/how-many-pearl-harbor-deaths-were-there/.

165   "19 U.S. Navy vessels": "Remembering Pearl Harbor: A Pearl Harbor Fact Sheet," National WWII Museum, accessed May 29, 2020, https://www.census.gov/history/pdf/pearl-harbor-fact-sheet-1.pdf.

166   "Oswald's supervisor… missing from work.": "Affidavit In Any Fact by Roy S. Truly #1," University of North Texas, accessed September 3, 2022, https://texashistory.unt.edu/ark:/67531/metapth338979/.

Chapter Fifteen: Schooled by Jimmy Carter

173   "'could be the world's second largest'": Kirby, Smith, Wilkins, "Field Review: Plains, Georgia – Jimmy Carter Peanut," RoadsideAmerica.com, accessed August 20, 2019, https://www.roadsideamerica.com/story/10409.

173   "recorded 776 residents": U.S. Census Bureau, 2010 Census of Population and Housing, *Population and Housing Units Counts,* CPH-2-12, Georgia (Washington, D.C.: U.S. Government Printing Office, 2012), 38, https://www2.census.gov/library/publications/decennial/2010/cph-2/cph-2-12.pdf.

173   "'Jimmy passes by… take it down'": Jeff, "Jimmy Carter Peanut," RoadsideAmerica.com, July 14, 2013, https://www.roadsideamerica. com/tip/5627.

175   "White House tennis courts": James Fallows, "The Passionless Presidency: The trouble with Jimmy Carter's Administration," *The Atlantic*, May 1979, https://www.theatlantic.com/magazine/ archive/1979/05/the-passionless-presidency/308516/.

176   "In December 1978": "Jimmy Carter, 'Establishing Diplomatic Relations With China,' Dec. 15, 1978," USC US-China Institute, accessed September 3, 2022, https://china.usc.edu/ jimmy-carter-%E2%80%9Cestablishing-diplomatic-relations-chi-na%E2%80%9D-dec-15-1978.

180   "'committed adultery'": Lee Dembart, "Carter's Comments on Sex Cause Concern," *New York Times*, September 23, 1976, https://www. nytimes.com/1976/09/23/archives/carters-comments-on-sex-cause-concern.html.

Epilogue

188   "still open to the public": Doug Delony and Chloe Alexander, "George H.W. Bush Presidential Library partially reopens during government shutdown," *KHOU 11 News*, updated December 27, 2018, https://www. khou.com/article/news/local/george-hw-bush-presidential-library-par-tially-reopens-during-government-shutdown/285-624575038.

188   "denied pay and furloughed": David Koenig, "5 Ways the Government Shutdown Is Affecting Air Travel," *TIME*, January 11, 2019, http:// time.com/5501117/airports-tsa-government-shutdown-effects/.

189   "cremated and the ashes returned": Dick Cheney and Jonathan Reiner, *Heart: An American Medical Odyssey* (New York: Scribner, 2013), 7.

189   "awaits interment in Minneapolis." Jennifer Brooks, "Walter Mondale's urn rich in family history," *Minneapolis Star Tribune*, May 7, 2022, https:// www.startribune.com/walter-mondales-urn-rich-in-family-and-histo-ry/600171376/?refresh=true.

189   "'managed to visit the graves'": George A. Christensen, "Here Lies the Supreme Court: Revisited," in *Journal of Supreme Court History* 33, no. 1 (February 2008): 17-41.

About the Author

KURT DEION is a public historian, author, guest speaker, and the presidential expert for RoadsideAmerica.com. He holds an M.A. in history. At age 14 he launched kurtshistoricsites.com as a means to both document his travels and to encourage others to visit gravesites and engage in hands-on history. His website and his cemetery pilgrimages were the subject of a 2015 interview on the C-SPAN show *Q&A*.

In 2023 he relocated from Rhode Island to Washington, D.C. to join the staff of Historic Congressional Cemetery. He concurrently became a next-gen leader with the White House Historical Association.

38°52'51.0"N 76°58'38.4"W